Unrecognized States in th International System

AF760660

Unrecognized states are territories that have achieved de facto independence, yet have failed to gain international recognition as independent states. These territories constitute anomalies in the international system of sovereign states and often present significant challenges to policymakers, as evidenced by the war in Georgia and the continued debate over Kosovo's independence.

This book draws on both theory and case studies to better understand the phenomenon of unrecognized states, demonstrating that the existence of such entities is less unusual than previously assumed. Moving away from an overt focus on case studies, the chapters present various themes that link the emergence, operations, and development of unrecognized states and assess how the established order of states responds to the challenges they present:

- How do unrecognized states interact with the international system of sovereign states? How does it shape their emergence, operations, and development?
- How do these entities develop in a context of non-recognition?
- Are we witnessing a new form of statehood, or are these entities better understood as states-in-waiting?
- What are the strategies available for dealing with unrecognized states? Could power-sharing or autonomy provide a solution, or are more innovative strategies necessary?

With contributions from leading scholars in a number of fields, this book will appeal not only to students and scholars of Political Science, International Relations, Geography, Area Studies, Sociology, and Conflict Resolution, but also to journalists, government bodies, and NGOs.

Nina Caspersen is Lecturer in the Department of Politics, Philosophy, and Religion at Lancaster University. Her research interests are primarily centred on ethnic conflicts in the Balkans and the Caucasus, dynamics within ethnic groups, and internal developments in unrecognized states. She has published a number of journal articles relating to this research and is a frequent presenter at international conferences and workshops.

Gareth Stansfield is Professor of Middle East Politics and Director of the Institute of Arab and Islamic Studies at the University of Exeter. His current research is on the political development of post-2003 Iraq, in particular the interaction of religious and ethnic groups and conceptions of nationalism and federalism. He is series editor of the Exeter Studies in Ethno Politics series with Routledge.

Exeter studies in ethno politics
Series Editor: Gareth Stansfield
University of Exeter, UK

Unrecognized States in the International System
Edited by Nina Caspersen and Gareth Stansfield

Unrecognized States in the International System

Edited by Nina Caspersen and Gareth Stansfield

Routledge
Taylor & Francis Group
LONDON AND NEW YORK

First published 2011
by Routledge
2 Park Square, Milton Park, Abingdon, Oxfordshire OX14 4RN

Simultaneously published in the USA and Canada
by Routledge
711 Third Avenue, New York, NY 10017

First issued in paperback 2014

Routledge is an imprint of the Taylor & Francis Group, an informa company

© 2011 editorial selection and matter, Nina Caspersen and Gareth Stansfield; individual chapters, the contributors

The right of Nina Caspersen and Gareth Stansfield to be identified as editors of this work has been asserted by them in accordance with sections 77 and 78 of the Copyright, Designs and Patents Act 1988.

Typeset in Times by Wearset Ltd, Boldon, Tyne and Wear

All rights reserved. No part of this book may be reprinted or reproduced or utilized in any form or by any electronic, mechanical, or other means, now known or hereafter invented, including photocopying and recording, or in any information storage or retrieval system, without permission in writing from the publishers.

British Library Cataloguing in Publication Data
A catalogue record for this book is available from the British Library

Library of Congress Cataloging in Publication Data
Unrecognized states in the international system/edited by Nina Caspersen and Gareth Stansfield.
p. cm. – (Exeter studies in ethno politics)
Includes bibliographical references and index.
1. Recognition (International law) 2. Sovereignty. I. Caspersen, Nina, 1976– II. Stansfield, Gareth R. V.
JZ4059.U57 2011
320.1–dc22 2010028609

ISBN13: 978-0-415-58210-0 (hbk)
ISBN13: 978-1-138-78895-4 (pbk)

Contents

Illustrations

Figure

Maps

Tables

Contributors

Liam Anderson is Associate Professor of Political Science at Wright State University, Ohio. He is the author of *Crisis in Kirkuk: The Ethnopolitics of Conflict and Compromise* (with G. Stansfield, UPenn Press, 2009).

Kristin M. Bakke is Lecturer in Politics and International Relations in the Department of Political Science at University College London. Prior to this, Dr Bakke held a research fellowship at Harvard University and was Assistant Professor in Political Science at Leiden University.

Helge Blakkisrud is Head of Department for Russian and Eurasian Studies at the Norwegian Institute of International Affairs. In 2009–2010, he has been Fulbright Visiting Scholar at the Institute of Slavic, East European and Eurasian Studies, UC Berkeley.

Nina Caspersen is Lecturer in Peace and Conflict Studies in the Department of Politics; Philosophy and Religion at Lancaster University. She is the author of *Contested Nationalism: Serb Elite Rivalry in Croatia and Bosnia in the 1990s* (Oxford: Berghahn Books, 2009).

Matan Chorev is Executive Director of the Future of National Security Project at the Belfer Center for Science and International Affairs at the Harvard Kennedy School. He holds a Master's of Arts in Law and Diplomacy from the Fletcher School, Tufts University, with a concentration on International Security Studies and Southwest Asia and Islamic Civilizations.

Stacy Closson was a Fellow at the Woodrow Wilson Center, Washington between September 2009 and May 2010, researching the international politics of Russian energy. From 2007–2009, she was a Trans-Atlantic Research Fellow at the German Institute for International and Security Affairs.

James Harvey is a Ph.D. student in Ethno-Political Studies at the Centre for Ethno-Political Studies (EXCEPS) at the University of Exeter.

Antje Herrberg is the Director of the European Forum for International Mediation and Dialogue. She is also working as Senior Mediation Advisor to the Crisis Management Initiative. She is a trained, certified, and practising mediator in intrastate and multicultural conflicts in the South Caucasus, South Asia and Asia, and Africa.

Pål Kolstø is Professor of Russian Studies in the Department of Literature, Area Studies and European Languages at the University of Oslo. He specializes in nationalism, nation-building, and ethnic conflict in general and in the former Soviet Union and the former Yugoslavia in particular. Monographs in English include *Russians in the Former Soviet Republics* (London: Hurst, 1995) and *Political Construction Sites: Nation-Building in Russia and the Post-Soviet States* (Boulder, Colorado: Westview Press, 2000).

Klejda Mulaj is Lecturer in Ethno-Political Studies in the Centre for Ethno-Political Studies (EXCEPS) at the University of Exeter. She is the author of *Politics of Ethnic Cleansing: Nation-State Building and Provision of In/security in Twentieth-Century Balkans* (Lanham, MD: Rowman & Littlefield, 2008) and editor of *Violent Non-State Actors in World Politics* (London: Hurst; and New York: Columbia University Press, 2010).

Francis Owtram has a Ph.D. in International Relations from the London School of Economics and is the author of *A Modern History of Oman: Formation of the State Since 1920* (IB Tauris, 2004). He is an Honorary Fellow of the Institute of Arab and Islamic Studies, University of Exeter and is currently teaching at the University of Kurdistan Hawler, Erbil, Iraq.

Gareth Stansfield is Professor of Middle East Politics and Director of the Centre for Ethno-Political Studies at the University of Exeter. He is also an Associate Fellow of the Middle East and North Africa Programme at the Royal Institute for International Affairs (Chatham House), London.

Stefan Wolff is Professor of International Security at the University of Birmingham. He has extensively written on international intervention in ethnic conflicts, including *Ethnic Conflict: A Global Perspective* (Oxford University Press, 2006) and *Ethnic Conflict: Causes, Consequences, and Responses* (Polity, 2009, with Karl Cordell).

Acknowledgements

An edited collection on the subject matter of 'unrecognized states' requires the bringing together of a group of academics from a relatively small pool of political scientists whose interests have taken them away from the more mainstream aspects of the field and who instead have chosen to delve into the complex and mercurial world of the 'unrecognized'. We are firstly grateful to our contributors for being among the trailblazers in a field that remains understudied, irrespective of its arguable importance.

Our ability as editors to bring together these contributors was enhanced by the awarding of research grants that supported our own research activities in this field from 2007–2010. Nina Caspersen wishes to acknowledge and thank the Economic and Social Research Council (ESRC) for supporting her project on *The Politics of Unrecognized States*, and Gareth Stansfield wishes to acknowledge and thank The Leverhulme Trust for the support provided by a Research Leadership Award to build a research group on *Ethnopolitics in a Globalized World*.

We would also like to thank Laura Newberry for her excellent administrative support that underpinned workshops held in Exeter and Lancaster, and Anaïd Flesken for assisting with copy-editing and map design. The excellent maps on display in this volume were created by Ian Cool.

Lastly, editing collections requires focus and effort that unavoidably places greater strains on the families of the editors than it does on the editors themselves. Nina would like to express her gratitude to Keith, as would Gareth to Lise and Amélie, for their support and patience, which we are sure we have tested to the full over the last year.

Introduction

Unrecognized states in the international system

Nina Caspersen and Gareth Stansfield

With the exception of the Arctic and Antarctic regions, the surface of the Earth is divided neatly into entities that are internationally recognized and control territories clearly delineated by internationally agreed boundaries. Or at least this is how the global state system is often presented. A more detailed evaluation of the territorial and political organization of the planet's surface uncovers anomalies that do not fit the idealized model which is fundamental to the academic study of political science and international relations. Evidence of these anomalies appears almost daily in news reports: the collapse of the state in Somalia; the Tamil–Sinhalese confrontation in Sri Lanka; the re-emergence of a Taliban 'insurgent' state in Afghanistan; state weakness in the periphery of Pakistan; the Kurds' demands for autonomy in Iraq; the continued existence of the Armenian enclave of Nagorno Karabakh; and the future of the Balkans. This is just a small sample of the range of issues that do not quite 'fit' into the neat model of 'recognized' states in the international system.

These specific regional/country problems also present specific policy predicaments for neighbouring states or for other states with national interests in the region. How does the international community respond to the security problem presented by unrecognized states that pose a challenge to the established regional security order, either because of their failings or, perhaps, their successes; that undermine the territorial integrity of sovereign states, whether purposefully (i.e. through an active secessionist dynamic) or merely by virtue of their existence; that could provide a territorial platform for insurgent groups; and that often have serious humanitarian problems associated with them? What challenges are posed by these 'states of concern', and how are they now viewed in a period that is, in many ways, in significant political flux following the opening-up of political space in a globalized world that is increasingly characterized by fragmented, rather than organized, authority and projections of power?

Unrecognized states, shadow states, states-within-states

Among the different entities that do not fit into the system of sovereign states, one type of entity stands out in particular: the so-called unrecognized states.[1] These are territories that have achieved de facto independence often, though not always, through warfare, but have failed to gain international recognition as independent states. Despite the challenge they present to the principle of the territorial integrity of established states, unrecognized states are not trying to undermine the *system* of sovereign states or create alternative forms of statehood; they are rather seeking a place in a system that does not accept them as constituent members. As such, there is no formally recognized mechanism by which an unrecognized entity can legally make the transition to 'recognized' state – after all, such a mechanism would logically require established states to agree upon principles that could result in their own territorial attenuation.

Many of these territories therefore exist in a state of limbo – in situations that have been characterized as being 'no war, no peace' (Walker 1998) – and have, for a long time, represented unresolved (for some observers, unresolvable) but also largely forgotten conflicts conducted at the geographical peripheries of states (Rutland 2007). Most people would be hard-pressed to locate territories such as Transnistria or Nagorno Karabakh on a map, and unrecognized states are, in more ways than one, the 'places that don't exist'; absent from the map and from the international agenda, until the tensions generated by them erupt in often spectacular fashion, taking by surprise observers whose interest had moved on to other, more accessible, problems. Recent events illustrate this tendency clearly. The outbreak of warfare in Georgia in August 2008 and in Sri Lanka in the spring of 2009 are just two examples of how situations involving unrecognized states can rapidly explode. Suddenly, these curious entities were back on the international agenda and journalists began to take an interest in the inner-workings of little-known places such as Abkhazia, South Ossetia and the now-collapsed Tamil Eelam. What they found was, however, a vacuum; very little is known about these entities, to the extent that they have been described as 'informational black holes' (King 2001).

Unrecognized states are ambiguous entities which are hard to pin down and, when trying to describe them, we are tempted to turn to Winston Churchill's famous characterization of Soviet foreign policy: 'a *puzzle* inside a *riddle* wrapped in an *enigma*.' With reference to his Soviet focus, Churchill believed that the key to unlocking the puzzle included an appreciation of the role played by Russian nationalism, and part of the key to understanding unrecognized states is similarly found in the mobilizing power of ethno-nationalism. Yet ethno-nationalism is not enough, in itself, to build an understanding of the dynamics of unrecognized states. They do indeed often emerge from ethno-nationalist mobilizations, but they are also very much the product of the international system, which constrains, shapes, and perhaps even enables these aspiring states. If we understand this interplay, then it is easier to understand these entities and easier to find ways of solving the puzzle; of making sense of unrecognized states in the international system.

This 'making sense' must also apply to the internal aspects of unrecognized states, in addition to the exogenous effects of them on their regional politics. Most reporting on unrecognized states has tended to view them through the prism of 'security threats'; they are often conflated with failed states, they are commonly associated with war and ethnic cleansing, and they tend to be viewed as the puppets of larger powers who use them to assert their regional influence (Lynch 2004a). More recent literature has, however, also pointed to the relative success of unrecognized states when it comes to state-building and even political reform (Caspersen 2008; Kolstø and Blakkisrud 2008). The case of Somaliland is often mentioned as an unlikely oasis of relative calm, stability, and democratization in the Horn of Africa (Hansen and Bradbury 2007), and the example of the Kurdistan Region of Iraq presents an interesting case study of socio-political development in a post-conflict setting (Stansfield 2003). Rather than viewing these analyses as polar opposites, they can be seen as illustrating different, even paradoxical, aspects of these entities, which occupy an uneasy in-between position in the international system.

So what is an unrecognized state and how does it differ from other anomalies in the international system? Unrecognized states are not the same as 'shadow states' (Reno 2000), 'black spots' (Stanislawski 2008) or 'insurgent states' (McColl 1969), even though many examples have emerged from these conditions. Unlike the Taliban-controlled parts of Afghanistan or the tribal areas of Pakistan, unrecognized states such as Nagorno Karabakh and South Ossetia control (most of) the territory they lay claim to and have managed to build at least some state institutions; they have, in other words, achieved a level of 'stateness' underpinned by a degree of de facto domestic sovereignty (as defined by Krasner 1999). Moreover, unrecognized states demonstrate, or are believed to demonstrate,[2] a clear aspiration for full independence; they do not seek invisibility (Stanislawski 2008) and want to become part of the world of sovereign states. This latter factor also distinguishes them from autonomous regions, states-within-states or various semi-dependencies such as Andorra and the Channel Islands. Unrecognized states are not satisfied with their current status and their current status is, moreover, under threat; their domestic sovereignty is not accepted by their, *de jure*, parent state. We, therefore, define unrecognized states based on three criteria:

1 They have achieved de facto independence, including territorial control, and have managed to maintain this for at least two years.[3] Unrecognized states control most of the territory they lay claim to, including the territory's 'capital' and key regions, and this distinguishes them from other separatist movements. But the territorial control is not necessarily absolute; they may aspire to more territory than they currently control and the extent of their control is likely to vary over time.
2 They have not gained international recognition, or even if they have been recognized by some states, they are still not full members of the international system of sovereign states. We consequently include what we could term 'partially recognized' states', such as Abkhazia and South Ossetia, which have been recognized by their patron state and three other states, and even Kosovo, which has been recognized by 70+ states.[4]
3 They have demonstrated an aspiration for full, *de jure*, independence, either through a formal declaration of independence, through the holding of a

referendum, or through other actions or declarations that show a clear desire for a separate existence.[5]

The first two criteria are fairly similar to other definitions of unrecognized states (for example, Pegg 1998; Kolstø 2006), although our criteria are a little more permissive and we, for example, include Kosovo, which Kolstø (2006) characterizes as a borderline case. However, the latter criterion differs from previous works and broadens the concept of unrecognized states to include entities that have not formally declared independence.[6] By not insisting on a formal declaration of independence, we are able to include entities such as Taiwan, the Kurdistan Region of Iraq, as well as Montenegro prior to its independence from Serbia-Montenegro. The absence of a formal declaration of independence can be a strategic attempt to increase room for manoeuvre and the prospect for international support. Such considerations were seen in Abkhazia, which only formally declared independence in 1999, even though it had been de facto independent since 1993. Eritrea, likewise, only declared independence in 1993 following an independence referendum, but it had been de facto independent since 1991 and its aspirations were clear. Table I.1 lists unrecognized states since World War II.

The dates identified for the beginnings and (in some cases) ends of unrecognized states should be regarded only as approximations. In some cases, Somaliland, for example, a formal declaration of independence accompanied by unambiguous political control of territory makes identifying the birth date

Table I.1 Unrecognized states since World War II

Unrecognized state	*Parent state*	*Dates*
Abkhazia	Georgia	1993–
Anjouan	Comoros	1997–2008
Biafra	Nigeria	1967–1970
Bougainville	Papua New Guinea	1975–1997
Chechnya	Russia	1991–1994, 1996–1999
East Timor	Indonesia	1999–2002
Eritrea	Ethiopia	1991–1993
Gagauzia	Moldova	1991–1994
Katanga	Congo	1960–1963
Kosovo	Serbia	1999–
Kurdistan-Iraq	Iraq	1991–
Montenegro	Federal Republic of Yugoslavia	2000–2006
Nagorno Karabakh	Azerbaijan	1994–
Northern Cyprus	Cyprus	1983–
Republika Srpska	Bosnia	1992–1995
Republika Srpska Krajina	Croatia	1991–1995
Somaliland	Somalia	1991–
South Ossetia	Georgia	1992–
Taiwan	China	1949–
Tamil Eelam	Sri Lanka	1986–2009
Transnistria	Moldova	1991–

relatively straightforward. In other cases, such as Montenegro, the process was more gradual and the absence of such a formal declaration of independence complicates the dating of the birth. In still other cases, Chechnya and Kosovo, for example, the on–off nature of the conflict makes it difficult to determine with precision when the 'de facto independence' criterion applied. During the time of the First Chechen war (1994–1996), for example, it would be difficult to argue that anyone really *controlled* the territory of Chechnya in any meaningful sense.

Cases that do not meet our criteria include the Mahabad Republic – the stillborn Kurdish state established in northern Iran in 1947, and the Republic of Crimea, neither of which satisfy the criterion for two-year duration. Less clear-cut are omissions such as Puntland (Somalia) and Adjara (Georgia). Although both entities clearly satisfy the requirements of de facto statehood in that both are (were) self-governing and in control of defined territory for periods longer than two years, neither expressed a desire to secede from their respective parent. Unlike some authors (for example, Geldenhuys 2009) we have also not included Western Sahara and Palestine. These entities are more widely recognized than most unrecognized states, but they do not meet the criterion of territorial control and the dynamics of their development, existence, and the potential for conflict resolution is therefore expected to differ. However, some contributors to this volume have decided to include them.[7] Also omitted are a significant number of insurgencies and uprisings that may have been inspired by a desire for independence, but in which the separatist movement has not managed to exert sufficient political control over the desired territory to qualify as de facto independence. Among these cases we are likely to find candidates for future unrecognized states and the category includes entities such as Aceh (Indonesia) and southern Sudan.

Despite such omissions, our definition allows for a high degree of fluidity in terms of territorial control, degree of recognition and demands made, and this is deliberate. Within the category of unrecognized states, we find a high level of variation and, despite being known for their intransigence, these entities are frequently characterized by a sense of flux and are, moreover, perceived as transitional. Non-recognition is not regarded as a permanent status, not by the outside world and not by the leaders and populations of these entities. Internally, non-recognition is seen as a necessary, and possibly painful, step on the road to recognition, and by the outside world it is frequently seen as a temporary anomaly before territorial integrity is restored – through negotiations, or through the use of force. And unrecognized states do indeed change form; for example, Chechnya went from an insurgent state in the early 1990s, to an unrecognized state from 1996 to 1999, to a black spot during the wars and now to a state-within-a-state (Pełczynska-Nałęcz *et al.* 2008). The ability to adapt is often crucial to their survival but it also hints at possible limits to their long-term viability.

Esoteric anomalies?

Unrecognized states are full of paradoxes and this makes them a practical challenge to policymakers and an intellectual problem for scholars; how do we make sense of these entities that do not fit into the international system, but are trying to create entities that imitate recognized statehood? How do they interact with the international system and how are the problems associated with these entities managed? The international system is still very much based on a clear division between sovereign states and non-sovereign entities, and in international relations theory, sovereignty has traditionally been seen as straightforward. As J.D.B. Miller put it, 'Just as we know a camel or a chair when we see one, so we know a sovereign state' (quoted in Sørensen 1999: 590; see also Pegg 1998). But the reality is considerably more complex and the global state system is not as neatly organized as we might think. Lack of external sovereignty does not necessarily equate disorder, neither statehood nor identities are fixed, and in-between entities are trying to carve out a niche for themselves in an international system predicated on external sovereignty.

Unrecognized states tend to be small, their chance of international recognition is often remote, and the exogenous and endogenous pressures on them are intense. One could, therefore, easily be led to conclude that they are doomed to be short-lived anomalies of no great consequence. But perhaps this form of statehood could take on a more permanent character. Unrecognized states are borne out of conflict; they exist in very volatile parts of the world, they are often founded on violence and ethno-nationalist mobilization, and they lack the protection provided by the norms of non-intervention. On the face of it, these aspiring states would therefore be the unlikeliest candidates for successful state-building, never mind democratization and good governance, yet they claim that statehood can exist without internationally recognized sovereignty, that recognition does not constitute states and that they have in fact managed to build institutions in conditions where recognized entities have failed. Their demand for separateness is not the dream of optimistic, or perhaps deluded, separatists; rather it presents the current reality, and herein lies a great challenge for policymakers. Can the leaders of unrecognized states be persuaded to accept less than full independence as currently understood – and can they bring their followers along? Can leaders of established states which have, within or across their borders, an unrecognized entity ultimately accept having paper sovereignty over the territory in effect controlled by others? Are there any alternatives to recognition if they cannot? Recent international developments suggest that non-recognition or indeed partial recognition could possibly acquire a more permanent status. There is little to indicate that Kosovo will be able to join the United Nations in the near future, and even less to indicate that Abkhazia and South Ossetia will, yet reintegration seems a very unlikely prospect in all three cases. Does this mean that we are witnessing a new form of statehood, or are these entities better understood as states-in-waiting?

Exploring and theorizing unrecognized states

A notable body of work focuses on unrecognized states, both in terms of case studies of particular situations and in terms of considering responses to them.

Valuable empirical work has forwarded our understanding of case studies, with some at times being comparative. Yet little has been done to theorize 'unrecognized states' per se: how they form, operate, and develop, and how they are placed in and interact with the 'international system'. It is our intention that this collection takes forward the study of 'unrecognized states' by moving away from an overt focus on case study analysis to one which presents various themes that link the emergence, operations, and development of them, in addition to assessing how the established order of states respond to the challenges they present. In so doing, this collection does not constitute a comprehensive coverage of 'unrecognized states' as appears in valuable works such as Pegg (1998), Bahcheli *et al.* (2004), Kingston and Spears (2004), and Geldenhuys (2009). Instead, the contributions to this volume each take a particular theme relating to the formation, operation, development, and existence of unrecognized states with the hope of presenting a new theoretical synthesis that allows such entities to be viewed as, if not 'regular' features of the international system, at least ones of a more perennial rather than anomalous nature.

The first part of the book explores the place of unrecognized states in the international system. Stansfield and Harvey contextualize the problematique of the 'unrecognized state', investigating how the language of abstraction used to describe and analyse these entities presents inherent limitations when it comes to understanding their developmental trajectories and positioning within the wider international system. Chorev finds that the emergence, survival, and viability of unrecognized states is closely tied to the process of globalization and argues that it is mistaken to see these entities merely as 'states-in-waiting'. Mulaj similarly examines how the actions and inactions of the international community have aided, but also hindered, the creation and survival of unrecognized states. Finally, Closson analyses unrecognized states in relation to different notions of sovereignty and asks if these entities challenge dominant conceptions of sovereignty.

The second part of the book examines the inner workings of unrecognized states; how they develop in a context of non-recognition and how it is portrayed to the outside world. This part highlights how the international system constrains and enables these entities, and also how their portrayal to external audiences is strongly affected by dominant discourses and norms. Caspersen analyses how unrecognized states try to imitate (recognized) democratic statehood and finds that, although statehood is possible without external sovereignty, it takes a specific form. Bakke focuses on a 'darker' side of unrecognized statehood: the propensity for internal violence. She analyses the types and causes of this violence and asks how it affects the viability of these entities. Kolstø and Blakkisrud explore how the perceived security threats emanating from unrecognized states are seen and securitized by their respective parent states; i.e. how they are portrayed to internal and external audiences. They find significant overlap in the rhetoric used, but also argue that this form of securitization has been relatively unsuccessful with international audiences. Owtram further examines this interaction between unrecognized states and the international system, by analysing the foreign policy of these entities; what are their goals and how do they try to achieve them?

Finally, the third part of the book focuses on conflict resolution and examines strategies for dealing with unrecognized states. Wolff addresses the limits of international conflict management in unrecognized states through an analysis of EU conflict management in Abkhazia and South Ossetia. Herrberg draws on her experience from the Crisis Management Initiative and examines the opportunities and limitations affecting mediation in conflicts involving unrecognized states. Anderson finishes the book by examining the range of 'alternative destinations' for unrecognized states, with a particular focus on options for reintegration with the parent state; could power-sharing or autonomy provide a solution or are other more innovative strategies necessary?

Notes

1 These entities have also variously been described as de facto states (Pegg 1998), separatist states (Lynch 2004a), almost-states (Stanislawski 2008), contested states (Geldenhuys 2009), or unrecognized quasi-states (Kolstø 2006).
2 This is a particularly important qualification to make. For some leaders of 'unrecognized states', their geopolitical situation is such that they are very cautious – to the point of denial – of declaring their aspirations for full independence. It is then the case that the aspirations of the leaderships of unrecognized states are outlined by neighbouring states in the region that remain fearful of the presumed intentions of their unrecognized neighbour.
3 Kolstø (2006) also uses two years as his criterion, while Geldenhuys (2009) opts for three years. The exact number of years is not decisive, but what is important is that we are looking at entities that are not completely transient, but have demonstrated a certain staying power.
4 What we refer to as 'partial recognition' includes what Geldenhuys (2009) has termed 'paltry recognition' and 'patron recognition'. 'Partial recognition' is in Geldenhuys' usage reserved for entities that have been recognized by a significant number of states. We appreciate the potential usefulness of more specific categories, but for the sake of simplicity we will stick to a single category.
5 This would, for example, include Abkhazia's Declaration of Sovereignty in 1990 and Montenegro's introduction of a separate currency (the Deutschmark) in 2000.
6 Scott Pegg mentions such a broadening of the definition as a potential improvement of his original work (2004: 38).
7 See, for example, Anderson's chapter.

Part I

Conceptualizing unrecognized states

1 Theorizing unrecognized states

Sovereignty, secessionism, and political economy

James Harvey and Gareth Stansfield

Introduction

Unrecognized states are anomalous features of the international system and international society. They are, in short, very odd, and their oddities present numerous challenges to the international system and those who study it. They are odd in terms of their very existence as spatial entities in a world already divided comprehensively into states and ordered by international boundaries. The awkwardness of juxtaposing unrecognized states alongside or, more accurately, 'over' or 'under' recognized states in terms of sovereignty is also clearly odd.[1] Never the easiest concept to define or theorize, nothing encapsulates the 'organized hypocrisy' of sovereign states quite so much as how domestic sovereignty may be held and exercised in unrecognized states which do not have international legal sovereignty compared with those which have questionable domestic sovereignty yet are recognized as international legal sovereign entities.[2] Stephen Krasner (1999) considers the 'muddle' that exists around the concept of sovereignty, identifying four different ways in which the term has been used: Westphalian, domestic, interdependence, and international legal. The majority of his analysis focuses on Westphalian and international legal concepts of sovereignty.[3] However, in the case of unrecognized states, the confusion – and even the hypocrisy – becomes starker when domestic sovereignty is given additional weight, as it is usually the case that unrecognized states begin from a starting point of enhanced domestic sovereignty vis-à-vis the international legal sovereign entity.

Yet unrecognized states are also anomalous in terms of how they exercise domestic sovereignty. With mostly limited resources and questionable legitimacy borne from political structures that had emerged under extreme circumstances, the manner in which unrecognized states exercise control over their territory can vary enormously. Often authoritarian or semi-authoritarian in nature,[4] dependent on considerable patronage structures,[5] yet relying on being seen as embracing democratization strategies in order to illicit support from the international community,[6] while usually trying to embarrass the parent state which holds international legal sovereignty over their domains, unrecognized states are often schizophrenic in terms of how they project their authority at home and present their legitimacy abroad.

The problematic language of abstraction

It is these oddities, and the ideal to make sense of them, that this chapter attempts to tackle. But this is a difficult task because unrecognized states are products of their immediate domestic and regional environment, conditioned by historical context and affected unevenly by wider international and globalized pressures. Significant among these pressures is the political economy of trade in resources and the needs of the market – economic dynamics which this chapter contends exert a profound influence, in many cases, upon the international politics of unrecognized states, secession, and territorial revision in the global state system. One of the biggest challenges facing anyone attempting to tackle theoretical and conceptual issues surrounding unrecognized states is the question of abstraction. Before any attempt is made to unpick the complicated politics and political economy of secession, self-determination, state-building, and survival in the international system, which goes hand-in-hand with the study of unrecognized states, one is forced to confront the very confused and confusing language of abstraction used to describe and analyse them.

A problem which has confronted scholars since unrecognized states began to attract significant attention in the 1990s, and continues to exert considerable influence today, can be rationalized as the problem of adding further conceptual abstractions to concepts – namely statehood and sovereignty – which are already abstract, enigmatic, and contentious. Put simply, the concept of an unrecognized state starts with properties that may be considered features of the continuum of states and statecraft in the international system, but through the dynamics of non-recognition, the politics of location, territorial disputes, and long-term legal ambiguities, these entities field a counterintuitive challenge to the concepts of statehood and sovereignty which then demands unrecognized states be approached as examples of something else completely. On the one hand, these abstractions of sovereignty and statecraft are loosely regarded as states, albeit unrecognized in international law, but on the other hand, many of the dynamics which sustain these de facto independent territories[7] can be said to militate against their inclusion in the same theoretical, conceptual and categorical space occupied by sovereign states in the international and interstate systems.

Theorizing unrecognized states?

This chapter attempts to explore the complex conceptual terrain surrounding unrecognized states and the theorizing of them. Its primary aim is to explore whether or not the problematic archetype of 'unrecognized states', as both a term and a concept deployed by analysts across disciplinary boundaries, contains sufficient conceptual flexibility and robustness to encompass the widely differing causal dynamics and political trajectories each case represents. In short, is it possible to consider unrecognized states at a level of abstraction that lends itself to theorizing their formative influences, developmental trajectories, political economy, and end-state? The concept of the unrecognized state, it is argued, is formed out of disciplinary perspectives and conventions that have built a rich and varied empirical understanding of a range of cases throughout recent history, but have struggled to do so in a systematized manner that would lead to a theoretical framework or conceptual understanding of the phenomenon encompassing emerging trends and realities on the ground in regions where these entities exist or have existed.

This failure exists with regards to the starkest element of many unrecognized states' existence. When required to accommodate the conceptually ambiguous and meta-theoretical implications of secession, or attempted secession, which leads to the creation of unrecognized political and territorial space in many cases, the concept of the unrecognized state as an explicitly *secessionist* entity becomes a site of analytical contention. How far should we render these territorial and ethno-political conflicts a direct product of the state-creation impulse? To what extent are de facto autonomy and de facto independence, not *de jure* recognition and sovereignty, the most likely outcomes for secessionist movements in these cases? What causal role did state fragmentation play in the creation of contemporary examples of unrecognized states? Can a political economy of unrecognized statehood be said to exist in the globalized international system? These, and other, questions remain unanswered largely because relevant conceptual research in this area has not been forthcoming – a situation which currently hinders our understanding of unrecognized states as an extant feature of international politics. By focusing on the empirical variance inherent within any discussion of unrecognized states as a continuum within international politics, the chapter highlights the paradoxical distance between the concept of 'unrecognized statehood' and the causal processes which have, for well over a decade, defined the phenomenon. This is achieved through an exploration of the problems inherent in developing a conceptual continuum which is capable of charting the evolution of the unrecognized state, and how the problems encountered during this process indicate a level of conceptual ambiguity which is rarely approached in terms of representing a workable set of abstractions.

The second half of this chapter introduces a relatively understudied aspect of unrecognized states – how those endowed with resources that have value to the international community of established states engage with them to their mutual benefit. Many unrecognized states reside in areas rich in natural resources or areas of considerable strategic and foreign policy importance to external actors and interests. For recognized states, their unrecognized counterparts can often provide access to resources which their own national economies have a desperate need for, but with economic gain coming with political risk. This risk is tied to the strengthening of the unrecognized state which brings with it a range of consequences that could include further consolidation of the entity and the weakening of the established parent state of which the unrecognized state is legally part. By engaging with unrecognized states for mutual benefit, recognized states also risk supporting the aims of ethnic separatists and would-be breakaway minorities, creating fertile ground for further ethno-political conflict and regional instability. The importance of the resource question, therefore, is one which, we contend, should be factored into any theoretical understanding of the development of unrecognized states, whether they turn into independent states or find an expedient form of accommodation within the broader contested frameworks of international society.

Exploring the causal continuum

Conceptual literature

The term 'unrecognized state' does not represent or embody a conceptual consensus.[8] Since the late 1990s, unrecognized states have assumed a range of conceptual guises, with most of them being driven by the need to rationalize conflicts and territorial revisions which occurred in the space previously occupied by the Soviet Union. Foremost among these is the 'de facto state', a term coined by Pegg (1998) in his studies of Eritrea before independence, Northern Cyprus, Somaliland, and Tamil Eelam, and who defined this political unit as 'a secessionist entity that receives popular support and has achieved sufficient capacity to provide governmental services to a given population in a defined territorial area, over which it maintains effective control for an extended period of time'. An interesting feature of Pegg's definition is its focus on secession as the primary causal dynamic preceding the emergence of the de facto state, rather than criteria of status in international law, which run parallel within his analysis as a reinforcement of his conceptualization of the 'secessionist entity'. By Pegg's definition, the de facto state *is* a secessionist entity, which explains why it was logical for the concept to be adopted for analysis of the breakaway republics that formed in Eurasia and the Caucasus following the decline of the Soviet Union.[9]

In his analysis of post-Soviet conditions, King referred to 'unrecognized states', 'de facto countries', 'de facto states', 'independent statelike entities', 'unrecognized regimes', 'separatists', 'surreptitious state building' and a wealth of other conceptual forms and dynamics in his article 'The Benefits of Ethnic War: Understanding Eurasia's Unrecognized States' (2001: 524–52). King's analysis provided a temporal framework for understanding the emergence of such entities by acknowledging a continuum of state weakness, external support, cultural legitimization, complicity of central governments, and the sometimes 'unwitting' assistance of international negotiators as potent dynamics surrounding the evolution of unrecognized states in the post-Soviet space (ibid.: 535). Importantly, King's analysis did not introduce new theoretical and conceptual abstractions to the concept of the unrecognized state, seeking instead to emphasize the expedient strategies pursued by armed groups and other actors operating within these entities, as well as those 'complex economic incentives' (ibid.: 524) which sustained conflict and subsequently enabled state-building and a political economy of de facto independence to emerge in the cases of Nagorno Karabakh, Transnistria, Abkhazia, and South Ossetia.

Again viewing events in post-Soviet space, but with a more prescriptive tone, Dov Lynch's book *Engaging Eurasia's Separatist States* (2004a) used the terms 'separatist state' and 'de facto state' interchangeably to explore a wide range of existential problems concerning post-Soviet unrecognized states, the conflicts from which they emerged, and future dialogue these entities could have with international society.[10] In the same year, the concept of the de facto state was re-internationalized with a greater level of generality in the co-edited work by Bahcheli, Bartmann, and Srebrnik entitled *De Facto States: The Quest for Sovereignty* (2004). This volume presented a diverse range of case material and forwarded a world view comprised of 'distinct nationalities and, as such, "states in waiting"' (ibid.: 246).[11] With the experience of the emergence of new states in the space previously occupied by the Soviet Union, and the collapse of the former Yugoslavia still very much in the minds of many, this world view of 'states in waiting' fitted neatly with the patterns and processes that had become, if not commonplace, then relatively unsurprising when they emerged. With the bulk of literary output during this period emphasizing the existence of unrecognized 'states in waiting' or separatist 'states in all but name', a particularly abstract state-centric narrative of self-determination – one in which the creation of new states by ethno-nationalists took centre stage – was promoted, despite the problematic praxis accompanying this new conceptual formula for state creation. Whilst many secessionist movements and impulses exist, as far as establishing states is concerned, very few ethno-national secessionist movements (and interest groups within these movements) succeed in fully rolling back the sovereign space(s) occupied by the international legal entity within which they reside to create new, *de jure* sovereign homelands or fully recognized states. Indeed, the argument that most new states formed over the past thirty years have been the byproduct of fragmentation and wider processes of territorial revision in the international system rather than secession (Hechter 1992: 279–80) remains persuasive, irrespective of the momentum that had built behind the 'states in all but name' approach.

This gap between how the problem of unrecognized states was viewed, particularly with reference to the trajectory they would take, as compared with empirical evidence that tended to suggest something quite different, was indicative of a deeper set of definitional problems that had begun to obfuscate the field. The study of unrecognized states had developed in a largely ad hoc manner, jumping from case study to case study, without having developed a terminological consensus aimed at filtering (or standardizing) the widely swinging meanings and nuanced usages which were emerging in the literature. Indeed, the problem was deeper than simply over-utilizing a range of terms inaccurately. The conceptualism contained in the literature seems to progressively work away from standard designations, resulting in a level of terminological confusion which persists to the present. Whether it was a result of reflective disciplinary distance or the absence of discussion and debate between practitioners engaged in the study of unrecognized states, by 2005 a plethora of terms were circulating within the literature. Kolstø's article 'The Sustainability and Future of Unrecognized Quasi-States' (2006) cleverly embodies a concerted attempt at tackling this conundrum. Kolstø argued that the term 'quasi-states', previously used by Jackson (1990) to describe *recognized* states which had failed to develop the necessary infrastructural capacity to function as states yet possess external recognition, should be reserved as a designation for unrecognized, de facto states, given the term's usage to describe 'less-than-real statehood' in other literature. His analysis included the proposition that 'if any of the unrecognized quasi-states of today's world should succeed in achieving international recognition, most of them will end up not as "normal" or fully fledged states but instead transmute into recognized quasi-states of the Jacksonian variety' (Kolstø 2006: 723–5).

This attempt to tackle the terminological confusion which developed in the study of unrecognized states defiantly balanced the numerous existing terms used to describe these phenomena by figuring the projection of an uncertain future for 'quasi-states' in the appropriated idiom of an existence lacking international recognition. Despite Kolstø's strong argument for clarification, the proliferation of terminology and new conceptual schema remains a distinct possibility, if not a necessity, given the preferences of authorship and evolving realities in international politics, and by dint of fresh approaches emerging in relevant fields of study and academic disciplines. In their location at the margins of the international system, unrecognized states continue to wilfully defy attempts at standardization and categorization in a manner which reinforces their contemporary significance to our understanding of the praxis of secession and state creation.

Causal dynamics

Dynamics of secession remain fundamentally tied to the study of unrecognized states, with secession usually being seen as the objective of the national movement opposed to a continued existence within the legal sovereign state, accompanied by political elites riding the wave of nationalism for their own political purposes. Whether this is an appropriate set of assumptions to make is an interesting question to ask – as it could be argued that many post-modern unrecognized states often find the ambiguous political and economic space provided by their anomalous status to be more attractive than the often highly romanticized option (if it is an option) of independent statehood. Yet secession is placed centre stage by many would-be theorists of unrecognized states, and this presents problems.

One of these problems is that the concept of secession is often instrumentalized; another is that it is often a problematic and inadequate causal explanation for the long-term predicaments experienced by unrecognized states. For example, incorporated into the definition of the de facto state was the requirement for the political object to be rationalized as a 'secessionist entity' (Pegg 1998). The problem then is that the object in focus is theorized as a secessionist entity at the same time as being considered as some form of state or state-like construct within pre-existing sovereign space(s). But one does not necessarily beget the other. To define a political entity in this way tethers the concept to a dynamic which:

- may not reflect the expedient strategies pursued by interest groups in unrecognized states over the long-term; and

- instrumentalizes secession as an enduring feature of political existence (albeit de facto independent and unrecognized), creating a theoretically abstract entity which perpetually secedes in theory but may not do so in practice.

Secession is, therefore, a particularly tricky and potentially misleading dynamic to incorporate into designations referring to unrecognized states because conflicts which once contained a powerful secessionist impulse can, as the cases of some unrecognized states attest, ossify into permanent de facto independence or autonomous federal existence just as easily as they can reinforce the power of the parent state and facilitate other outcomes, such as gradual reabsorption. Consider the Kurdistan Region of Iraq, for example, a region that is commonly described as 'secessionist', yet was the leading force in the creation of a federal constitution, legalizing the place of the Kurdistan Region within it.[12] Much also depends on the economic and political strength of the parent state, the presence of an external patron (Kolstø 2006: 737), structural limitations and institutional experimentation by the parent state/federation with federal designs to accommodate ethnic and territorial diversity (Hughes 2001: 61), and the ability of the secessionist movement to overcome problems of group sentiment, loyalty, regional group identification, and regional collective action (Mayall 1992; Hechter 1992: 269–75). Furthermore, secession rarely happens. The international system favours the interests of sovereign states and is regulated in such a way that relatively few secession movements ever succeed in gaining de facto independence.[13] Those which have formed unrecognized states have clearly made a transition to a political existence which is as different from secession as it is from *de jure* sovereignty. Hence the inclusion of secession as a dynamic may not only be confusing, it may also serve to limit the cases from which wider generalizations can be made and subsequent theorizing may enjoy heightened explanatory value.

Secession, as a causal dynamic facilitating the formation of unrecognized states, is arguably more significant when understood as a phase in the creation of de facto independence when combined with processes of fragmentation and rupture in the fabric of the state system itself. In effect, secession should be factored into analyses of failures of the international system of sovereign states, with it then being a product of this failure, rather than as a bottom-up dynamic of forced territorial attenuation of states, resulting in a secessionist movement achieving its aims.[14] This is because secession, for secessionist movements, is very difficult to achieve as they have to contend with opposition from not only the legally sovereign parent state itself but, more often than not, the international state system of which the former is a constituent. On its own, secession is not necessarily feasible if the parent states and political structures to which the movement agitates against have a proportional strength which favours the longevity and contiguity of nationally bounded sovereign space. The wars of Soviet succession (King 2001: 525), the Kurdish insurgencies against the government of Iraq (Stansfield 2003), and the conflict between Somalia and Somaliland are all examples of conflicts which, in the 1990s, resulted in the creation of de facto independent territories. It is arguably the case that state weakness and instability in the parent unions and sovereign arrangements both paved the way for conflict and provided the necessary openings for secessionist movements to secure territory and engage in processes of separation – the formation of new political institutions, identities, ideologies, and methodologies of state-building – rather than the secessionist movement itself taking the risk of making the first move and being represented as a belligerent force.

The ability for secession movements to create new states should therefore not be taken for granted or separated from the expedient role which state failure, rupture, and fragmentation plays in enhancing the formation of unrecognized states. The historical continuum of territorial revision in the international system is noted as having had four phases, or 'waves', with each wave being distinctly broad in geographic scale:

- in Latin America in the nineteenth century;
- in Europe after World War I (1914–1918);
- in Asia, Africa, the Caribbean, and the Pacific after World War II (1939–1945); and
- in Eastern and Central Europe after the break-up of the Soviet Union (1989) (Guibernau 2000: 28).

This continuum of territorial revision is predominantly marked by the collapse of imperial structures, but importantly the inclusion of the Soviet Union's collapse introduces the breakdown of 'hegemonic system[s] of economic and political influence' into this nexus of fragmentation and fracture in the international system (Guibernau 2000). Events such as the collapse of the Soviet Union's multinational hegemonic structures and the crisis which unfolded in the Balkans during the 1990s, or the temporary collapse of the Ba'thist state in Iraq in 1991, underscore the historical contingency of geopolitical failure which allows secessionist parties to form in regions which had once been effectively controlled by the centre. These historical examples demonstrate the existence of geopolitical forces which enable secession and promote the fragmentation of states (Hechter 1992: 276–9). Hence, the global map of nations is heavily populated by secessionist movements whose desires for self-determination have remained in a state of abeyance for decades, in some cases centuries, due to their inability to challenge the status quo, given that secession constitutes a standing challenge to an international order based on the sovereign state (Guibernau 2000). All things being equal, the aforementioned wars of self-determination which occurred during the 1990s reveal just how much the fate of secession movements (who seek to create independent states rather than regimes of autonomy) is tied to the latent stability of nationally bounded sovereign space, and the ability of that sovereign space to withstand fragmentary pressures from within, rather than any notion of secession movements possessing the ability to determine the creation of new political entities without consideration of the wider geopolitical and global forces arrayed in opposition to them.

Given the significantly small incidences of state creation through secession since the early 1990s, the question of unrecognized states as a metaphorical tool for describing a range of processes and phases of ethno-political mobilization comes to the fore. The historical case of Iraqi Kurdistan provides many insights into the problems of prescriptive analysis and the designation of conceptual features of statehood to unstable political scenarios of the type often encountered in unrecognized states. Between 1961 and the present, a wide array of Kurdish political systems have theoretically operated in the northernmost provinces of the Iraqi state. This range of political systems presents us with a continuum which challenges the unitary notion of the 'secessionist entity' as conceptually fixed, thereby bringing many of the values and properties associated with the contemporary image of the unrecognized state into critical focus. It can be argued that, since the early 1960s, the predominantly ethnic Kurdish areas of northern Iraq represented, at one time or another, an insurgent state (as defined by McColl 1969; Rich and Stubbs (eds) 1997), an autonomous region (McDowall 1996; Stansfield 2003), an insurgent state/proxy (Dunér 1981), and, from the 1990s onwards, a range of state-like forms such as a de facto state, de facto *states* (due to the division of the Kurdistan Region of Iraq following civil war), an unrecognized state, a 'recognized unrecognized' state, as well as a regional state of federal Iraq (2005–). Furthermore, the extent to which the autonomy regimes which have existed in Iraqi Kurdistan can be described as overtly secessionist is also highly debatable, given the numerous pitfalls which territorial revision in this case could engender, even though a common view exists in the media and in academic literature that the Iraqi Kurds are irreconcilably tied to a secessionist agenda. The Kurdish example is, in fact, a useful case study in not taking nationalist rhetoric focused upon independence at face value.[15] As stated by Meadwell (1999) '[r]hetorical moves are an integral part of the political game set in motion by a claim to independence, and the languages of justification – including the language of rights – can have causal force'. This 'causal force' of rhetoric, emanating from all sides of these disputes, largely accounts for the perfunctory perception of unrecognized states and the low appetite for state creation through secession exhibited by the international community.

So, unrecognized states may not be so closely tied to secessionist tendencies beyond mere rhetoric. As controversial as it may seem, they may also not be as independent from other international legal sovereign states as is often supposed. Evidence suggests that similarly elastic and counterintuitive developmental and political trends can be charted in those post-Soviet unrecognized states which emerged in Eurasia and the Caucasus during the 1990s (notably Abkhazia, Transnistria, and South Ossetia). Recent analysis of political developments in these de facto independent entities, which have long been regarded in the literature as de facto states and unrecognized states, highlights that, far from being de facto independent, they have instead significantly outsourced (or have had outsourced for them) high levels of independence and administrative autonomy to Russia through the securitization of their borders by Russian peacekeepers, the use of the Russian rouble as an official currency (Abkhazia, South Ossetia), the outsourcing of governmental functions to Russia (South Ossetia),[16] and the politics of recognition by Russia, which, it has been argued, not only contributes to their continued isolation in the international system but increases levels of reliance and dependency on their former parent state, thereby rendering them 'de facto Russian regions' (Popescu 2006b). At the conceptual level, there is a growing need to acknowledge tendencies within territories described as unrecognized states that challenge the continued designation of them as states – an arrangement which increasingly appears excessive to the basic needs of autonomy, security, and survival encountered in most cases.

There are, then, problems with generalizing the manifold experiences of unrecognized states. Yet it is still possible to do so, to a degree. The political trajectory of many unrecognized states, for example, can be plotted on a continuum which originates with geopolitical contingencies and openings for territorial revision, allowing for the pursuit of independent statehood through secession, but which later solidifies into long-term de facto independence and outcomes of autonomy which remain distant from any legal recognition of independent status in international law. In practical terms, autonomy and the maintenance of de facto independence under other arrangements (such as federal agreements) represents the optimal outcome for many of these territories, given the low probability of ascent to statehood in the majority of cases. This may signify a rejection of the commodity status of statehood in favour of more rational preferences, which, in turn, would indicate a radical move away from notions of these entities pursuing isolated secessionist existences as unrecognized states. To think of unrecognized states primarily in terms of a unique secessionist object marginalized in the international system, is to further isolate them from the dynamic relational, political, geopolitical, and economic interplay without which they could not exist. Whilst the conceptual and terminological usefulness of the designation 'unrecognized state' is clear, its metaphorical properties should be balanced against the potential for realistic political transformations in cases where the political movements themselves have opted for limited autonomy and functional de facto independence as a means of regulating drawn out, territorially antagonistic disputes and negotiations where a more equitable solution lies in compromise, allowing for experimentation with nascent and regionally appropriate alternatives to sovereign statehood.[17] In the next section, we explore how political economic factors, particularly trade in and strategic access to resources, play an often critical role in shaping the emergence and subsequent political development of unrecognized states in a globalized international system.

Rethinking the international presence of unrecognized states

The continuum of international integration and the needs of the market

So far the argument has been presented that unrecognized states have been understood through a range of related causal dynamics surrounding secession which, until now, have determined the designations and terminologies used to define the political entities in question. The task remains, however, of finding new conceptual means by which to understand the outcomes other than statehood which challenge existing notions of these entities as unrecognized 'states in waiting' or separatist 'states in all but name' – designations which place considerable emphasis upon nascent statehood which, more often than not, remains in a state of perpetual abeyance. The analytical problems involved in rethinking paradigms of territorial revision associated with unrecognized states are considerable given the disciplinary and scholastic preference to rationalize the territorial autonomy of ethno-nationalist movements as evidence of nation- and state-building which, by default, must somehow be related to a determined push for *de jure* sovereignty. The problem with this depiction of the ethno-politics of unrecognized states is that it tethers abstractions of a legitimacy deficit in international law, and a peripheral existence in the international system, to more tangible processes of autonomy and de facto independence which do not require the ornamentation of independent statehood for their sustenance.[18]

In this section, the relationship between unrecognized states and the international system in which they exist will be examined in terms of compound factors which allow these entities to function and transform without any recognition of *de jure* sovereignty – a goal which has long been posited as their peak ambition. We follow the argument made by King (2001: 552) that 'seeing ethnoterritorial confrontations as a security problem can blind researchers to the deep political and economic incentives that sustain disputes and fossilize networks of war into institutions of de facto states' and frame the question of unrecognized states against the political economy of global resource trade and the needs of the market – a hitherto understudied dynamic which brings the question of unrecognized states and territorial revision by would-be secessionists into sharp focus.

It is meaningless to discuss a political entity such as an unrecognized state as though it operated in isolation, unconnected to other international dynamics and processes. Through political ties and interactions with governments and international actors, unrecognized states are often politically and economically socialized through means which reconcile abstractions of legal non-recognition with the needs of states, markets, and a range of commercial interests. Pegg raised the issue of the de facto state's impact on the global political economy, arguing that, although generally modest, business is done with these entities:[19]

> Charles Taylor's 'Greater Liberia' was France's third-largest source of tropical timber. Taylor earned an estimated US$8–10 million a month from a consortium of North American, European, and Japanese companies interested in extracting diamonds, gold, iron ore, timber, and rubber from the areas he controlled. Taylor's forces also allegedly reached an agreement with Firestone to cooperate in rubber production and marketing. The Khmer Rouge in Cambodia and UNITA in Angola are two other examples of non-sovereign groups exercising effective territorial control which have been able to finance their operations through the sale of mineral resources they

> control – diamonds in UNITA's case and an assortment of gems and hardwood forest products for the Khmer Rouge.
>
> (Pegg 1998: 3)

When factoring unrecognized states into international relations and the global political economy, there is a tendency to situate strategic issues of trade and the politics of natural resources as an adjunct to issues of state-building, conflict resolution, and status. Though general economic and more specific resource questions are deeply interwoven into the international relations of unrecognized states, they are rarely approached as a unique geo-economic paradigm. For example, unrecognized states in the Caucasus are situated at the heart of the complex geopolitics of oil in the Caspian basin, where cases such as Nagorno Karabakh have influenced international negotiations concerning pipeline routes, US foreign policy in the Caucasus, and the commercial strategies of oil companies operating in the region (Garcelon *et al.* 1998). The geopolitics of oil is also a major factor in the case of Iraqi Kurdistan. The de facto independent provinces which make up the Kurdish unrecognized state are situated alongside sites of immense hydrocarbon wealth, including the undeveloped oilfields in the Kurdish region, and those surrounding the town of Kurkuk – a place outside the Kurdish region but which remains the site of long-standing ethno-political tension between Arabs and Kurds in Iraqi politics (see Anderson and Stansfield 2009). The Kurdistan region, in its current borders, possesses five oilfields (estimated to contain 3.1 billion barrels) and two large gas fields in Suleymaniya province – assets vital to the economic future of the unrecognized state and the political options available to actors within it, and a focus for tense future negotiations between the Kurdistan Regional Government (KRG) and the government of Iraq.

The geo-economic paradigm of resources which surrounds unrecognized states and state-building through dynamics of secession, conflict, and de facto independence can be extended to the case of Kosovo and territorial revision in the former Yugoslavia. Concentrations of mineral wealth in the Trepča mining complex (located in the Kosovska Mitrovica municipality of northern Kosovo) were historically a key asset of both socialist Yugoslavia and the Milosevic regime, with mines in this region yielding highly valuable commodities, such as zinc, lead, magnesium, nickel, and a range of precious metals, as well as coal (Rogel 2003: 172).[20] Described as 'the most valuable piece of real estate in the Balkans' (Hedges 1998), the presence of such incredible mineral wealth at the heart of the Albanian Kosovar push for self-determination, and the creation of an independent state, is seldom acknowledged. The importance of this, and other cases, is that they introduce a political economy of resource conflict and expediency to examples of secession, separatism, self-determination, autonomous government, and de facto independence, which has significant implications for understanding how secession movements, which achieve physical autonomy and independence from their parent states, are subsequently socialized into the global political economy and the wider international society of states. Historically, the linkage between resources, conflict, and secession is well documented:

> Rather than resulting from the greed of rebels, as emphasized by recent literatures, the existence of natural resources may be an incentive for third parties – states and corporations – to engage in or indeed foster civil conflicts. Hence, for example, the escalation of the civil war in the Democratic Republic of Congo has resulted in part from the involvement of neighboring states seeking raw materials. The secessionist bid in Katanga in Congo was supported if not instigated by the Belgian firm Union Minière du Haut Katanga. And evidence suggests that the French oil corporation Elf took actions that led to an escalation of the conflict in the Republic of Congo.
>
> (Humphreys 2005: 511)

Where commercially significant resources exist, either in or around unrecognized states, the presence of this geo-economic dynamic represents an important issue for policymakers and central governments across the globe, especially those concerned with issues of foreign policy, conflict resolution, regional security, risk, and global trade. Foreign support for separatist movements and the policies of neighbouring states exert a direct influence on the duration of conflicts through the levels of logistical support given to insurgent groups, and the facilitation of mediation depending on the 'optimal benefits they can expect to achieve during wartime relative to those they could gain in a negotiated settlement, a feature that can often depend on the resource endowments of their neighbors' (Humpreys 2005: 517). Conflicts and disputes surrounding unrecognized states are no different. The dynamic of dependence on an external patron (exhibited in many cases) strengthens the governments of unrecognized states and gives crucially important support, which increases the survival chances of the de facto independent territory dramatically (Kolstø 2006: 733–4).

Conceptually, resource conflict and subsequent trade plays a significant role in determining the future feasibility and ability of secession movements to strike out on their own and create de facto independence and control over a defined territory. The ecology of unrecognized states in the international system is greatly influenced by variables of (1) strategic importance, and (2) resource importance. The capacity for part recognition (recognition by one or more central governments) without international legal consensus on status, such as in the cases of Taiwan, Kosovo, the Turkish Republic of Northern Cyprus, South Ossetia, and Abkhazia, gives unrecognized states a self-installed geopolitical (and geo-economic) importance in the international system, which is reinforced through strategic location and the presence of resources. However, the importance of resources should not be overstated in political terms as the experience of many unrecognized states proves that resource wealth alone is often a weak basis for presenting political demands. The case of the Karabakh conflict proves that resource politics (in this case, pipeline routing and oil transportation) neither builds peace nor brings states on either side of the dispute to the negotiating table (Garcelon *et al.* 1998). Iraqi Kurdistan's attempts at forging a decentralized oil regulation system has created a difficult political position for the KRG, with disputes over resource legislation helping to 'awaken the sleeping giant of Iraqi nationalism' and foster the creation of a nationalist bloc in the Iraqi parliament to oppose the passage of hydrocarbon legislation which favours Kurdish interests in the north (Khalil 2009: 1).

Conclusion: the relevance of the natural resource factor

Whilst the international community remains cautious of the issue of resource expediency in unrecognized states and separatist regions, the interests of secessionists and autonomy movements often presuppose economic self-sufficiency through access to revenue generating resources over which central governments have de facto control. In this way, the question of resources becomes a key site of contestation, not only at the point of political mobilization for a secessionist agenda, but also in terms of the mapping of future independence. Independence movements in Alaska, East Turkestan, Caucasus/Eurasia, Kurdistan, and Kosovo are all examples of zones of contestation where sovereignty over natural wealth plays a considerable role in shaping the agendas and policies of central governments and the demands of independence movements alike. Calls for greater rights of self-determination by national minorities and distinct ethnic groups is often accompanied by a key awareness, on both sides of the issue, of territorially specific questions, such as access to natural resources. Whereas natural resources can be a factor for empowering the independence and secessionist aspirations of regional and ethnic groups, when physical de facto independence is attained through conflict and territorial revision, the attention of policymakers is inevitably drawn to the fact that unrecognized states alter the boundaries of regional trade and usher in political dynamics, which cannot necessarily be countermanded by their sovereign parent states and the contributions of international negotiators. To this extent, unrecognized states often make geopolitical history by exploiting regional stalemate over territorial revision alongside the needs of 'an impatient international community looking for any symbol of "progress", regardless of whether it actually contributes to resolution of the dispute' (King 2001: 549).

The importance of natural resources in such a scenario is that they can reinforce the organic, bottom-up desire for independent statehood and increase the requirement for unrecognized states to be factored into international relations as not only a regional security issue but also a distinct geo-economic paradigm of territorial autonomy; one which is increasingly of high geopolitical and strategic importance for central governments and the twenty-first century global economy as a whole.

Notes

1 In the words of Dominik Zaum:

> As Sovereignty is an institution comprising several sometimes conflicting norms, and is associated with a basket of properties such as territory, population, autonomy, authority, control, and recognition, it is a contested concept, with both legal and political attributes. Because of the apparent complexity of sovereignty, it is

difficult to provide a definition that is sufficiently broad to encompass all its different meanings, yet specific enough to be analytically useful.

From D. Zaum, *The Sovereignty Paradox* (New York: Oxford University Press, 2007), p. 28.

2 For analysis of states which possess only *external* or *negative* sovereignty, see Robert Jackson, *Quasi-States: Sovereignty, International Relations and the Third World* (Cambridge: Cambridge University Press, 1990). Many related works on *quasi-states* focus on post-colonial Africa. For instance, A.G. Hopkins, 'Quasi-States, Weak States and the Partition of Africa', *Review of International Studies*, 26, 2000, pp. 311–20; and A.J. Christopher, '"Nation-states", "quasi-states", and "collapsed-states" in contemporary Africa', *GeoJournal*, 43, September 1997, pp. 91–7. Jackson's usage of the term *quasi-state* was subsequently refigured in Kolstø (2006).

3 On the problematic dimensions of Westphalian conceptions of sovereignty, see, for instance, Darel E. Paul, 'Sovereignty, Survival and the Westphalian Blind Alley in International Relations', *Review of International Studies*, 25, 1999, pp. 217–31; K. Burch, 'Changing the Rules: Reconceiving Change in the Westphalian System', *International Studies Review*, 2:2, 2000, pp. 181–210; A. Claire Cutler, 'Critical Reflections on the Westphalian Assumptions of International Law and Organization: a Crisis of Legitimacy', *Review of International Studies*, 27, 2001, pp. 133–50; and Andreas Osiander, 'Sovereignty, International Relations, and the Westphalian Myth', *International Organization*, 55:2, Spring 2001, pp. 251–87.

4 For a rare analysis of an unrecognized state's internal situation from a human security perspective, see Félix Buttin, 'A Human Security Perspective on Transnistria – Reassessing the Situation Within the "Black Hole of Europe"', *Revue de la Sécurité Humaine/Human Security Journal*, 3, February 2007, pp. 13–28.

5 See Kolstø (2006), pp. 733–7.

6 An example of such a framework for international support was the 'standards before status' policy initiated for Kosovo by the United Nations in 2002. See U.N. SCOR, 57th Session, 4528th Meeting, 24th April 2002; and UNMIK, 'Standards for Kosovo', Pristina, 10th December 2003, www.unmikonline.org/standards/docs/leaflet_stand_eng.pdf (accessed 7th June 2010).

7 In an effort to avoid confusion, the term 'de facto independent' is used throughout this chapter to denote the exercising of domestic sovereignty, territorial security, autonomous governance, and related attributes of independence, alongside an absence of legal recognition from other nations and institutions within international society.

8 As noted in Kolstø (2006) and Kolstø and Blakkisrud (2008).

9 Examples of unrecognized states which still exist in territory once occupied by the Soviet Union are Transnistria/Pridnestrovskaya Moldovskaya Republika (PMR) in Moldova, the Republic of Nagorno Karabakh (NKR) in Azerbaijan, and the Republic of Abkhazia and the Republic of South Ossetia in Georgia.

10 As Lynch (2004a: 141–3) argues, the Eurasian unrecognized states will 'hold out as long as they can' provided the status quo of non-recognition favours the maintenance of de facto independence. In this context, Lynch argued that the international community should set aside the ineffectual and 'piecemeal' policies of the past in favour of conflict resolution strategies which create 'a new logic on the ground that addresses the dynamic processes driving the self-declared states'. In addition, the warning is also given that '[t]he conflicts will not resolve themselves, and the de facto states will not disappear of their own volition', echoing Edward Walker's conclusion that secessionist wars 'do not end easily' and more often than not attrition, impasse, a lack of trust on both sides, and an absence of progress at the negotiating table are all factors which lend themselves to a 'no peace, no war' scenario surrounding unrecognized states; see Walker (1998).

11 Case studies within this collection include the Republika Srpska; relations between

Montenegro and Serbia; Albanian and Serb rivalry in Kosovo; the political development of Transnistria; Chechnya; Abkhazia; the Turkish republic of Northern Cyprus; Palestine; Somaliland; and Bougainville.

12 For a more detailed discussion of the role of Kurdish politicians and political parties in contemporary Iraqi politics, see, for example, Gareth Stansfield, *Iraq* (Cambridge: Polity, 2007); Reider Visser and Gareth Stansfield (eds), *An Iraq of Its Regions: Cornerstones of a Federal Democracy?* (London: Hurst, 2007).

13 Hechter (1992: 278) contends that geopolitical factors may inhibit secession given the multinational makeup of most states and the fact that many states contain potential secessionist movements. This fact, he argues, provides an incentive for a universal discouragement of secession given that 'the net benefit to be gained by courting secessionists tends to be negative' except when expedient in times of war.

14 Indeed the opposite may also be applicable. The concept of 'central secession' or 'secessionism by the centre' has been proposed by Conversi, who argues that political literature customarily defines secession as a movement developing in the periphery against the centre, whereas the possibility exists that secession may actually be propelled by the centre in certain cases. For further discussion of centrally propelled secession, see Daniele Conversi, 'Central Secession: Towards a New Analytical Concept? The Case of the Former Yugoslavia', *Journal of Ethnic and Migration Studies*, 26:2, April 2000, pp. 333–55.

15 For a general overview of the history, politics, and complex geopolitics of Iraqi Kurdistan, see Carl Dahlman, 'The Political Geography of Kurdistan', *Eurasian Geography and Economics*, 43:4, 2002, pp. 271–99.

16 See Nicu Popescu, '"Outsourcing" de facto Statehood – Russia and the Secessionist Entities in Georgia and Moldova', *Centre for European Policy Studies (CEPS)*, Policy Brief, 109, July 2006.

17 For the sake of simplicity, we have confined our analysis to examples where well-defined de facto independence is completely analogous to unrecognized statehood.

18 Considered in relation to the need for long-term survival as balanced against the need for recognition from international society. It is argued that one does not necessarily beget the other, given evidentiary tributaries which suggest that some unrecognized states may have abandoned the quest for external legitimation in the face of evolving geopolitical realities, new political priorities (both internal and external), and the reduced value of legitimacy given the alternative means by which dialogue is created and business done with these entities.

19 Although it may be debatable whether the examples Pegg refers to directly fit the definition of an unrecognized state as outlined in the introduction to this collection by Caspersen and Stansfield.

20 See also Milovan Vukovic and Ari Weinstein, 'Kosovo Mining, Metallurgy, and Politics: Eight Centuries of Perspective', JOM, 54:5, 2002, pp. 21–4.

2 Complex terrains

Unrecognized states and globalization

Matan Chorev

The policy and theoretical conundrums posed by unrecognized states – territorial entities that possess many of the attributes associated with the modern nation-state but devoid of international recognition as independent sovereigns – are derivative of the broader yet fundamental questions about what James Rosenau calls the 'underlying nature of world affairs' (2002: 261). The forces of modern-day globalization have revolutionized the modes of production, communication, and conflict in ways that have elementally reshaped the contemporary system of nation-states. Power has shifted. New political spaces have emerged. Destructive forces heretofore the sole reserve of states now rest in the hands of individuals.

This seemingly dramatic restructuring of global politics is not unique to the modern era. Indeed, the evolution of sovereignty makes up the central narrative thread of modern political history (see Bobbitt 2002: xxx).[1] As Rosa Ehrenteich Brooks contends, 'the idea of a territorial state as the locus of authority, within a system of formally equivalent similar states, is of recent vintage' (2005: 1169). Nevertheless, the currents of globalization and the concomitant shifts in the patterns of modern conflict have raised the consciousness of scholars and policy-makers about the fragility of the modern state and its impact on the nature of the international system. Robert Rotberg's warning is illustrative of the mainstream discourse: 'in a modern era when national states constitute the building blocks of world order, the violent disintegration and palpable weakness of selected African, Asian, Oceanic, and Latin American states threaten the very foundation of that system' (1996: 2).[2]

The 11 September 2001 al-Qaeda attacks on the United States raised the threat of weak and failing states to a top-tier national security issue. The 2002 United States *National Security Strategy* states that 'weak states … can pose as great a danger to our national interests as strong states' (National Security Strategy of the United States 2002: iv).[3] Nine years after the 9/11 al-Qaeda attack, the US and its allies remain consumed by the threat emanating from the group's safe haven in the ungoverned tribal frontier straddling Afghanistan and Pakistan.[4]

The stark bipolarity of 'strong' and 'weak' states, however, is misleading. As the phenomenon of unrecognized states demonstrates, the central geostrategic fault-lines in today's world run through murky waters of contested sovereignties that do not fit neatly on the state strength continuum. In spite of the emergence of new and distinct socio-political cartographies, much of the academic discourse remains plagued by the deeply entrenched 'conceptual jails' (Rosenau 2006: 22) of political science, encumbered by a 'territorial trap' (Agnew and Corbridge 1995: 79) and, in John Ruggie's words, 'reposed in deep Newtonian slumber' (1998: 194).

The scant attention to the phenomenon of unrecognized states is emblematic of this hidebound approach. Yet, as will be demonstrated, even within the unrecognized state literature, scholars operate largely within the 'state in-all-but name' construct. This chapter seeks to redress this shortcoming by highlighting the divergent impacts of globalization's underpinnings on the emergence, survival, and viability of unrecognized states. It will argue that the 'logic' of unrecognized states as well as their internal dynamics and statecraft are a consequence of, or at least amplified by, globalization, and will demonstrate that a failure to account for this 'logic' imperils policy mitigation approaches.

Globalization and 'the state of the state'

Scholars have tied the transformation of the 'state' as the fundamental unit of global politics to the determined forces of 'globalization.' However, as numerous and diverse as the definitions of 'state' are (in his 1981 article in *Political Theory*, David Easton identified over 140 definitions for the term (1981: 307)), the seemingly infinite conceptions of 'globalization' have nearly rendered the term meaningless.[5]

To pierce through the conceptual fog, Robert O. Keohane and Joseph S. Nye offer a helpful distinction between globalism as a 'phenomenon,' and globalization as a 'process':

> Globalism is a state of the world involving networks of interdependence at multicontinental distances. These networks can be linked through flows and influences of capital and goods, information and ideas, people and force, as well as environmentally and biologically related substances ... Globalization and deglobalization refer to the increase or decline of globalism.
>
> (Keohane and Nye 2000: 2)

At its most rudimentary, the process of globalization is composed of two layers. The first describes an increase in networked interdependence linked through flows, or what David Held *et al.* characterize as 'the enmeshment of national and societal systems in wider global processes' (1999: 27–8). The second layer highlights the rapid reconfiguration of political space that transcends official sociopolitical demarcations, where '"local," "national," or even "continental" political, social, and economic space is re-formed such that it is no longer necessarily conterminous with established legal and territorial boundaries' (ibid.). The two layers of this phenomenon result in 'increased density of networks, increased "institutional velocity," and increased transnational participation' (Keohane and Nye 2000: 7).

Manuel Castells' concept of the 'network society' describes this social structure. He argues that the emergence of the network society was driven by the revolution in information and communication technologies, the 'crisis and restructuring of industrialism and its two modes of production, capitalism and statism,' and the political and social movements of the 1960s and 1970s.[6] This society is 'constructed around flows' of capital, information, technology, organizational interaction, images, sounds, and symbols. In a networked society, the 'power of flows takes precedence over the flows of power. Presence or absence in the network and the dynamics of each network vis-à-vis others are critical sources of domination and change in our society' (Castells 2000: 501).[7] Therefore, Castells argues that the central analytic lens for analyzing global politics should no longer be premised on the rigid territoriality of the state system but rather on the 'spatial form' that characterizes modern-day social practices (2000: 441–2).

Keohane and Nye concur with the view that the state may be in 'retreat' (Strange 1996). 'The "image of the state,"' they argue, 'may become increasingly misleading as agencies of states are linked in networks to private and third sector actors. Transgovernmental networks will become more important, as will transnational relations of all kinds' (Keohane and Nye 2000: 19). This 'power shift' (Mathews 1997) has resulted in what Saskia Sasses describes as 'a new institutional spatio-temporal order' (Ferguson and Jones 2002: 14) and Held *et al.* describe as a 'deterritorialization and reterritorialization of socio-economic and political space' (1999: 27). Rosenau takes it even further in his conception of the world as a 'globalized space – a space that is not disaggregated in terms of specific geographic territories so much as it consists of a wide range of fast-moving, boundary-spanning actors whose activities cascade erratically across amorphous ethnoscapes, mediascapes, ideoscapes, technoscapes, and financescapes' (2002: 263).[8]

The impact of this de-territorialization and democratization of global communications is far from unidirectional. As Castells emphasizes, 'The relationship between the space of flows and the space of places, between simultaneous globalization and localization, are not predetermined in their outcomes' (2004: 458). Rosenau argues that these drivers often act in opposition:

> The dynamics of globalization, taken together, contend that the new, post-Cold War arrangements have lessened the role of the state, that a central feature of the arrangements is a continuing disaggregation of authority in all parts of the world and all walks of life, and that consequently the salience of local phenomena has been heightened. Put differently, the global-local nexus underlies tensions between worldwide forces pressing for integration and those fostering fragmentation, an interaction that I have sought to capture in a label ('fragmegration') that combines the two forces.
>
> (2006: 2)[9]

These forces have fueled not only a 'crisis of the nation-state and the explosion of nationalisms' (Castells 2000: 306)[10] but a broader legitimacy crisis of the modern state, accelerating the proliferation of alternative spheres of authority on the international domain through intergovernmental institutions as well as in the sub-domestic sphere through fragmentation to more local collectivities – a world where Doha Rounds, Swat Valleys, and unrecognized states co-exist.

Understanding unrecognized states

Article I of the 1933 Montevideo Convention on Rights and Duties of States lays out four basic qualifications the state must possess – a permanent population, defined territory, government, and a capacity to enter into relations with other states. This definition applies to a host of entities, from neutralized states to vassal states and trusteeships. All of these, and many other state forms, possess degrees of international legitimacy, if not full sovereignty (Hannum 1996: 16). This is why J.P. Nettl's conception of 'the state' as a conceptual variable as opposed to a generic unit of analysis is apposite. This approach allows for:

> a more discriminating theory of the state, one that treats politics not as either states or nonstates but as merely more or less statelike – in other words, in which the question is not 'to be [a state] or not to be,' but to have more (of 'stateness') or less of a certain political structure and concomitant logic of political behavior.
>
> (Ben-Dor 1988: 83)

Some states that fall short of virtually all performance-based criteria of internal legitimacy retain their international recognition, or 'juridical statehood' as equal sovereigns (external legitimacy). These 'quasi-states' possess only 'negative sovereignty' (Jackson 1987: 529). In other words, they hold to their legal protections from intervention and interference but lack the capacity or will to provide the services and resources its citizens demand of it. Today, these are commonly called failing states.

In contrast, some entities can demonstrate the fulfillment of the four features of Montevideo but lack the international personality of quasi-states. These are called de facto or 'unrecognized states' (Pegg 1998: 4). As Scott Pegg explains, 'The quasi-state is legitimate no matter how ineffective it is. Conversely, the de facto state is illegitimate no matter how effective it is' (ibid.: 5).[11]

For Robert Jackson and Pegg, both the quasi and the unrecognized state derive their existence from the outcome of the decolonization process. Territories that, on their surface, lacked the basic attributes articulated by Montevideo were granted wholesale legitimacy and protection from foreign interference. Their legitimacy, in other words, was not derived from their ability to govern effectively, but instead from a perceived just outcome of a struggle against foreign domination and predation. Conversely, many entities that could provide these basic requirements for statehood, but that were otherwise losers in the dramatic cartographic reshuffling of the post-colonial period, were deprived recognition as sovereign states because of the normative bias against further dismemberment of existing borders. As Pegg explains, 'International norms which support existing quasi-states also deny the legitimacy of any would-be challengers' (1998: 5). Similarly, Pål Kolstø contends that 'the community of recognized states has thus, in principle, been closed at both ends. While no members are thrown out, the entrance gate has been strictly guarded and new applicants are routinely turned away' (2006: 736). Richard Rosecrance *et al.* note that, although the number of states has increased substantially in the last two centuries from fifty in 1900 to about 200 today, 'international opinion and Great Power support for self-determination and creation of new states has lessened' (2006: 4–5). Samuel Huntington puts it more bluntly: 'The bias against political divorce, that is secession, is just about as strong as the nineteenth-century bias against marital divorce' (quoted in Bahcheli *et al.* 2004: xi).[12]

While Jackson's account is persuasive, it fails to place the phenomenon within the dynamics of today's globalizing world. The normative attachment to the state as the supreme unit of analysis at times has led scholars to label a proliferating reality an ongoing anomaly. What does one make of Somaliland, Nagorno Karabakh, South Ossetia, Abkhazia, Transnistria, and other territories that lack formal international personalities, yet maintain a relatively effective capacity to provide for their denizens that eclipses that of many recognized states? Are these simply 'frozen conflicts' waiting for a ripe moment to settle their disputes with the central government under which they are 'officially', if only nominally, attached to? Or are we witnessing the emergence of the new, post-modern concept of sovereignty that is both durable and permanent?

These territories are at the heart of the most strategic regions in today's security environment. They have been involved in some of the most deadly conflicts that humanity has witnessed in the last century and the possibility of future conflict over these territories remains distinct. Unfortunately, there has been a dearth of any secular examination of these territories. How do these entities function in the absence of international recognition? What impact did the dynamics of conflict and political development under such conditions have on the nature of the unrecognized state? How does its survival at the margins of the international system impact its worldview and statecraft?

Pegg's volume on unrecognized states is one of the major contributions to this rather under-researched area. He defines an unrecognized state, or in his terminology the de facto state, as one that:

> exists where there is an organized political leadership which has risen to power through some degree of indigenous capability; receives popular support; and has achieved sufficient capacity to provide governmental services to a given population in a defined territorial area, over which effective control is maintained for an extended period of time. The de facto state views itself as capable of entering into relations with other states and it seeks full constitutional independence and widespread international recognition as a sovereign state. It is, however, unable to achieve any degree of

> substantive recognition and therefore remains illegitimate in the eyes of international society.
>
> (1998: 26)

Pegg takes care to distinguish the unrecognized state from state-less entities, criminal, terrorist, or other networks, puppet states, peaceful secession movements, quasi-states, and other sovereign entities with greater international legitimacy. This leaves a description where an unrecognized state is 'a state in all but name,' seeking to govern as a 'legitimate,' democratically accountable government would. Thus, its political goal is 'sovereignty as constitutional independence.'

His definition and the ten associated dimensions of unrecognized statehood face two inter-related deficiencies.[13] First, Pegg's analysis does not take into consideration whether the 'state' making project of these entities might yield a product that is, in some important ways, different from the 'classic' state model. For example, in the absence of international recognition and facing formidable governance challenges, many of these entities engage in the kind of 'illicit' activities and behaviors akin to those of criminal networks. While Charles Tilly's seminal 1985 essay 'War Making and State Making as Organized Crime' argues that state-making, through war making and its associated resource extraction imperatives, is not all that different from the activities of organized crime, the methods of governance, by necessity if not by design, in many of these mercurial state entities, are radically different than recognized states. This carries important implications for the functioning of the state, its political and economic development, and the nature of instability emanating from it. It also could help explain the disadvantages and potential benefits of non-recognition and why these anomalies remain in protracted states of ambiguity.

Pegg's linear and somewhat deterministic 'state in all but name' approach fails to tie the unique endogenous political development process in these entities with the substantial impact of globalization's underpinnings on the capacity of unrecognized states. For example, Charles King's study of Nagorno Karabakh, Transnistria, Abkhazia, and South Ossetia – unrecognized states that have arisen in the aftermath of the Eurasian wars of the 1990s – demonstrates the 'beneficial economies of stalemate' (2001: 548). The limbo status of unrecognized states serves to satisfy the interest of several major groups. He shows how the 'basic networks, relationships, and informal channels that arose during the course of the violence, can replicate themselves in new, state-like institutions in the former conflict zones.' The impact of replication to the internal dynamics and statecraft of the unrecognized state is profound. Unfortunately, Pegg's construct leaves little room for such analysis.

Second, the manner with which Pegg deals with the question of recognition eliminates some important state-like entities from his conceptual framework. He argues that 'although the de facto state seeks widespread recognition as a sovereign state, it is unable to achieve any degree of substantive recognition' (1998: 37). The criteria for 'substantive recognition' includes recognition by the major powers of the day, a juridical state that the unrecognized state seeks to leave, neighboring countries, the United Nations General Assembly, and the invitation to participate by other global and regional international organizations. Pegg argues that Taiwan, which enjoys formal and informal relations with dozens of state, regional, and international bodies, lacks the prerequisite degree of substantive recognition, but that the post-1992 Kurdish 'safe haven' in north Iraq, which lacked any formal representation in any regional or world body, 'does appear to have secured a much greater degree of international acceptance (due to its however tenuous origins in UN Security Council 688 of 1991) than any of the de facto states discussed [in this book]' (1998: 38). This definitional requirement does not match the historical record. In fact, the United Nations went to great lengths to ensure that its efforts in north Iraq would not be construed as undermining Iraq's territorial integrity or Baghdad's administrative authority. The UN would not transition from an emergency humanitarian mission to a more sustainable, long-term development program, principally because it did not want to grant Iraqi Kurdistan the degree of acceptance Pegg assumes it received.[14]

In addition, the degree of international acceptance and engagement varies between unrecognized states and across time. The degree of legitimacy that ensues from such recognition is problematic for it is highly politicized. Some of these entities – Abkhazia, for example – are seen as weak or failing, while Kosovo, before it was granted independence in 2008, was understood in far more positive terms and enjoyed the support and expenditure of political capital by major regional and global powers. The divergent attitudes cannot be explained by secular variables alone. Thus, the standard set by Pegg is perhaps too restrictive.

Further exploration of unrecognized states must overcome the limitations of Pegg's definitional framework (see Chorev 2007). In *Shield of Achilles*, Philip Bobbitt raises the impact of the interdependence of law and strategy on the development of the modern nation-state: 'Each state develops its own constitutional order (its inward-facing profile) as well as its strategic paradigm (its outward-turned silhouette), and these two forms are logically and topologically inseparable' (2002: xxvii). Since the 'constitutional order' and the 'state-building' project of unrecognized states was undertaken under dramatically different conditions than recognized ones, it is important to avoid falling into the trap of viewing these entities as emerging modern nations, whose growth was simply stunted or unfulfilled.

The 'logic' of unrecognized states

The 'logic,' or the dynamics that sustain the ambiguous state of unrecognized states, is in large measure a consequence of, or at least amplified by, globalization. Edward Walker and King both suggest that an equilibrium of sorts has been reached between the unrecognized state leaders and the leadership of the government from which they are trying to gain autonomy.[15] Walker describes this as a 'no peace, no war impasse that keeps the national government from exercising its authority in the separatist area while preventing normalization of life for the separatists' (1998: 40). The reasons for the prolonged status quo include the notable military achievement of the separatist state, ceasefire terms favorable to them, and a shared reluctance by both sides to reach compromise on status issues. King contends that the persistence of the disputes can be explained by the benefits that both parties accrue from stalemate:

> It is a dark version of Pareto efficiency: the general welfare cannot be improved – by reaching a genuine peace accord allowing for real reintegration – without at the same time making key interest groups in both camps worse off. Even if a settlement is reached, it is unlikely to do more than recognize the basic logic and its attendant benefits.
>
> (2001: 526)

He adds to Walker's assessment a crucial factor – the centrality of the state building project in the breakaway region. These projects not only propagate a nationalist discourse across all sectors of the population but also lead to the creation of a host of institutions and associated bureaucracies and interest groups. In Iraqi Kurdistan, for example, these factors combined with the rapid emergence of the 'space of flows' to help fill the knowledge gap created by the unwillingness of the United Nations to engage in long-term development and institution building in Iraqi Kurdistan. For Mohammed Ihsan, the first minister of human rights in the Kurdisan Regional Government and currently its Minister of Extra Regional Affairs, the very existence and survival of a unrecognized state in north Iraq is a factor, first and foremost, of the revolutionary moment in history in which it was born. The end of the Cold War dramatically shifted the course of world politics in a manner that greatly facilitated the formation of a grand coalition to counter Saddam's invasion of Kuwait as well as the post-war protection of Iraq's Kurdish population. In an earlier era, 'we [the Kurds] would not have been able to rule a de facto state let alone rule a village.'[16] In particular, the role of the diaspora and the informational networks that connected it to Iraqi Kurdistan were crucial:

> Since the early 1990s influential Iraqi Kurdish diasporic communities have become engaged in transnational nationalism, exporting their nationalist ideas, skills, and financial support to their homeland. Legitimated as victims of Saddam's regime, recognized internationally in host-country systems, and free to return to the autonomous North, politicized Iraqi Kurdish communities in Europe and the United States have sponsored cultural and educational activities. They have improved research centers in Iraqi Kurdistan by donating materials for schools, libraries, and laboratories.
>
> (Natali 2005: 164)

The cumulative result has an injurious effect on any efforts to negotiate terms with the central government. The role of the central government, which is typically rather weak, and the role of external actors, which range from patronage to predatory and destabilizing activities, help explain the 'logic' of these ambiguous territorial entities' existence and perseverance.

Pål Kolstø identifies five factors that contribute to the viability of unrecognized states (or what he terms 'quasi-states') in the absence of strong state structures. First is that 'even in the absence of effective state-building, most quasi-states have succeeded reasonably well in their nation-building efforts' (2006: 730). This has been largely due to the common experience of conflict with the state from which they are trying to secede, the existence of a common external enemy, and the relative homogenous population that exists within the separatist state, or Robert McColl's 'insurgent state' (1969: 614)[17]:

> All quasi-states have adopted a state flag, a national anthem, a state coat of arms, new national holidays, and other symbolic attributes of statehood. They also build museums, erect statues, rename streets, and frequently create a cult of personality around their leader in order to inculcate in the population a sense of common past and common allegiance to the same state.
>
> (Kolstø 2006: 731)

Unrecognized states possess more than mere 'symbolic' attributes of statehood. Absence of recognition is not preclusive to their securing, for example, the revenue to sustain the statehood project. Indeed, the 'space of flows' facilitated the acquisition of knowledge and material to function in the global economy. For example, within several years of its declaration of independence, Somaliland was able to recover livestock and crop production to pre-war levels. In 1999, the volume of imports and exports in its central trading hub and economic capital was estimated to be double the pre-war figures (Edmundson 2005: 47).

Kolstø's second factor is that the unrecognized state remains a militarized society – the armed forces play a crucial role in deterring the parent state and, in turn, military leaders have become political and economic figures as well. The armed forces' access to the globalized arms market and technologies that typically would be unavailable to non-industrialized societies allows them to pose a formidable challenge.

The weakness of the parent state is a third reason for the territory's perseverance. Typically, the parent state either is too weak to retake the separatist state or fails to attract the breakaway population to return to its domain: 'Even those citizens of the quasi-state who are thoroughly disgusted with their self-proclaimed leaders have few reasons to wish for reunification with a miserable parent state' (Kolstø 2006: 733). The legitimacy crisis fueled by globalization's fragmagrative dynamics contributed to parent-state weakness that exacerbated the drivers of ambiguity. Fourth, support from an external patron increases the chances of survival by an exponential function. Finally, the role of the 'international community' is key: it either serves as an external patron or, more commonly, plays an important arbitrage role. Graham Allison argues that the globalization of information is a critical causal mechanism for the 'international community's' attention and intervention in these conflicts. As he explains, '"CNNization" allows citizens who are connected to a global television network to see for themselves events occurring almost anywhere around the world – and thus to judge that their interests are threatened or values offended' (2000: 81).[18]

The work that Rosecrance *et al.* have done on factors that facilitate or retard the emergence of new states sheds further light on the role of globalization in sustaining the status quo. Their theoretical model demonstrates that the bond between the parent-state capital and the 'dissident province' is strengthened when the dissident province's position on globalization was similar to that of the metropolitan capital and of leading international actors. Even when there are distinct cultural or ethnic differences between the regions, the 'characteristic outcome' is the one in which all three sets of actors are in favor of globalization. Furthermore, 'if the dissident province favors globalization, its independence is in a degree unnecessary' (Rosecrance 2006: 12–13). Since favoring globalization is a survival imperative, the unrecognized state must plug into the 'network of flows' from which it can sustain itself in absence of the more formal channels available to recognized states.

Dov Lynch's comprehensive comparative study of Eurasia's unrecognized states offers another framework for analysis. He asserts that, despite their individual peculiarities (largely influenced by the context of their relations with the parent state), unrecognized states share common characteristics: they remain isolated in international relations, suffer from deep internal problems and existential external threats, and are often dismissed as 'criminal strips of no-man's land or as the puppets of external states' (Lynch 2002: 832).

Lynch divides his analysis into external and the oft-ignored internal (political, ideological, military, and economic) factors (2004a: 42). He highlights three internal drivers common to the unrecognized states of Eurasia: absolute sovereignty, fear and insecurity, and subsistence syndromes. The leaders of these entities 'explicitly adhere to an empirical definition of statehood and sovereignty along the lines of the 1933 Montevideo Convention' (ibid.: 43). 'These governments maintain that recognition does not *create* a state but rather *reflects* an existing reality' (ibid.: 47). This existing reality is legitimized by popular elections and referenda and the passing of legislation and constitutional documents that 'enshrine what are seen as popular and democratic resolution on independence and sovereignty' (ibid.: 49).

Understanding this 'discourse of legitimacy' is crucial to developing a fine-grained knowledge about the internal politics of unrecognized states. In the case of Iraqi Kurdistan, the globalized discourse of human rights, democracy, and 'good governance' served to diminish, rather than amplify, Kurdish nationalism. As Natali explains, 'Instead of linking their nationalist project to socialist ideology or talking about a free Kurdistan like they did immediately after the 1990s Gulf War, Iraqi Kurdish officials have reframed their nationalist project as a democratic one' (2005: 164). Thus, the Kurdish struggle is no longer exclusively, or even primarily, 'separatist' but one that has a stake in ensuring that the

Baghdad government protects the interests of the Kurdish community in a federal and democratic Iraq.

Unrecognized states are also driven by fear and insecurity. Like King, Lynch cites Tilly's assertion that 'war and the necessity of war making were formative features of the state-making process in modern Europe. These forces play a similar role in the post-Soviet declared states' (2004a: 57). Lynch claims that the unrecognized states are racketeer states wherein the 'discourse of insecurity makes reconciliation and notions of power-sharing very difficult to accept, as it has primordialized and totalized the conflicts with the metropolitan states' (ibid.: 59). Finally, Lynch argues that these territories suffer from 'subsistence syndromes.' These pathologies, 'which are based on a combination of firm political determination, deep economic weakness, and extensive criminalization, are a key part of the internal logic sustaining the de facto states' (ibid.: 64). Kolstø also pays particular attention to the economic weakness of unrecognized states. He identifies several reasons why they fail to develop self-sufficient economies: the destruction wrought by the protracted insurgency and conflict with the parent state, the inability to construct a favorable investment climate due to uncertain legal climate (what Pegg refers to as the 'economic cost of non-recognition'), and the presence of a substantial illicit economy and its linkages with the ruling elite, all of which are exacerbated by the absence of international monitoring and accountability (2006: 729).

The internal drivers interact with the direct and indirect external roles of the central government or parent states, regional and global powers, diaspora groups, as well as the international government organizations and non-governmental groups operating within their borders. Actors' divergent engagement strategies with the unrecognized states pull in opposition to one another. However, the plurality of the explanatory variables share a strong link with drivers that are a direct consequence of the current era of globalization.

Beyond cartographic entrepreneurship

The degree to which the identified logics of unrecognized states apply to specific cases will vary. Indeed, one would be hard-pressed to find more seemingly divergent cases than Somaliland and Taiwan. However, preventing a festering problem from becoming a crisis requires policymakers to base prescriptions on sound comprehension of the internal and external drivers propelled by these 'illegitimate states.' For example, the pervasive view of the Iraqi Kurdish leadership as inherently 'separatist' has undermined the United States' management of the 'Kurdish problem' from the onset of the 2003 invasion to the ongoing negotiations over Kirkuk and other disputed territories (see Natali 2008). This is indicative of how little is understood about these entities. Since they will continue to play an outsized role in global politics in the coming years, the ongoing effort to explore the policy and theoretical puzzles posed by unrecognized states is both timely and urgent.

In part because of their chaotic neighborhoods, unrecognized states are often portrayed in paradisiacal fashion. There is indeed little doubt that many of them have performed remarkably well on both economic and political indicators in comparison to their neighbors, at times exponentially so. It is also true that with all the challenges of their disposition, unrecognized states enjoy some important advantages as well. Primary among these is the construction of a governance mechanism that was authentic to the people of the region and could not have been replicated by an externally driven process. The imprimatur of international recognition does not guarantee progress. Witness, for example, the at-times unconstructive role of international financial institutions in improving the situation of the developing world or the present state of a variety of countries that, despite all the international funding, expertise, and engagement, remain on the verge of state failure.

The effects of functioning as an anti-state in a protracted state of ambiguity have greatly undermined the long-term sustainability of many of these unrecognized states as independent entities. Kolstø judges that:

> there are strong reasons to believe that, if any of the unrecognized quasi states [semistates] of today's world should succeed in achieving international recognition, most of them will end up not as 'normal' or fully fledged states but instead transmute into recognized quasi-states of the Jacksonian [Robert Jackson] variety.
>
> (2006: 725)

The 'logic' of unrecognized states is likely to hold for quite some time. This implies that the economic and political dilemmas that undermine their sustainable development are likely to persist and, in turn, cause the kind of crisis of authority typically associated with the deficient internal legitimacy of weak and failing states. Thus, while unrecognized states have shown 'impressive longevity,' one should be skeptical of the notion that they are 'states in waiting' (Bahcheli *et al.* 2004: 246) or that they present the new post-modern form of sovereignty.[19] Some scholars, like Kolstø, posit that the most likely conflict resolution outcome is a federal settlement[20] because it is 'the solution that creates the lowest number of people who are so disgruntled that they will work actively to overturn it. In addition, the factors that militate against the alternative outcomes are clearly stronger' (2006: 738).[21]

Moving beyond the 'territorial trap,' however, might offer some creative and credible alternatives. Gidon Gottlieb's 'states-plus-nations' approach is one that is worth exploring in greater depth. This framework of self-determination is 'less territorial in character and more regional in scope … it does not preclude territorial compromises; it widens the menu of options when territorial changes do not suffice or when they are altogether ruled out' (1994: 100). The requirements of Gottlieb's recommended approach include:

> functional spaces and special functional zones across state boundaries, the creation of national home regimes in historical lands, the grant of recognized status to national communities that have no state of their own, the design of unions between peoples, as distinct from territories, as well as an

> approach to issues of national identity and rights that differentiates between nationality and state citizenship.
>
> (ibid.)

Gottlieb and others are correct in pointing out that recognition of independence will remain a most unlikely scenario. Furthermore, it will neither solve the conflict with the state from which these entities seek to separate nor accelerate the development internally within the separatist state. In fact, recognition, absent a host of other engagement methods, might exacerbate both problems.

What does the existence of unrecognized states tell us about the future of the state-based international system? The manner in which they have survived and the ability of their neighbors and regional players to accommodate them suggests that the international system is resilient to broader degrees of 'stateness' than is often assumed. Any effort to manage the instability presented by the phenomenon of unrecognized states must, therefore, account for the ways in which the system of states is transforming and update the policy tool-kit.

As this chapter demonstrates, the drivers of globalization and the dilemmas posed by unrecognized states go far beyond the issue of recognition and the redrawing of state borders. Such solutions might provide short-term stability but also sow the preconditions for future conflicts. An essential prerequisite to a broader thematic discussion of the topic is a realization that the drivers that sustain the ambiguous status of unrecognized states require a much more sophisticated approach than the cartographic entrepreneurship that brought about this reality in the first place.

Notes

1 Bobbitt provides a history of the modern state and its constitutional orders from the Princely States that preceded the 1648 Treaty of Westphalia to the Kingly States, Territorial States, State-Nations, Nation-States, and the modern Market State. He argues that 'once one sees that there have been many forms of the modern state, one can appreciate that though the nation-state is in fact dying, the modern state is only undergoing one of its periodic transformations.'

2 For data that demonstrates that internal conflicts have become far more prevalent than interstate ones, see Hewitt, Wilkenfeld and Gurr (2010). For definitional nuances between weak, failing, and failed states, see Snow (1996: 98–102). For a glimpse into how the US government has approached the subject of ungoverned areas, see Lamb (2007).

3 See Brooks (2005) for a criticism of the proposition that state frailty is a new phenomenon: 'Weak, failing, and failed states are not the exception in many parts of the world. They are the norm, and have been since their inception.'

4 Chairman of the Joint Chiefs of Staff Admiral Michael Mullen testified in June 2008 that 'if the United States is going to get hit, it's going to come out of the planning that the leadership in the [Federally Administered Tribal Areas] is generating, their planning and direction.' See Spiegel (2008). The Failed States Index, compiled by *Foreign Policy* Magazine and the Fund for Peace, tracks the countries on the verge of collapse. Afghanistan and Pakistan both rank in the top ten most failing states. See 'The 2009 Failed States Index,' *Foreign Policy*, July/August 2009.

5 According to the US Library of Congress catalogue, in the 1990s, about 500 books were published on globalization. Between 2000 and 2004, there were more than

4,000. In fact, between the mid-1990s and 2003, the rate of increase in globalization-related titles more than doubled every eighteen months (cited by Ghemawat 2007). As Graham Allison quips, 'distinguishing between globalization, on the one hand, and globaloney, on the other, is a major challenge' (2000: 2).

6 For a succinct summary of the 'network society,' see Castells (2004: 3–45).

7 Castells does not pretend that globalization is inherently democratic – indeed he seems quite sensitive to what Allison calls the 'inequality of an unwelcome connectedness' (2000: 76).

8 Rosenau credits Arjun Appadurai for the 'scapes' formulation (1996: 33). In his study of terrorism, Allison demonstrates the manner in which globalization has provided 'the infrastructure for terrorism' by multiplying 'networks that both enlarge destructive capacity and reduce barriers and borders to delivery' (2006: 99).

9 Mary Kaldor writes about 'a deepening and widening, a move away from state-centered approaches combining more concern with individual empowerment and person autonomy, as well as territorial restructuring of social and political relations in different realms' (2003: 6).

10 Though a 'nationalist resurgence' has challenged many of these entities, it has not led to the emergence of new states. In fact, as Richard Rosecrance *et al.* demonstrate, 'globalization has proven to be a force for restraint in creating new nation-states' (2006: 7). The authors contend that 'few new states will form in the next generation.' Also see Pegg (1999) for an earlier critique of alarmism about the coming 'proliferation of states.'

11 King rightly notes that to 'live inside a recognized state (especially beyond the capital cities) is little different from life in one of the unrecognized ones. In some cases it is worse' (2001: 551).

12 To be sure, some new states have emerged since the end of the Cold War (for example, the former Soviet and Yugoslav republics, East Timor, Eritrea, and Kosovo), suggesting that, though the entry barriers to secession are high, they are not prohibitively so.

13 For an explanation of the ten dimensions, see Pegg (1998: 29).

14 Denise Natali, who worked for the Office of Federal Disaster Assistance (OFDA) at the United States Agency for International Development (USAID) during Operation Provide Comfort, recounts that staff members were forbidden to use the word 'development' in official cables so as not to give the appearance of US support for greater autonomy, and possibly independence, to Iraqi Kurdistan. Author's interview (Erbil, Iraq, December 2007).

15 Much of the academic literature on this subject is framed by the cases of Eurasia's 'separatist states.' Though numerous variables exist across regional cases, one should be careful not to generalize exclusively from the Eurasian sample.

16 Author's interview (Erbil, Iraq, January 2007).

17 McColl contends that 'modern national revolutions have accepted as a basic tactic the creation of a territorially based anti-state (insurgent state) within the state.' Such an entity will work to attain the attributes of a 'legitimate' state, 'namely a *raison d'être*, control of territory and population and, particularly, the creation of its own core areas and administrative units as well as a power base in its guerilla army.'

18 A former National Security Advisor for President Jimmy Carter, Zbigniew Brzezinski, has credited the advances in information and communication technologies with ushering a 'global political awakening' wherein 'the masses of the world are politically activated' (Brzezinski *et al.* 2008).

19 See also Caspersen's and Closson's chapters in this volume.

20 See also Anderson's chapter in this volume.

21 The Iraqi Kurdistan case substantiates his claim, although the federalization of Iraq was brought about by the overthrow of the parent-state regime and a complete overhaul of its constitutional framework.

3 International actions and the making and unmaking of unrecognized states

Klejda Mulaj

In a recent contribution, Richard Rosecrance and his collaborators considered the question: 'Who will be independent?' They reached the conclusion that the process of political subdivision is not likely to continue unabated, and that the process of (new) state formation has largely run its course. This is so, not because demands for self-determination do not exist, but because metropolitan governments are being more efficient in buying off the discontented parties or in compelling them to submit, and because Great Power support for self-determination and creation of new states – in general – has lessened. Moreover, the net effect of globalization dwarfs political units in so far as it renders them dependent on the outside world for technology, markets, raw materials, and trained manpower. Such dependency impacts all polities but it impedes in particular smaller political units, especially so independence movements (seeking or) just gaining autonomy (Rosecrance *et al.* 2006: 3–22; Rosecrance 2006: 279–92).[1] It follows, therefore, that lack of self-sufficiency is a key attribute which puts a break on the creation of new states. This last point has relevance in understanding why some political entities survive the process of state formation, whilst others are subjected to unrecognized statehood.

Despite strong national aspirations to sovereignty, the term 'state' is somehow problematic for an adequate characterization of the entities analysed in this chapter and volume. In addition to limited economic and strategic self-sufficiency, entities defined here as 'unrecognized states'[2] lack political clout as a result of absence of international recognition and concomitant benefits which come with it, as well as facing strong impediments posed by what once was – or is – their 'parent' country. In addition to (likely) failing to fully meet legal requirements of statehood as laid down in the Montevideo Convention,[3] at issue for any 'unrecognized state' is (deficiency of) a key attribute of statehood, namely sovereignty.[4] Perhaps 'quasi-states' or 'de facto states' might be more accurate depictive notions, but they are likely to offend aspirations for statehood on the part of national elites and their followers, as well as their political actions to this end. With this caveat in place, and for the purpose of consistency, this chapter follows the terminology adopted throughout this volume and therefore refers to 'unrecognized states' to describe political entities that show resemblance of statehood but lack the formal acceptance of the international community.

The non-state status – in conventional terms – of the political entities interrogated in this volume does not imply that they exist and evolve outside a discourse of international standards and norms. In fact, a survey of the emergence and evolution of such entities shows that their claims to statehood have been couched in terms of some key principles and practices of the society of states, such as protection of group rights (in particular, cultural rights – including use of language, the right to education, employment, and protection from discrimination on ethnic grounds), the right to self-determination, the right to security, as well as the right to freedom and human dignity. When using force to achieve their aims, the leaders of unrecognized states have been keen to distance themselves from claims of separatism and/or secessionism and have stressed instead their right to self-determination and aspirations for sovereignty. Moreover, they have sought to distance themselves from terrorism and they have claimed that they fight for freedom. Observing the international political background and evaluating the prospects of their cause, the leaders of unrecognized states have shown capacity to adapt by – sometimes – transforming their claims from demands for outright independence from their 'parent' state to claims for confederal arrangements on equal basis. They have consistently stayed on the point – however – that their actions far from challenging the society of states aim, in fact, to join it (Mulaj, 2010: 6).

The irony is, nevertheless, that whilst unrecognized states strive to utilize some international practices and norms to justify their existence, the persistence of certain international norms – such as inviolability of territorial boundaries, priority of maintenance of peace and security, specific interpretation of self-determination, and especially collective non-recognition – poses formidable challenges to the capacity of entities analysed in this volume to eventually join the society of states.

Thus, the existence of unrecognized states in the international system is conditioned by a conflictual impact of dominant standards and norms, some of which may serve to justify demands for independence, whilst others frustrate and suppress them. This impact is also asymmetrical, in the sense that the interpretation of international standards and norms – as they may pertain to the circumstances of unrecognized entities – is done and implemented by the society of states which is not, normally, sympathetic to new candidates, due to (perception of) them being a threat to peace and stability (for instance, because of consequences connected with change of boundaries or regional balances of power, or because of organized crime or illicit trade). In other words, unrecognized states are not necessarily active participants in the normative debate over international reactions to their pleas. In fact, unrecognized states are bound to depend on the international system for support and recognition of any sort that might enable their survival and evolution of their status from non-state to state. The asymmetry hinted at above, therefore, has to do with the fact that the success or failure of unrecognized states does not necessarily depend on their effective actions but rather it depends on the international society – particularly actions or inactions of its member states, in selective or collective form. Whilst unrecognized states may exist and operate within the contours of the international system, it is the acceptance or the denial into the international society that holds the key to their ultimate survival or demise.[5]

International actions as facilitators of the emergence and existence of unrecognized states

Whilst their origins lie in incompatible nationalisms and irreconcilable claims to domination and subordination, the term 'unrecognized states' disguises the fact that the emergence and the survival of such entities owes a great deal to the action – or inaction – of international actors, including individual states or groups of states, and international organizations. As the following analysis will demonstrate, explicit or implicit support of a foreign – frequently a neighbouring – power has had direct impact on the emergence of an unrecognized state, but so has inaction of the international community – for instance, in the form of 'neglecting' or 'ignoring' the existence of a given unrecognized entity. Frequently, the absence of concerted international action to actively challenge or suppress the existence of unrecognized states has implied their passive – if frustrated – existence. However, it is conscious policy on the side of foreign powers – in terms of action, inaction and/or both – which has had a more decisive and prolonged impact on the emergence and survival and/or demise of unrecognized states, as evidenced in such cases as the Tamil State (Eelam) in Sri Lanka, the Turkish Republic of Northern Cyprus, Republika Srpska Krajina in Croatia, Republika Srpska in Bosnia, and Abkhazia and South Ossetia in Georgia.[6] These cases provide a range of examples where the international factor holds explanatory power regarding the emergence, evolution, and/or demise of the unrecognized states concerned. The following proceeds to consider the international impact on the creation of the above unrecognized entities, as well as the international impact on their survival or extinction. A basic consideration of their emergence and evolution is also in order. The closing section of the chapter sums up the argument and emphasizes that collective non-recognition is the greatest obstacle to unrecognized states' aspirations to legitimate statehood.

The Tamil State (Eelam)

One of the first entities to acquire attributes of an unrecognized state is also one of the least known. Attempts to establish a Tamil State, Eelam, primarily associated with the political and military agenda of a violent non-state actor – the Liberation Tigers of Tamil Eelam (LTTE) – are best understood in the context of tense inter-ethnic relations in Sri Lanka, concomitant efforts to minimize tensions on the part of the Colombo government, and reactions – sometimes in the form of inaction – of international actors, or the international community at large. Previously known as Ceylon (until 1972), Sri Lanka is a multicultural country of about 20 million people, of which 74 per cent are Sinhalese, whilst the second largest group is of Tamil background.[7] Governed by the British since 1815, the country gained independence in 1948 when the ruling powers were transferred to the Sri Lankan people. Concerned about the prospects of fair treatment, the Tamils, who had provided a large share of professional services under the British rule, demanded an equal share of power with the Sinhalese majority. These concerns were addressed on paper – at British insistence – by provisions in the country's constitution, which stated that no discriminatory legislation against ethnic or religious groups would be enacted by Parliament (Hussain 2010: 388–9).

However, strains in the tense relations between the Sinhala majority and the Tamil minority were soon to appear. The post-independence government in Colombo acted swiftly to pass legislation that denied about one million Plantation Tamils the right to acquire Ceylon citizenship and advocated their compulsory return to India. Moreover, the existing two-language policy was abrogated and Sinhalese was declared the sole official language with the advent to power of Prime Minister SWRD Bandaranaike in 1956, who implemented his Freedom Party's pre-electoral pledge. It is in this year that Tamil members of the Parliament formed the United Front, with the aim of preserving the Tamil language, culture, freedom and identity. They also issued calls for the creation of a Tamil State, which could federate itself with the Sinhalese state on equal terms (Hussain 2010: 390).

The continuing discrimination against the Tamils gave fuel to their resolve to oppose the government in Colombo. The suppression of the Tamil language continued in the 1960s and 1970s, encompassing grievances in relation to insufficient access to higher education, lack of economic opportunities, and discriminatory land distribution. Some figures provided by Robert Rotberg in his study *Creating Peace in Sri Lanka* illustrate the scale of discrimination against the Tamils: for instance, the share of Tamils in professional employment in state administration fell from 60 per cent in 1948 to under 10 per cent in 1970, whereas their employment in the armed forces fell from 40 per cent in 1948 to less than 1 per cent by 1970 (Rotberg 1999: 19).

Frustrated that peaceful means were not securing rights of their people, the Tamil elite spoke openly about the benefits of the establishment of a Tamil State. The ruthless crushing by the Sri Lankan military of the 1971 armed insurrection by the People's Liberation Front enhanced militant feelings amongst the Tamils, especially the youths who came to see violent action as the answer to their discrimination. Influenced by the success of the armed struggle of the Bengalis in East Pakistan, which led to the independence of Bangladesh in December 1971, and reacting to the ultra-nationalist rhetoric of Tamil parties, Tamil youths began joining militant organizations in large numbers. Building on a tradition of armed resistance, the Liberation Tigers of Tamil Eelam (LTTE) was formed in 1976. It gradually laid claim to being the sole representative of the Tamil people and took upon itself the task of waging armed struggle on their behalf, with the view of achieving sovereign statehood (Hussain 2010: 393, 396).

The LTTE leader, Velupillai Prabhakaran, justified the use of force as a response to what he saw as a 'calculated programme of genocide' on the side of the Colombo government. But he refused to classify his movement as separatist:

> It is wrong to call our movement 'separatist'. We are fighting for independence based on the right to national self-determination of our people. Our struggle is for self-determination for the restoration of our sovereignty in our homeland. We are not fighting for a division or a separation of a country, but rather, we are fighting to uphold the sacred right to live in freedom and dignity. In this sense, we are freedom fighters not terrorists.
>
> (Pratap 1984; Hussain 2010: 401)

Considering itself to represent grievances of the Tamils, the LTTE employed violence against the Sinhala-dominated government in Colombo as a 'parallel process of state building primarily by military means' (Uyangoda 2007: 42).[8] On the civic front, the LTTE established a parallel civil administration within the territory it controlled in the north and east of Sri Lanka, together with an army, police force, law courts, postal services, banks, and a TV and radio station. Moreover, despite their armed struggle against the Colombo government, the LTTE participated – with the Sri Lankan government – in a number of rounds of peace talks in 1985, 1989–1990, 1994–1995, and 2001–2002. The idea of Eelam did, however, not find broad support in these talks (Iyer 2007). Despite many setbacks in the more than three decades of struggle for statehood, LTTE leaders and their cadres did not stop thinking of Eelam as a state of their own.

What deserves emphasis in the context of this chapter is that, in the course of the LTTE fight for the establishment of Eelam, Indian support was crucial, especially in the initial stages. Between 1983 and 1987, the LTTE received material and financial assistance from neighbouring India, and more than 20,000 Sri Lankan Tamil insurgents were offered sanctuary, training, and weapons by Indian officials. Moreover, during this time period, the LTTE operatives moved freely between India and Sri Lanka (Hussain 2010: 402–3). Such was the scale and impact of India's assistance that analysts agree that the fact that the LTTE emerged as the dominant Tamil fighting force by 1986–1987 can be attributed to the massive support it received from New Delhi (see, for example, Bose 2003: 634).

India's support for the LTTE was conceived as a means to pressure Colombo into distancing itself from China and Pakistan, two adversaries of India at that time. Moreover, the Tamils of India had been very concerned over the discriminatory treatment meted out by Colombo to the Tamils in Sri Lanka, and India's support for the LTTE was intended to appease the Indian Tamil community. However, New Delhi's stance towards the insurgent movement changed following the 1987 Indo-Sri Lanka accord when its peacekeeping forces were attacked by LTTE following attempts by the Indian Army to disarm them. Confronted with armed insurgency in Kashmir and Punjab, New Delhi could not afford a prolonged deployment in Sri Lanka. Having suffered heavy casualties at the hands of the LTTE, Indian forces eventually withdrew from Sri Lanka in 1990, opening the way for renewed fighting between Sri Lankan forces and the insurgents but also for new rounds of peace talks. These were organized by the Colombo government and the LTTE were a party.

The creation of Tamil Eelam was an issue on which the LTTE was reluctant to budge. However, in February 2002, a ceasefire agreement (CFA) between the Sri Lankan government and the LTTE was brokered by Norway, which called for a federal solution to Sri Lanka's crisis, proposing a semi-autonomous province to be ruled by the Tamil leadership. Six rounds of talks were facilitated by Norway, at the end of which – despite tensions over continuing incidents of violence – both the Colombo government and the LTTE agreed to a federal solution. Exhausted militarily and deprived of external support, the LTTE had consequently given up its longstanding demands for a separate state. Following the coming to power of Prime Minister Mahinda Rajapaksa in 2005, the terms of the CFA were revisited, leading yet again to escalation of violence. With violations of CFA provisions by both sides, the agreement was unilaterally denunciated by the Colombo government in January 2008. This plunged the country into a full-scale war by spring 2009, which the Sri Lankan army eventually won, following a military offensive accompanied by enormous manpower losses on the side of the LTTE and claims of massive violation of human rights on the side of the government forces.[9] The LTTE was banned as a terrorist organization by the United States of America and the European Union (EU), which eased operations of Sri Lanka's government, as did the LTTE's reluctance to admit that state-making by military means had become an untenable strategy, given the very large-scale military loses suffered at the hands of the Sri Lankan army. Having no realistic chance of political endorsement by the international community, the military defeat of the LTTE marked the demise of over 30 years of struggle for a Tamil Eelam.

Turkish Republic of Northern Cyprus (TRNC)

A former British colony, Cyprus became independent in 1960, but two out of its three political movements (the National Organization of Cypriot Fighters and the Turkish Defence Organization) sought unification of the island with Greece and Turkey respectively.[10] In what can be described as conflict by proxy, the clash between these movements resulted in the establishment of a 'Green Line' between Greek and Turkish Cypriot communities in Nicosia. This was initially supervised by the British and later by the United Nations (UN). Eleven years of skirmishes followed by Greek-supported, pro-unification attacks on the Cypriot presidential palace prompted Turkey to occupy northern Cyprus in 1974.[11] Directly related to Turkey's military intervention, the establishment of the Turkish Republic of Northern Cyprus (TRNC) (on 15 November 1983) was conceived as a means of protecting the rights of Turkish Cypriots and overcoming their polity's inferior status in the international arena. Couched in ambiguous terms, the rationale of the TRNC was interpreted not as an act of secession – strictly speaking – but rather as 'an important step in a process of political and administrative evolution'. The Turkish Cypriot leadership stressed that the TRNC would not unite with Turkey but would be committed to unification with their southern co-patriots on an equal, sovereign basis, which could lay the grounds for a common confederal state (Geldenhuys 2009: 178).[12]

Facts on the ground, nonetheless, proved to be more conducive to the division of the island rather than its confederal organization. The Green Line provided a hard border, with Turkish Cypriots controlling the north and Greek Cypriots controlling the south. Indeed, the presence of the United Nations Force in Cyprus (UNICYP), which patrolled the buffer zone between the two entities, eventually froze the situation, thereby enabling the existence not only of the Republic of Cyprus but also that of the TRNC. UNICYP has been praised for keeping a delicate peace in a divided island, but this has been done at the cost of the existence of an unrecognized state. As one scholar has put it: 'the preservation of peace at the price of a de facto state [is not] the worst option available. Indeed ... it [is] preferable to renewed conflict and bloodshed' (Pegg 1998: 166). Nonetheless, peacekeeping has not resulted in peacemaking in Cyprus. Because the status quo has offered advantages to both sides of the divide, none of them has had strong incentives to search for a more lasting peace (Doob 1986: 385).

The TRNC, nevertheless, was subjected to existential crises from the very beginning. The United Nations Security Council condemned the TRNC on the grounds that it purports 'secession of part of the Republic of Cyprus' and has called on the international community 'not to recognize any Cypriot state other than the Republic of Cyprus'.[13] However, collective non-recognition has not yet translated into TRNC's death, thanks to vigorous protection and continuous support granted by Turkey, which is also the sole country to have recognized the TRNC. Faced with economic isolation, including an economic embargo sanctioned by the Greek Cypriot government – joined by Greece and other European countries – as well as denial of substantial aid available to the Greek Cypriot government (Bahcheli 2004: 170, 174), the TRNC has survived economically, (primarily) thanks to Ankara's support (International Crisis Group 2006a: 27).[14]

The 1990s brought about new dynamics in the life of the TRNC, as the Republic of Cyprus embarked upon the process of joining the European Union (EU). The benefits of joining the EU contrasted sharply with the deprivation caused by the TRNC's international isolation, and this encouraged Turkish Cypriot leaders to pursue rapprochement with their co-patriots and seek the benefits of EU citizenship via a federal arrangement with the Greek Cypriots.[15] The European Union, for its part, wished to promote a settlement in Cyprus, realizing the potentially destabilizing impact of the conflict. Supported by the UN, Brussels proclaimed that it preferred that the island as a whole joined the European Union – as advocated in the Annan Plan. Not coincidentally, 2003, the year before the Republic of Cyprus' accession to the EU, saw 'the most concerted and comprehensive international effort to achieve a settlement since the independence negotiations of 1959–60' (International Crisis Group 2006a: 3). Following a number of revisions, a referendum was held on the Annan Plan, which saw 76 per cent of the Greek Cypriots rejecting it and 65 per cent of the Turkish Cypriots approving it (International Crisis Group 2006a: 4). The result of the referendum reflected the fact that concerns over state security and sovereignty were central to Greek Cypriots' reluctance to accept the willingness of their Turkish counterparts to give up their unrecognized polity and integrate themselves into a united Cyprus in the hope of enjoying the benefits of EU membership.[16] Ironically, despite UN and EU efforts to base a Cyprus settlement on increased security for both Greek and Turkish inhabitants of the island, a zero-sum conception of security has ensured the *anomalous* continuance of the TRNC – in so far as it survives but is internationally unrecognized. At the same time, it is ironic that, by failing to enforce the plan of unification, the UN and the EU – (even if) unintentionally – have become complicit in the TRNC's continued existence.

Republika Srpska Krajina in Croatia and Republika Srpska in Bosnia

Not geographically far removed from Cyprus lies the region of the former Yugoslavia where the questions of secession, irredentism, and independence have been fiercely contested in recent times. Prior to the present political configuration, the region experienced great upheavals related to the re-organization of the political space and concomitant attempts to create new states or consolidate or aggrandize existing ones. Two central features have characterized this process of state formation, namely mass violation of human rights – including ethnic cleansing – and intensive courting of international support on the part of the national elites (Mulaj 2008). Ultimately, however, international support has been the key factor in determining the viability of prospective polities and their eventual recognition.

Unrecognized states have been part of the process of nation-state creation, but they are nevertheless a recent phenomenon in the region. Their emergence in the 1990s was closely related to a process of state disintegration and reformation, as the Socialist Federal Republic of Yugoslavia became inoperative and new states emerged in the wake of its dissolution.[17] The Yugoslav federation was adversely affected by the end of the Cold War. For example, the strategic importance which it enjoyed for several decades at the behest of the Non-Alignment Movement dissipated, as did the preferential financial treatments it used to get from the International Monetary Fund and the World Bank. Economic decline impacted unproportionally upon various republics, enhancing the disparities between the rich and poor regions, and creating serious tensions in the federal-republic relationships, as politicians were unwilling to compromise (Woodward 1995: especially 15, 40).

The formation of new states in the aftermath of the dissolution of the Yugoslav federation was a violent affair, centred on control of territory, borders, and the rights of national groups in emerging new entities. Moreover, kin-state involvement and support has been a key feature of the conflict (Mulaj 2008; Gow, 2003). For instance, the war in Croatia was preceded by extensive Belgrade-sponsored activities to mobilize the Serbian community in Croatia to adopt a programme suitable to Belgrade's agendas. Despite being alienated by Franjo Tuđman's policies, initially, Croatia's Serbs did not embrace a nationalistic plan of action. In fact, in the 1990 elections, they voted for parties with civic programmes. Within a year, however, their stance hardened: after forming paramilitary groups and staging a rebellion, in the summer of 1990, they held a referendum on the issue of autonomy, proclaiming themselves first an autonomous region of Croatia. Then, in March 1991, the self-proclaimed autonomous region of Krajina was declared to be part of Serbia, preceding the declaration of Croatia's independence on 25 June 1991.

A six-month war (July 1991–January 1992), which was initiated by Serbian forces in Croatia with the aim of securing de facto control of territory and delineating the borders of Republika Srpska Krajina, acted as a prelude to war over control of Serb-claimed territory in Bosnia (1992–1995). Preceded by a referendum, a declaration of autonomy, and then independence by Bosnian Serbs, the ensuing fighting – in which the Bosnian Serbs received substantial support from neighbouring Serbia – aimed to cement the ethnic division of the territory and ensure Serb control.[18] The extensive international efforts to deal with these conflicts had a direct impact on Republika Srpska Krajina and Republika Srpska, and three initiatives deserve special mentioning.

First, considering the consequences of the conflict, the European Community (EC) established, in August 1991, a commission of jurists – known as the Badinter Commission – to advise the EC on the situation in the former Yugoslavia and especially so on the prospect of recognition of emerging entities. In doing so, the commission appealed to key international principles, namely uti possidetis and self-determination, to underpin the rationale of the international community with regard to recognition of new polities. Referring to a principle of international law under which new states emerging from the fracturing of larger ones are recognized within their federal administrative borders, uti possidetis implied that only former federal republics could be entitled to statehood, i.e. Croatia and Bosnia but not the statelet entities in their midst. Moreover, the Badinter Commission invoked the principle of self-determination to *restrict* the emergence of the new states in the region. Intent to avoid setting a legal precedent, the commission recommended that the disintegration of the federation of Yugoslavia should be limited exclusively to federal units (i.e. republics). In its second opinion, delivered on 11 January 1992, the commission acknowledged 'the right to self-determination of the constituent peoples of Yugoslavia (e.g. Serbs and Croats) but argued that this right must not involve changes to existing frontiers' (cited in Caplan 2005: 69). Thus, the commission did not support the unilateral establishment of Republika Srpska Krajina in Croatia and Republika Srpska in Bosnia. In using the Badinter Commission's recommendations as a legal justification for its recognition policy in former Yugoslavia, the European Community sought to avert creating a legal precedent: statehood for Croatia and Bosnia would not mean statehood for Catalonia, or statehood for the Turkish Republic of Northern Cyprus.

Second, deployment of UN peacekeeping forces in Croatia kept the peace at the cost of the existence of Republika Srpska Krajina. Aware that a ceasefire would enable the Serbs to consolidate their gains by freezing the situation, Yugoslavia's (i.e. Serbia's) representative to the UN on 26 November 1991 made the formal request to the Security Council for a peacekeeping operation in

Croatia (UNPROFOR).[19] Concerns about Serbian rationale were raised by the then UN Secretary-General, Boutros Boutros-Ghali, who in his 16 March 1994 report to the Security Council stated: 'The Serb side has taken advantage of the presence of UNPROFOR in its efforts to freeze the status quo, under UNPROFOR "protection", whilst establishing a self-proclaimed "state" of "the Republic of Serb Krajina" in UNPROFOR's area of responsibility.'[20]

Republika Srpska Krajina existed until 1995, when Zagreb – concerned about loss of territory and sensing no international opposition – launched two operations, in May and August, which, with relative ease, recovered the Serb-held areas of Croatia (Žunec 2001: 67–83). These operations ended the life of Republika Srpska Krajina. Its fall has not been contested by virtually anyone in the international arena given the widely held perception that it was illegitimate, being a creation of war and ethnic cleansing. Criticism that UNPROFOR failed to protect the Serb population of this region overlooks the fact that, by the time of the Croatian offensive, Republika Srpska Krajina had been transformed into a garrison society where 90 per cent of the Serb population was employed in the police force.[21] Long-term maintenance of peace and security trumpeted concerns for violation of human rights of people displaced by the 1995 offensive.

Third, the peace accord that ended the war in Bosnia – yet again – kept the peace at the expense of the existence of an unrecognized polity, namely Republika Srpska. Under the terms of the Dayton Agreement which ended hostilities, Republika Srpska is one of the two constitutive parts of the Bosnian Federation.[22] The reason for this – as stated by the international mediator and peace broker Richard Hoolbroke – centres on the need to accommodate Serbia and secure the support of President Slobodan Milošević for the peace deal, which in turn would secure the support of the Bosnian Serbs (Holbrooke 1996, 1998). Dayton, therefore, left the new federation in a state of limbo by tying Bosnia's uncertainty with the existence of a state-like entity within its midst.

Republika Srpska has undergone a curious evolution over the last decade. Surviving international isolation, it has gradually been strengthened due to receiving support and investments from neighbouring Serbia, and also from Russia and some Eastern European countries. Functioning as a unitary entity and managed by one political party – the Alliance of Independent Social Democrats and, ultimately by its leader, Milorad Dodik – Republika Srpska poses a threat to the survival of the Bosnian state. The nature and degree of this threat is not universally agreed by analysts. A recent International Crisis Group (ICG) policy briefing states that fears that 'the RS [Republika Srpska] will try to secede unless checked by strong international policy' are 'unrealistic'. 'An RS breakaway would very probably fail to obtain any recognition. Russia and Serbia, RS's staunchest supporters, strongly oppose a breakup.'[23] But a long-term observer of Bosnian affairs – Matthew Parish – begs to differ. In his view, Dodik's agenda is one that detaches Republika Srpska from its institutional dependence on Sarajevo:

> Dodik's plan for the RS is incremental. Independence will be pursued piecemeal, as one tie to the central state after another is sequentially cut. By the

time the RS is de facto independent, already not far off, the international community will barely have noticed.

(Parish 2009)

There is already some evidence of this strategy: law courts in Republika Srpska owe their allegiance to Dodik and are not inclined to jeopardize Republika Srpska's interests by applying (Bosnian) state laws. Having its own police, courts, legal regime, and tax system, Republika Srpska does not experience real control of state police and state courts. Republika Srpska's border services with Bosnia are manned exclusively by Serb officials, whilst Republika Srpska's borders with Serbia are virtually unnoticeable. Ironically, Dodik's agenda is facilitated by the Bosnian Constitution, incorporated in the Dayton Agreement, which provides that decisions at the central level can be taken by consensus of the country's three ethnic groups, giving Serbs (and Bosniaks and Croats) the right to veto decisions at the state level, as a consequence of which Bosnia has suffered constant stalemates.[24] As Louise Arbour – the current president of the International Crisis Group – recently observed, the political turmoil in Bosnia is very real. Whether Bosnia avoids fragmentation – from which Republika Srpska stands to benefit – depends on continuing international, and especially EU and US, commitment to reinforce Bosnia's stability and membership in NATO and the European Union (Arbour 2009). If that commitment is not forthcoming, the international community could – inadvertently – aid Republika Srpska's claim to independence.

Abkhazia and South Ossetia in Georgia

Abkhazia and South Ossetia in Georgia provide other examples of recent cases of unrecognized states resulting from the disintegration of a larger political constellation, namely the Union of Soviet Socialist Republics (USSR). Experiencing only a brief time of statehood – from March to December 1921 – for the most part of the twentieth century, Abkhazia was part of the state of Georgia, which in turn was a constitutive republic of the USSR. This, however, has not been an easy union. Abkhazia suffered badly under Stalin's rule, its people being subjected to cultural discrimination and even ethnic cleansing.[25] Policies of discrimination against Abkhazians were reversed after Stalin's death, but the ensuing liberalization and capital investment, far from appeasing Abkhazians, fuelled demands for political reform and gradually, with the weakening of the Soviet Union, fuelled demands for sovereignty. The latter were bound to clash with Georgia's own aspiration for statehood and secession from the Soviet Union – eventually asserted in 1989. The ensuing confrontation resulting from Georgia's and Abkhazia's incompatible claims for control of territory and full sovereignty – including the 1992–1993 war, as well as the violence in May 1998 – has been documented in several studies (see, for instance, Human Rights Watch 1995; Goltz 1993; Mihalkanin 2004). Despite massive use of force – and concomitant violations of human rights – Georgian forces, which invaded Abkhazia in August

1992, did not manage to retain control of her territory due to Russian military support offered to Abkhaz forces. A peace agreement facilitated by the UN and Russia, and a peacekeeping force of the Commonwealth of the Independent States (CIS) – comprising mostly Russian troops – deployed between Georgian and Abkhazian territory, froze the situation and gave a lease of life to the de facto state of Abkhazia. This owed a great deal to Russia's military and economic assistance, as well as the international community's reluctance to confront Moscow. Whereas for the Georgians the 1992–1993 war hardened their belief that confrontation in Abkhazia reflected Moscow's ambitions for regional hegemony, for the Abkhazians the war hardened their sense of vulnerability and distrust of Georgia, as well as Sukhumi's determination to attain statehood.

Strategies for legitimizing the Abkhaz entity have included not only the application of traditional symbols of statehood such as a flag, a national anthem, a constitution, and a head of state, but also claims to the creation of democratic institutions, provision of public services, and internal stability (Caspersen 2008: 113–36). Survival and imitation of statehood have been possible due to a dependent relationship with Russia, which has proceeded to the extent that Abkhazia pursues a common defence and foreign policy with Russia, relies on Russian forces to protect its borders, receives Russian pensions, and uses the Russian currency and Russian passports.[26]

Not unlike the case of Abkhazia, historical interpretations of group origin and territorial control of the territory of South Ossetia differs between Ossetians and Georgians (International Crisis Group 2004). Following the dissolution of the Russian Empire (1918), South Ossetia was forcefully incorporated into Georgia, being granted the status of an autonomous region in 1922, which nevertheless did not appease South Ossetians' aspirations for republican status.

The disintegration of the USSR provided the opportunity for pursuing sovereignty claims, which the South Ossetian Popular Front did in 1990 with a view to securing secession of South Ossetia from Georgia but not necessarily from the Soviet Union.[27] Responding to such secessionist demands, the Georgian government abolished the autonomous status of the region and declared a state of emergency, followed in January 1991 by deployment of Georgian troops in Tskhinvali. Just like in Abkhazia, the Russian army stepped in to support South Ossetia. In the aftermath of the fighting – as a result of which about 1,000 people were killed and thousands were displaced, the majority of whom were Georgians – some Russian military personnel were reportedly appointed in key government positions in the new polity. Moreover, following the Russian intervention, South Ossetians used the Russian rouble and benefited from Russian pensions, as well as Russian arms, equipment, and military training. By 2004, approximately 90 per cent of South Ossetians were officially Russian citizens (International Crisis Group 2006e: 3, 4–8, 18; Lynch 2004a: 115–16).

It is not surprising that for Tbilisi conflicts in Abkhazia and South Ossetia reflect a political crisis between Georgia and Russia.[28] The international dimension of the conflict was apparent in the Sochi accord – which was signed between Georgia and South Ossetia (following ending of hostilities) in Sochi

(Russia) in June 1992. The accord provided, amongst other things, for a Joint Control Commission (with representatives from Russia, Georgia, North and South Ossetia, and the Organization for Security and Cooperation in Europe – OSCE) to supervise the peace deal, plus a Joint Peacekeeping Force, consisting of units from Georgia, Russia, and South Ossetia, noticeably operating under Russian command (Geldenhuys 2009: 81). The peace deal, by depriving Georgia of control of South Ossetia, enabled the latter to exist as an unrecognized state, thanks to Russia's support and also the wider international community's reluctance to deal with the ongoing incompatible claims over Georgian territory, as well as Russian interference.

Peace in the region was, however, fragile and eventually broke down in 2004, ostensibly due to an anti-smuggling operation led by Georgian forces with the aim of cutting supplies to South Ossetian regime (International Crisis Group 2006e: 11–14). It is interesting to note that the ensuing initiatives to promote peace in the aftermath of the conflict – undertaken by the EU, OSCE, and the United Nations Development Programme (UNDP) – were not intended to promote independence for South Ossetia but rather contribute to its integration within Georgia (Geldenhuys 2009: 83). It is curious, however, that such initiatives did nothing to undermine either South Ossetia's aspirations for statehood or its dependent relationship with Russia. Unintentionally, therefore, the international community enabled the existence of South Ossetia as an entity, which was trying to adopt a semblance of statehood and somehow coped with the lack of international recognition.

Georgia, nonetheless, did not give up hope of resuming control of its breakaway regions. To this end, its military invaded South Ossetia in August 2008, underestimating prospects of a Russian counteroffensive, which in the event was ruthless: not only defeating Georgian forces in South Ossetia but attacking targets in Georgia proper, as well as chasing Georgian forces out of Abkhazia.[29] Within two weeks of an EU-mediated peace deal between Georgia and Russia, which did not end Russian troops' control of South Ossetia (and Abkhazia) and which made no explicit reference to protecting the territorial integrity of Georgia, Moscow declared its formal recognition of South Ossetia's and Abkhazia's statehood, justifying its decision on the ground of protecting 'Russian citizens' and preventing 'genocide' allegedly intended against them by Georgia.[30]

Russia's recognition of the statehood of Georgia's breakaway regions has been met with criticism by Western powers and the larger international community. Revitalizing the discourse of state-making and international recognition, Russia's action has, at the same time, pushed further away prospects of the integration of Abkhazia and South Ossetia into Georgia, therefore providing support for their state-like existence – although deprived of meaningful independence, sovereignty, and international recognition.

Conclusion

This chapter has suggested that the actions and/or inactions of the international community have had a crucial impact on the emergence, survival, or extinction of unrecognized states. Contextualising this claim through a number of case studies, the analysis has suggested that the non-state status – in conventional terms – of unrecognized entities is conditioned by the conflictual impact of dominant international standards and norms, some of which (such as protection of group rights, the right to self-determination, and the right to freedom and security) have been used to justify demands for independence, whilst others (such as inviolability of territorial boundaries, maintenance of peace and security, and specific interpretations of self-determination) have imposed formidable challenges to efforts of unrecognized entities to obtain access to the international society of states. Their unrecognized statehood has implied also that, in the normative debate of the international society about reaction to unrecognized polities, the latter have not necessarily been active and direct participants.

This notwithstanding, unrecognized states have taken advantage of various forms of international attitudes, including international inaction, kin-state protection, ceasefires, and deployment of peacekeepers, in order to freeze the situation and establish control over their claimed territory. Moreover, imitating strategies of state-building, they have aimed to project an image of statehood – and therefore survival – on the basis of which they have lobbied for international support and assistance.

However, one nut they have not managed to crack is international recognition. The experience of de facto states suggests that criteria of recognition, in reality, are more complex than they appear to be on paper. Indeed, the factual basis of statehood stipulated in the 1933 Convention on Rights and Duties of States (the Montevideo Convention) – namely, a permanent population, defined territory, government, and capacity to enter into relations with other states – does not suffice to secure international recognition. This is similar to the fact that claims to self-determination alone do not constitute a (sufficient) political criterion for statehood. The process through which self-determination claims are made public impacts on the granting or the withdrawal of recognition.

Moreover, as Richard Caplan notes in relation to the EC's recognition policy for new states emerging from the Yugoslav federation: 'to be lawful recognition cannot be extended in violation of peremptory norms.... [I]nternational law prohibits any act committed in violation of peremptory norms (jus cogens)' (Caplan 2005: 54).[31] Although the corpus of peremptory norms is not specified in the Vienna Convention, in light of state practice, many legal experts are of the opinion that they include the prohibition of massive violations of human rights. Whenever granted, recognition should not violate jus cogens norms. In our context, this means that when state creation exhibits illegal features, such as massive violations of human rights and humanitarian law, non-recognition of the new entity serves to sanction the offence. It is by virtue of non-recognition that a 'state' conceived through illegal processes is deprived of *de jure* statehood.

Inaccessibility to the international society is a key factor that undermines the prospects of survival of unrecognized states. Recognition is crucial because of its impact upon the viability of unrecognized entities. As Edward Mihalkanin notes: '[R]ecognition is vitally important because it allows access to the public goods that the international community doles out via institutions such as the International Monetary Fund and the World Bank.' In addition, '[t]he community of states in its decisions on recognition acts as a gatekeeper for the private sector as well'. Unrecognized states, therefore, have great difficulty obtaining loans, capital investment and other necessary resources for a functioning economy (Mihalkanin 2004: 157). Hence, their deficient viability.

Lastly, recognition is pivotal due to its direct correlation to legitimacy, which is due to recognition being a form of legitimation. Conversely, collective non-recognition denies unrecognized states' external legitimacy, in so far as the legitimate existence of such entities in the international arena depends on their acceptance as *states* by the international community. Moreover, in so far as unrecognized governments of de facto states – in their constituencies – can get away with deficits of democratic governance, transparency, provision of security and rule of law, and independent decision-making in the name of pursuing statehood, non-recognition can diminish also the internal legitimacy of unrecognized governments. Therefore, it is not unreasonable to suggest that collective non-recognition is the most fundamental impediment to unrecognized states' aspirations for legitimate statehood.

Notes

1 Rosecrance and his colleagues suggest that a limited number of independence movements may eventually succeed, like those in Palestine and Southern Sudan, but they are likely to be exceptions.
2 See the definition adopted in the introduction to this volume.
3 The 1933 Montevideo Convention on the Rights and Duties of States provides a definition of statehood in Article 1 as follows: 'The State as a person of international law should possess the following qualifications: (a) a permanent population; (b) a defined territory; (c) government; and (d) capacity to enter into relations with other States.' The Montevideo Convention is available at www.cosmopolitikos.com/Documents/Montevideo%20(1933).pdf.
4 See Closson's chapter in this volume.
5 It is useful to recall at this juncture the distinction between an 'international system' and an 'international society'. As posited by Hedley Bull, an international system consists of a number of states which 'have sufficient contact between them, and have sufficient impact on one another's decisions, to cause them to behave – at least to some measure – as parts of a whole'. In contrast to this, an international society consists of 'a group of states, conscious of certain common interests and common values' which 'conceive themselves to be bound by a common set of rules in their relations with one another, and [which] *share in the working of common institutions*'. (2002: 9, 13). Emphasis added.
6 This is not an exhaustive list of cases. For Transnistria, Nagorno Karabakh, and Kurdistan, for example, see some of the other chapters in this volume. See also Stansfield (2003).
7 The non-Sinhalese population consists of 12 per cent Sri Lankan Tamils, 5 per cent Indian Plantation Tamils, 7 per cent Muslims, and 2 per cent Burghers and aborigines. See Peebles (2006).
8 On the military front, the LTTE assassinated central and local government officials as well as moderate Tamils and attacked targets of strategic importance, such as the airport, sacred temples, military centres, naval ships, and oil tankers. In addition,

suicide terrorism has been a potent tool for the LTTE, claiming hundreds of casualties. See, for example, de Mel (2007: especially page 194).

9 In the course of the thirty years of conflict between the Colombo government and the Tamil rebels, both sides have been accused of committing violations of human rights. The closing episode of the conflict in 2009, however, appears to have been characterized by massive violations of human rights and humanitarian law on the side of the Colombo government. Amnesty International has documented such violations at www.amnesty.org/en/region/sri-lanka.

10 Given that there are numerous English sources that elaborate on the origins of the conflict which led to the emergence of the TRNC, consideration of those causes here is – by design – going to be economical. See, for instance, Necatigil (1993), Stephen (2001), Mallinson (2008), Hakki (2008), and Michael (2009).

11 In the course of the war, some 180,000 Greek Cypriots and 37,000 Turkish Cypriots fled their homes. In the aftermath of the war, a further massive population swap took place: 20,000 Turkish Cypriots went north, whilst some 200,000 Greek Cypriots headed south (Schaeffer 1990: 240–4; Stephen 2001: 21–51).

12 This was a double-edged rationale, however. On the one hand, it alienated Greek Cypriots who viewed Turkish Cypriots' aspirations for confederal arrangements as excessive. On the other hand, by envisaging no long-term future for the TRNC, such rationale thwarted the prospects for the entity's international recognition.

13 UN Security Council Resolution 541 (1983), adopted on 18 November 1983, is available at www.un.int/cyprus/scr541.htm.

14 The TRNC is heavily reliant on external assistance, but so is the Republic of Cyprus. Scott Pegg cites a 1979 article in *Maclean's*, which states that Greek Cyprus ranks:

> as one of the most subsidized nations in the world. With a population of only half a million people, it receives something like $54 million annually in grant aid from the United States, Greece, the United Nations, Britain, Germany and other countries, as well as an average $12 million a year in soft loans … Foreign aid and loans approach a fifth of all government revenues, and the over-all contribution to the economy, including military spending, may be of the same order.
>
> (Pegg 1998: 152)

15 This suggestion was the gist of a 2002 UN Plan, known as the Annan Plan, which foresaw the establishment of a federal state – United Cyprus Republic – in which the Greek Cypriot territory and the Turkish Cypriot territory would be constituent units. The Annan Plan can be accessed at www.hri.org/docs/annan/Annan_Plan_Text.html.

16 Central to these concerns were demographic considerations (Loizides and Antoniades 2009: 611–22).

17 The Socialist Federal Republic of Yugoslavia (established in 1945) was constituted of six republics (Slovenia, Croatia, Serbia, Bosnia, Montenegro, and Macedonia) and two autonomous regions (Kosovo and Vojvodina), which were assigned to the republic of Serbia.

18 On 9 and 10 November 1991, Bosnian Serbs voted to establish an independent Serbian Republic within the border of Bosnia Herzegovina. Then, after announcing that the republic of Bosnia no longer existed, in January 1992, the Bosnian Serb leaders declared the 'Serbian Republic of Bosnia Herzegovina' (later renamed Republika Srpska) to be a part of the rump Yugoslavia (Andrejevich 1992: 9–13). For military and other forms of assistance Bosnian Serbs received from Serbia proper, see *Prosecutor vs. Duško Tadić*, opinion and judgement of 7 May 1997, case no. IT-94–1-T, paragraphs 84–97, printed in Klip and Sluiter (1999: 309–11). See also *Prosecutor vs. Duško Tadić*, Appeals Judgement of 15 July 1999, case no. IT-94–1-A, paragraphs 83–162, printed in Klip and Sluiter (2001: 783–806). See also Gow (2003: chapters 6 and 7).

19 Letter dated 26 November 1991 from the Permanent Representative of Yugoslavia to

the United Nations, addressed to the president of the Security Council, UN Doc. S/23240, 26 November 1991.

20 Report of the Secretary-General Pursuant to Resolution 871 (1993), UN Doc. S/1994/300, 16 March 1994, paragraph 8.

21 This figure comes from Glenny (1992: 29).

22 The Dayton Agreement (signed in November 1995) provided for two distinct entities within the Federation of Bosnia Herzegovina: the Bosnian-Muslim Federation, holding 51 per cent of the territory, and Republika Srpska, holding the remaining 49 per cent. The merits of Dayton remain disputed and some have criticized the accord for de facto partitioning Bosnia and legitimizing ethnic cleansing. See, for instance, Kumar (1997: especially pages 35–7, 104–5).

23 International Crisis Group (2009: 6). Citing Serbia's President Boris Tadić and Russian Ambassador Aleksandar Bocan Harcenko in *Dnevni Avaz*, 29 October and 14 October 2009, respectively.

24 For a concise and up-to-date review of events in Republika Srpska, see ICG (2009) and Parish (2009).

25 Abkhaz population shrunk from 26 per cent (of Abkhazia's population) in 1926 to 13 per cent in 1950 (Geldenhuys 2009: 70). Abkhazia is now estimated to have a population of just over 200,000 (International Crisis Group 2006d: 1).

26 Deon Geldenhuys notes that, by 2006, 80 per cent of the Abkhazians used Russian passports. This has further severed ties between Tbilisi and Sukhumi. Georgian authorities have declared the policy of 'annexation by passportisation' illegal – concerned about repercussions of having a large number of 'Russian citizens' residing in Georgia's territory (Geldenhuys 2009: 75–6). See also International Crisis Group (2006d: 8–10).

27 According to the 1989 census, the overall population of South Ossetia was then about 99,700 people, of whom 65,000 were Ossetians and 26,000 were Georgians. 98,000 Ossetians lived in the rest of Georgia (International Crisis Group 2004: 5).

28 This is exacerbated by two conflicting dynamics: Russia's preoccupation with control over its 'near abroad' – a region historically under its sphere of influence; and Georgia's aspiration to join Western structures, including NATO and the EU.

29 The Russian–Georgian war of August 2008 has been the subject of an extensive EU report which, amongst other things, stated that Russia's actions reflected long-term ambitions to impose her influence in her near abroad (European Union 2009). See also The Economist (2009).

30 Nicaragua, Venezuala, and Nauru are the only other states to have recognized the independence of Abkhazia and South Ossetia. Russia's rhetoric also used the 'Kosovo precedent' – namely that Kosovo's declaration of independence in February 2008 against Serbia's wishes was recognized by Western countries – to try and justify Moscow's decision to recognize the statehood of South Ossetia and Abkhazia. Nonetheless, parallels between Georgia's provinces and Kosovo are dubious since Tbilisi has not threatened the populations of South Ossetia and Abkhazia with large-scale violations of human rights such as those committed by Serbian forces in Kosovo. Kosovo's independence has been a long process, supervised by the international community under the umbrella of the United Nations. The latter have insisted that developments in Kosovo are not meant to set any precedent.

31 The Vienna Convention on the Law of Treaties defines a peremptory norm in Article 53 as 'accepted and recognized by the international community of States as a whole as a norm from which no derogation is permitted and which can be modified only by a subsequent norm of general international law having the same character'. The Vienna Convention is available at http://untreaty.un.org/ilc/texts/instruments/english/conventions/1_1_1969.pdf.

4 What do unrecognized states tell us about sovereignty?

Stacy Closson

In the classical sense of the state gaining sovereignty through recognition by a majority of existing states based on established principles, it would be enough to say that unrecognized states have no sovereignty. Most international legal experts would agree. And yet, since the 1980s, two fundamental debates in international relations that question the state and sovereignty suggest that there could be something gained from asking: *what do unrecognized states tell us about sovereignty?*

The assumption of a state, its sovereignty, and the functioning of a specific kind of state sovereignty are often taken for granted. This places certain restrictions on the possible variations on stateness and sovereignty that occur in practice. Testing the traditional notion of sovereignty are three strands of literature that engage with sovereignty in a post-modern context. They include political scientists questioning the changing normative context of state recognition, critical theorists challenging the traditional notion of sovereignty, and, most recently, constructivists taking a 'linguistic turn' on sovereignty. This chapter engages with this literature and accepts the idea that sovereignty is an evolving concept.

To this end, several questions are posed, pertaining, first, to the relationship between recognition and membership in the international state system and, second, to sovereign-like attributes of unrecognized states. It is accepted that the absence of recognition denies juridical statehood, but does it necessarily deny sovereignty? Can we distinguish between the practice and rhetoric of sovereignty? If so, how has the discourse of sovereignty been incorporated by unrecognized states into their quest for legitimacy in the eyes of the international community? What options, if any, short of internationally granted *de jure* statehood, are available to unrecognized states?

The first section will argue that recognition has followed a political path, changing according to the normative situation at that time. From self-determination to democratic principles, unrecognized states have sought to fulfil changing criteria for recognition. Following on from this, the second section will explore the theoretical debates on the notion of sovereignty in international relations. There is an increasing divide in the literature between those who argue for the staying power of sovereignty and those who argue that the state is being challenged by new forms of political authority. The third section will examine the linguistic turn in the notion of sovereignty and how this may relate to unrecognized states. In particular, the post-positivists have suggested that the simulation of sovereignty calls into question the location and exercise of traditional sovereignty. The chapter concludes by reflecting on how the three theoretical debates inform the meaning of sovereignty for unrecognized states. Despite theoretical challenges to the notion of sovereignty, recognition as a state by entities appears to reinforce sovereignty as the primary legal and political order. Nevertheless, this will only remain so long as the legitimization of the recognition process is not undermined.

The politics of recognition

Sovereignty is most often associated with the modern nation-state. In political terms, sovereignty refers to the political structures projecting power within and beyond boundaries, while legalistically the state is the sovereign source of political authority, establishing internal and external prerogatives (Adler-Nissen and Gammeltoft-Hansen 2008: 201). Conventional readings of sovereignty focus on a class of properties essential to statehood, qualifying differences that allow for the granting of sovereignty in certain cases. According to the practice of international law, a state has sovereignty through recognition by other states in the international community. Sovereignty is granted under customary international law, based upon the principles of the 1933 Montevideo Convention on the Rights and Duties of States. These four-fold principles require that a state has a permanent population, a defined territory, a government, and capacity to enter into relations with other states in the international community. Aalberts (2004: 250–1) argues that sovereign statehood does not exist independent of and prior to state practice and international law, and is, as such, the medium and outcome of the practices of states. At the same time, the classical notion of sovereignty accepts that empirical sovereignty exists before it is given. Thus, sovereign states are such because other states allow them to, and accept them as equals. This renders recognition a pivotal element for the existence of sovereign states within international society.

In practice, recognizing an entity as a sovereign state is inherently political. The context in which the claim of sovereignty occurs, to whom the sovereignty claim is addressed, the normative structures used to determine the legitimacy of a claim to sovereignty, and the consequences following from acceptance of a sovereignty claim depend on individual cases (Werner and De Wilde 2001: 286). In particular, whose recognition is required to be a sovereign state and the criteria necessary for recognition have changed according to the historical context. It is unclear if it must be a majority of states, major powers, a core of elites, or a hegemonic power. The matter of criteria is also subjective. It is often written that states are recognized as sovereign when they can demonstrate the ability to defend their authority against domestic and international challengers. However, there are recognized states that cannot do this (e.g. Sudan, Somalia, and Afghanistan), and there are states that can demonstrate their authority but have not been recognized (e.g. Somaliland). Likewise, there have been several instances in history when states met the Montevideo Convention criteria but they were in violation of the right to self-determination, or they violated some other norm of international relations (e.g. South Rhodesia), or recognition was politically too sensitive (e.g. Taiwan).

The basis of recognition has evolved from self-determination of the post-colonial period to secession based on communal identity and historic continuity, often combined with allegations of human rights violations.[1] However, territorial integrity of the state has almost always been upheld and there are very few successful cases of secession: Bangladesh, Eritrea, East Timor, and parts of the former Yugoslavia. Unsuccessful attempts at secession are more numerous: Tibet, Kashmir, Katanga/Shaba, Biafra, Karen and Shan States, Bougainville, Chechnya, and Republika Srpska. But secession has been deemed a final resort solution, followed only when federalism, autonomy, and minority rights cannot prevent injustice and the central government is deemed illegitimate due to its authoritarian and repressive nature. In this case, a group should have historic claims over a territory and should constitute a new state based on democratic norms. This has worked best when a state dissolves into several states, such as Czechoslovakia, the former Soviet Union, and Yugoslavia (see Geldenhuys 2009: Ch. 2).

The 2008 recognition of Kosovo by mostly Western states is evidence of the political nature of upholding self-determination of peoples over the territorial integrity of states. It is unclear if this will become a precedent in international law due to its non-compliance with the previously stated reasons for secession, the limited number of states thus far to recognize Kosovo, and opposing countries affected by separatist movements themselves (Krueger 2009). Nonetheless, it was tested when Russia recognized Abkhazia and South Ossetia in the wake of the August 2008 war between it and Georgia. In Russia's argument for recognition, it did not refer to a legal foundation, nor did any states other than Nicaragua initially join Russia in recognition. Instead Russia declared that, as Kosovo was an exception, so too were Abkhazia and South Ossetia. Prior to this, Russia's official position on Kosovo and the unrecognized states had been based on the sovereignty of the parent states, the implementation of United Nations Security Council resolutions recognizing this fact, and deference to norms of international law. In response, the European Union report on the 2008 war between Georgia and Russia over South Ossetia made clear that self-determination was not recognized in international law as a basis for the unilateral creation of a new state 'outside the colonial context and apartheid', and that much of international state practice 'and the explicit views of major powers such as Russia in the Kosovo case stand against it'. They concluded that Georgia, not its sub-units of Abkhazia and South Ossetia, was eligible for independence in case of dismemberment of a larger entity such as the former Soviet Union (European Union 2009: 18).

For the Western states, Kosovo's recognition was partly based on 'earned sovereignty', as per the EU and US foreign policy agendas promoting democratic principles (William and Pecci 2004). The European Community's Badinter Commission on Yugoslavia emphasized the rule of law, democracy, and human rights in recognizing the former Yugoslav republics. The 1991 *Recognition of New States in Eastern Europe and the Soviet Union of the European Community (*European Community 1991) added to the Montevideo criteria the nature of their political structures and practices, including respecting established borders, observing human rights and democracy, upholding the rule of law, guaranteeing minority rights, committing to settle disputes peacefully, and accepting nuclear non-proliferation. This culminated in the 2003 'standards before status' Western policy in Kosovo, suggesting that recognition could be awarded to entities that succeeded in building effective democratic institutions.

Hence, the context for recognition has changed over time according to the political climate and has not always followed the original principles attributed to a sovereign. As Tozun Bahcheli *et al.* opine, in some cases recognition is granted or maintained in spite of the actual conditions within the state. In other cases, recognition is withheld even though the realities on the ground support the principle of territorial integrity (Bahcheli *et al.* 2004). They go on to write:

> We are thus faced with an absurd combination of states and would-be states existing in a legal fog: some widely-recognized states can claim only the rudimentary conditions for statehood; indeed, in some instances, even those minimal conditions seem ephemeral and random. In other cases, full-functioning and self-contained states are guaranteed as pariahs, excluded form the mainstream channels of international diplomacy, existing in conditions beyond the pale of normal international intercourse.
>
> (Bahcheli *et al.* 2004: 12)

Given the changing context for recognition and its political nature, the credibility of the international system in assigning sovereignty to an entity is called into question. As Bartelson (2006) argues, it makes normative problems intrinsically hard to settle and it is this impasse, he predicts, that will prove to be a major challenge for legal and political theory in the future.

Contesting sovereignty

The second trend in the literature has been for critical theorists to contest the traditional notion of sovereignty. In the 1990s, the limits of benign juridical sovereignty and the legitimacy of certain sovereigns was an increasingly contestable factor. The post-Cold War international debate on issues such as the proliferation of intrastate conflict, humanitarian disasters, and genocide increasingly called into question the problematic nature of sovereignty in hindering intervention by the international community. Given that sovereign states were both democratic and totalitarian, developed and undeveloped, stable and unstable, sovereignty appeared to be both contestable and informative of political power arrangements (Weber 1995). Ilgen (2003: 9) argued that 'sovereignty resists a simple and static definition because it is to be found in a wide variety of changing social and political relationships'. In particular, scholars recognized that the formal equality of post-colonial states was not matched by practical and substantial equality within the states (Sørenson 1999). That is, many of the newly recognized states in the post-colonial period lacked internal legitimacy and were susceptible to external coercive forces.

Jackson (1990) was one of the first to suggest that post-colonial states possessed neither internal coherence nor credible governments to be granted the status of full sovereignty, labelling them instead 'quasi-states'. He argued that weakness persisted in African states because they were granted juridical sovereignty by the international community, despite lacking sufficient empirical sovereignty (internal legitimacy). Likewise, a post-structuralist reading of sovereignty by Walker distinguished inside from outside sovereignty (1992: 169–74). Sovereignty from the inside referred to the tensions between power and authority or between state and civil society. Sovereignty from the outside was the presence of sovereign states as primary actors, marking the absence of a sovereign power/authority governing the system itself (anarchy). While the absence of a domestic authority did not necessarily challenge the international legal sovereignty of a state, it produced a situation in which some states served as an arena for activities not conducive to state-building (Krasner 2001: 7).

Jackson's theory of 'quasi-state' broke the link between the right to sovereignty and the capacity to handle sovereignty. In fact, he reversed the neo-realist/neo-liberal consensus on the role of anarchy in international relations. Contrary to the neo-neo view, Jackson argued that there was stability in the international system through the acceptance of the juridical sovereignty of the state, while anarchy reigned within what he called 'quasi-states' at the domestic level. Jackson's discussion of a lack of empirical sovereignty should not be construed to mean that a state necessarily lacks institutions or the capacity to govern. Rather, it is the lack of authority existing within the state to wield effective control over the state due to an absence of will. Thus, authority depends on recognition, while control depends on concrete capabilities to monitor and enforce compliance with rules that are made under the authority. While there still may be an authority at the helm of the state, the loss of control over territory or other responsibilities of the state would signify the weakening of domestic sovereignty (Krasner 1999: 10).

There are those who critique Jackson for blurring the notion of sovereignty for quasi-states, rather than clarifying it. That is, his analysis is entrenched in the conventional sovereign discourse and he participates in the reconstitution of its descriptive fallacy. Jackson assumes, critics argue, that at some point empirical sovereignty will have to be developed in quasi-states. Werner and De Wilde (2001) argue that this approach towards quasi-states assigns too narrow an understanding to sovereignty as a part of international law and international society. They write:

> Sovereignty is not equivalent to the right to freedom from interference and respect for immunities as such; rather, a successful claim to sovereignty

> establishes a link between a status and certain rights, power and responsibilities that the sovereign entity possesses.
>
> (Werner and De Wilde 2001: 301)

Moreover, they argue, Jackson's separation of norm and fact misunderstands the institutional character of sovereignty. Sovereignty is not the brute exercise of power but a specific form of legitimization whose reality consists in its being accepted by relevant audiences. Bartmann (2004) argues, likewise, that the internal basis of legitimacy reflects the extent to which the state is identified with primary community loyalties. The international judgment of a state's legitimacy is based, in part, on the assessment of this evidence.

In addition to the juridical/empirical debate concerning sovereignty, others have argued that sovereignty is problematic as it is constantly challenged by supra- and sub-state entities. Debate among realist and liberal theorists on the concept of sovereignty has developed over the past 20 years, moving on from the fields of international law and political philosophy to a problematic concept with practical implications for international relations. For liberal theorists, sovereignty has traditionally been defined in terms of the state's ability to control actors and activities within and across its borders, which is being eroded by globalization, economic interdependence, and modern technology. For realists, sovereignty is about the state's ability to make authoritative decisions. Contrary to liberal theorists, realists argue that state control over important external flows has not eroded relative to state control over internal flows. Hence, the debate is split between those who view the sovereign state as challenged by new authorities and communities dividing the domestic and international spheres, eventually creating new forms of political life, and those who believe that sovereign states will remain a force of authority and community well into the future.

Bartelson (2006: 466) argues that, in reality, the divide in the debate appears to be more of a philosophical point than reflective of the political world today. Sovereignty, he argues, is regularly divided and shared among state and non-state actors at all levels of governance, at the supra- and sub-state levels. This view is shared by Walker (2008: 21–3), who suggests that sovereignty is relocated in a less state-centred world to new functional sites. Indeed, sovereignty is rarely monopolized by the state, but is shared among state and non-state actors at all levels of government, depending on the issue. For example, much is made of sovereignty ceded by the member states of the European Union to a supra-sovereign. However, an equally important movement in Europe is the decentralization and downward devolution of sovereignty within states, such as increasing Welsh, Scottish, and Irish control over economic development in Great Britain. Ilgen (2003: 2) writes that 'boundaries between national and regional or local sovereignty have been in flux and, more often than not, this movement has been towards greater sovereignty for sub-national layers of governance'. He attributes the causes of this reconfiguration and dispersion of authority to other levels of governance, to *inter alia*, ineffective or dysfunctional central governments coupled with external economic pressures.

Linguistic turn on sovereignty

The third debate on sovereignty has been a largely constructivist one. That is, the concept of sovereignty is just a general name to constitute an object (the state) into a class by which we create the world. By the 1980s, there was general agreement that sovereignty, conventionally understood as equally distributed across all states, was a contested concept (Buzan 1983: 68; Biersteker and Weber 1996). Moving away from positivism, it was argued that the meaning of sovereignty was dependent upon its use. The practices and discourses underlying and constituting the institution of sovereignty should be appreciated. 'In effect, sovereignty is a practical category whose empirical contents are not fixed but evolve in a way reflecting the active practical consensus among co reflective statements' (Ashley 1989: 272). Hence, the universally accepted definition of sovereignty with a fixed meaning was being challenged by inter-subjective actions within a normative framework and how these practices reconstructed state sovereignty (Biersteker and Weber 1996: 11).

Bartelson (2006) argued that this linguistic turn actually strengthened sovereignty's purpose in the legal and political discourse. He wrote:

> The very moment that scholars decided that the meaning of sovereignty lies very much in what we make of it through our linguistic conventions and rhetorical practices, they also opened up a new field of inquiry within which this concept could survive and thrive, albeit now as an object of inquiry rather than as its uncontested foundation.
>
> (Bartelson 2006: 464)

Sovereignty, then, plays an important role in normative discourses by imaginarily bridging the gap between what exists and what could be. A successful claim to sovereignty establishes a link between an institutional fact of 'being' sovereign and the rights and duties that follow from the existence of this institutional fact.

Sovereignty becomes important when the perceived ability of states to ensure effective internal rule and freedom from external interference is called into question. 'Sovereignty is a speech act to re-establish the claimant's position as an absolute authority, and to legitimize its exercise of power' (Werner and De Wilde 2001: 287). This way of interpretation resembles the 'linguistic turn' in studies of international security, such as the Copenhagen school's process-oriented securitization of issues, examining how an issue is transformed by an actor as a matter of security and how it is accepted (Buzan *et al.* 1998). Sovereignty also has to do with belief. In three recent examples – the former Socialist Federal Republic of Yugoslavia, the German Democratic Republic, and the Soviet Union – as soon as the belief in their existence waned, institutional facts ceased to exist. So, too, can institutional facts be believed into existence (Werner and De Wilde 2001: 293). Aalberts (2004: 255) writes:

> For sovereign statehood, both in its 'classical' and 'quasi' variants, is a discursive fact which depends on the constant maintenance, defence, attack,

> reproduction, undermining and relegitimation through widely circulated practices by diplomats, scholars and the like, which in turn settle its empirical contents. Both classifications depend on an inner subjective understanding of entities, which are constituted by this very agreement.
>
> (Aalberts 2004: 255)

Part of this linguistic turn has examined a society that does not adhere to the authority of a state, but rather to another political entity (Thomson 1995: 228). Cynthia Weber (1995) applies a post-modern approach to capture the debate on empirical sovereignty. She argues that sovereignty can be 'simulated' by state elites, or the regime, for the purposes of survival. State and society can also 'simulate' sovereignty in their efforts to undermine the state. Moreover, sovereignty can be constructed from the bottom-up; from the inter-connections among societal formations and the trans-national forces that penetrate them. Weber suggests analysing state sovereignty through a series of questions (1995: 30). Who or what is the foundational authority figure for each interpretive community? Where, if anywhere, does sovereignty reside in each distinct historical period and for each particular inter-subjective community? What, if anything, does sovereignty mean for each community?

Weber explains that simulated sovereignty is the result of the act of constituting a state. Like Walker, she argues that it should therefore be viewed as a continual process, 'repeated in various forms at numerous spatial and temporal locales' (1995: 3). In a later work, Weber clarifies how the study of sovereignty should be approached:

> While the word sovereignty denotes a state of being – an ontological status – sovereignty in fact expresses a characteristic way in which being or sovereign statehood may be inferred from doing or practice. It is not possible to talk about the state as an ontological being – as a political identity – without engaging in the political practice of constituting the state.
>
> (Weber 1995: 3)

Critics of the linguistic turn suggest that some scholars fall prey to a fallacy when they insist that sovereignty denotes the actual power or capacity a state possesses to exercise full control internally and to remain independent externally. These scholars often subsequently find that sovereignty is in decline. Adherents to the linguistic turn argue, in response, that sovereignty is not in decline; rather it is not a measurable percentage of effective power or independence (Werner and De Wilde 2001).

Sovereignty for the unrecognized

The three previously discussed developments in the study of sovereignty – the politics of recognition, contesting sovereignty, and the linguistic turn – combine to provide some insights into what the unrecognized states tell us about sovereignty. Post-modernists argue that power and politics have moved away from the strict definitions of state institutions towards the process of engaging in political activity. Simultaneously, sovereignty is problematic and continually being constituted. Compounding these uncertainties is a seemingly inconsistent pattern of state recognition since World War II. Given these developments, this last section will explore how the discourse of sovereignty has been incorporated by unrecognized states into their quest for legitimacy in the eyes of the international community and what options, short of internationally granted *de jure* statehood, are available to unrecognized states.

Unrecognized states can be comprised of state-like institutions and political processes, simulating empirical and juridical sovereignty. Authorities in unrecognized states believe they must convince their polity as well as the international community that they are capable of governing a state. The leadership of unrecognized states go to great lengths to present themselves as de facto sovereign. The de facto governments of unrecognized states have understood that it is important to appear democratic in order to earn their juridical sovereignty, following the 'standards before status' process observed in the case of Kosovo. They have passed constitutions with articles declaring their sovereign, democratic, and rule-of-law based statehood. De facto governments have opened themselves up for scrutiny, inviting observers to elections and foreign journalists to cover events. Their leaders insist that they are not just functioning democratic states, but also nation-states that command the loyalty of their population. To this end, they have held multiple referenda confirming that the majority of their populations support independent statehood. Increasingly, these republics have called for recognition of their sovereign status when meeting with representatives of the Europe Union and the United Nations. Additionally, they have adopted rhetoric that reflects the current support for recognition, from self-determination to human rights and, in the case of South Ossetia in 2008, aggressions by Georgian forces against Russian peacekeepers and the civil population.

Sometimes the exercise of sovereignty can be problematic within an unrecognized state. As unrecognized states undergo a transformative process, empirical sovereignty fluctuates. Penetrated by new global forces, open to traversing unprotected territorial and financial zones, and perhaps artificially divided from a dominant community, sovereignty is in flux within a certain period. Sovereignty for a community actually can mean very little if the community does not identify with the state, the regime, or the nation, but rather is fixated on survival and undermining authority to these ends. Moreover, the act of authority in an unrecognized state can be simulated by elites or the regime, for the purposes of survival. As Caspersen (2008: 122) notes, there is tension between the political competition entailed by democracy and the nationalist claim to unity and homogeneous interests. Nationalist leaders tend to present a united front, papering over internal divisions within a society. Indeed, non-recognition can actually enhance the legitimacy of the less desirable regimes in unrecognized states. The governments in these entities can get away with ruling less fairly, transparently, and democratically all in the name of 'embodying the quest for sovereignty' (Broers 2005).[2]

There are also issues of legitimacy of authority as several actors within the territory may vie to be the sovereign. In an unrecognized state, the foundational authority figure for the community can be conceptualized as shifting, often unidentifiable, and even illegitimate. For example, in Abkhazia most ethnic communities (Abkhaz, Armenian, Greek, and Russian) are loyal to the Abkhaz-led government in Sukhumi. However, the Georgian citizens (Mingrelians) living in the eastern Gali district bordering Georgia are mostly allegiant to local Georgian leaders. Moreover, as in recognized states, the sources of legitimacy in societies can be varied, including a council of elders, local leaders, and the family clan. This competition for legitimacy can be particularly troublesome in what tend to be small, isolated entities facing external challenges to their viability. This legitimacy can also be tested by an external state, whose influence appears to test the authority within the unrecognized state. Tensions have risen around election time in Nagorno Karabakh concerning the undue influence of Armenian elites from Yerevan. More recently, the authority of South Ossetia has been challenged by the Russian government's frustration with the weak and corrupt leadership in Georgia's breakaway region. Ossetians have called on the Russian government to hold their Russian designated leadership responsible for deplorable economic conditions in the post-war environment as a result of misappropriated aid.

Unrecognized states also engage in a competition with the parent state, seeking to discredit the democratic qualifications of, for example, Georgia in the case of Abkhazia. Why should they, the Abkhaz argue, join Georgia, an autocratic and unstable state? In response to this, the parent states have mobilized their populations, particularly displaced persons from the regions declaring independence, to exercise their claims of sovereignty in their former lands. The most striking example has been the establishment by the Georgian government of provisional administrations in South Ossetia and Abkhazia. These administrations were chosen either by presidential appointment (Abkhazia) or election (South Ossetia) and were provided federal funding for the construction of governmental and other buildings, as well as the payment of employees' salaries. Western leaders met with these alternative regimes, who expressed their desire to remain autonomous entities within Georgia. As a result, there were two governments simulating sovereignty with competing claims for recognition from the international community as the representative of an autonomous community.

Over time, non-recognition can create a feeling of 'condemnation' upon the part of the unrecognized authorities. Leaders of unrecognized states deal with such questions as to whether they are denied recognition because they do not comply with certain standards or they are judged unfairly against other states (Geldenhuys 2009: 7). Often an unrecognized state remains weak, hampered by sanctions, limited financial resources, isolation from the international community, and overshadowed by the parent state. Moreover, states upholding the territorial integrity of the parent state tend not to provide financial or other forms of development assistance to unrecognized states over concerns that this would legitimize the regime's claim to independence. This tends to keep the unrecognized state dependent on non-transparent means of economic welfare, including smuggling and remittances.

There are several suggested sovereign arrangements for unrecognized states. Short of outright recognition as juridical sovereigns, they can be included into the external patron state as a sovereign entity, unite with the parent state outright, or unite with the parent state in a federal arrangement, splitting sovereign duties.[3] There has been progress in boundary arbitration in several recognized states, allowing for qualified sovereignty of a people. These include the former Yugoslavia (Brčko within Bosnia-Herzegovina), Sudan (North and South pursuant to the Comprehensive Peace Agreement), and Somalia (Somaliland and Putland). Suggestions have also been made that an unrecognized state becomes a condominium between two states; that is, sovereignty is shared between two neighbouring states. One scholar has gone so far as to call for consolidating and partitioning already existing states to reflect the realities of relations (Herbst 1996). In reality, very few of these options are exercised. Rather, unrecognized states seek the support from a neighboring state or external entity for financial assistance. This allows some unrecognized states that are *de jure* part of recognized states to acquire de facto independent status.

In conclusion, despite all of the post-modern theoretical turns regarding the concept of sovereignty, most of the debates appear to reinforce the importance of the international system defined by a group of territorial entities, or states, recognized as sovereign. The struggle for recognition by unrecognized states only reinforces the system of sovereign states. Thus, although scholars may debate about the meaning and the concept of sovereignty, they are in agreement that the concept of sovereignty does have stable core connotations that make theoretical and empirical inquiry meaningful. They also agree that sovereignty will remain the main source of political authority in the near future (Bartelson 2008: 37). As states remain the ones defining the other, they will tend to support a vertical and rigidly hierarchical political architecture. Sovereignty is never granted to non-state entities or heterarchical systems of governing arrangements (Walker 2008: 26–7). Likewise, the international community of states has neither thrown out any states, nor has it been open to readily accept new states, only in exceptional circumstances, such as the break-up of empires, whose members have a constitutional right to independence.

That said, it is still unclear if sovereignty can be considered to be the domain of individuals or other forms of social organization beyond the state, or if sovereignty is exclusive to the party that is granted it initially, or whether it can be shared with another entity, such as between the parent state and an autonomous region. It remains to be determined whether sovereignty is, or will be, reshaped, and if this will ultimately contest the notion of sovereignty as currently understood in legal terms. The danger is that sovereignty will become so contested that it will lose its credibility. This can be done not just by theorists, but also by practitioners. 'Not only does the contemporary debate on sovereignty revolve around factual questions, such as the makeup of the political world, but there is always also a short step from explaining political phenomena to actually justifying them' (Bartelson 2008: 34). As a consequence, sovereignty seems to be an inescapable precondition of political authority and order. Whether other forms of political authority and social organization are deemed sovereign is something for continued debate.

Notes

1 The right to self-determination is cited in three sources: Article 1.2 and Article 55 of the United Nations Charter and Article 1 of both Covenants of Human Rights. Claims of secession are compliant with international law if it is based on a decision made by the entire population against the parent state or if it is anchored in the national law of the parent state and follows the respective secession procedure. It is also legitimate if a region annexed by another state in circumstances contrary to international law declares its secession from the annexing state (Cassese 1995; Kohen 2006).

2 For further analysis of how unrecognized states imitate effective, democratic statehood, see Caspersen's chapter in this volume.

3 Georgia has favoured asymmetrical federalism, granting Abkhazia a higher level of autonomy than South Ossetia. The Abkhaz and South Ossetians, in response, have supported independence in the first instance, and a confederation as a last resort. Under the confederate model, their sovereignty would be internationally recognized and would give them the right to secede when desired.

Part II

The interactions of the recognized and the unrecognized state

5 States without sovereignty

Imitating democratic statehood[1]

Nina Caspersen

> Pridnestrovie is an independent republic with a well-functioning democratic government.
>
> Government of Pridnestrovie[2]

The above statement, from a website which promises to teach you '10 things you didn't know about Europe's newest country', Transnistria, illustrates the effort, and occasionally considerable skill, that the leaders of unrecognized states put into raising their international profile and conveying an image of stability and acceptability. From Abkhazia to Somaliland, these entities emphasize not only their right to self-determination, and their alleged suffering of human rights violations, they also proclaim the creation of effective statehood, and this has become a central part of their claim to independence. For example, when asked why Abkhazia should be recognized, one of its leaders responded that it had proven itself viable as a state.[3] These entities are hoping to be recognized as independent states; therefore, trying to build something that looks like a state appears to be an obvious strategy. The unrecognized states are, however, not content with merely the symbolic attributes of statehood, such as a flag, a national anthem, national holidays, a head of state, etc.; they are making more ambitious claims to statehood. They are claiming to have created viable entities with state-like structures that enable them to defend the territory to which they lay claim and provide basic public services to their populations. They are, in effect, claiming that they have all the necessary attributes of statehood *except* international recognition. But can statehood exist without sovereignty and, if so, in what form?

Moreover, as part of their strategy for gaining recognition, unrecognized states are also claiming that they embody democratic values. The regimes are keen to emphasize that they enjoy popular legitimacy and hence do not represent what Walter Kemp (2005) has termed 'selfish determination'. In the past, the basis for this claim would usually be an independence referendum, and it would therefore be directly linked to the claim to self-determination, but over the last decade these entities have increasingly been proclaiming the creation of democratic institutions. Thus, the speaker of the Nagorno Karabakh parliament argues that the entity has 'a serious basis for the international recognition of our sovereignty'; 'we have held free elections for 16 years, law-enforcement bodies are formed, powers are divided, [the] army is under civil control…' (Karabakh Open 2008). Such claims may be meant mainly for an external audience, but the question is whether they can be reduced to this and are, therefore, entirely without substance. Can democratization co-exist with lack of recognition?

In some unrecognized states, this rhetorical commitment to effective, democratic statehood has in fact been accompanied by the building of relatively effective state institutions and a gradual movement away from rule by authoritarian war heroes. However, in other cases, the proclaimed statehood remains embryonic and a few unrecognized states, notably Chechnya and Republika Srpska Krajina, never really managed to move away from the anarchical badlands that dominate the popular imagination of such entities. While they all share the context of non-recognition, and the accompanying uncertainty and isolation, and although their legitimizing strategies are strikingly similar, we find considerable variation in the kind of entity that is created when it comes to both state effectiveness and regime type. Such differences are of course found among recognized states as well, and the question is therefore whether there is something qualitatively different about states without sovereignty. Are they just like other states, merely unrecognized?

This chapter focuses on the internal dynamics of these international anomalies: what kinds of entities tend to develop in the context of non-recognition? It examines the driving forces behind these processes, including the significance of external and internal legitimacy, and argues that the creation of effective, democratic statehood in unrecognized states is both constrained and enabled by the lack of recognition. The factors that may enable its creation also constrain the emerging statehood. The struggle for recognition and for maintaining de facto independence can, under the right circumstances, enable these anomalies to make a significant move away from chaos and disorder. Non-recognition provides powerful incentives for imitating democratic statehood – for imitating what good, recognized states look like – but unrecognized states are not just like other states, merely without the added bonus of recognition.[4] The context of non-recognition and the path of their creation set them apart from their recognized counterparts and make the claim to viable democratic statehood, at best, a claim filled with tensions and contradictions, and moreover affect their long-term sustainability. The specific dynamics of unrecognized statehood therefore affect whether we are dealing with something new in the international system *and* whether it is merely a transient phenomenon or something more permanent.

Creating statehood: overcoming infighting warlords

When we compare the kind of statehood that has been created in unrecognized states, the variations are immense and it may seem that we are comparing entirely different entities. Taiwan, for example, has a per capita GDP of $16,030 and is the world's leading producer of a range of IT products,[5] while most unrecognized states fall closer to a case such as Somaliland, whose economy is largely based on livestock and where the GDP per capita was estimated at only $226 in 2003 (Bradbury 2008: 162).[6] These differences, to some extent, reflect the different starting points for these entities – in particular, their access to resources and the depth of destruction wrought by the wars that, in most cases, preceded their creation. Some unrecognized states, such as Abkhazia and Nagorno Karabakh, experienced devastating warfare, while the violence in other cases, such as Transnistria, was on a much smaller scale. The cases also differ in terms of their geography (including access to natural resources), population size, pre-existence of institutions, and degree of international isolation. State-building is therefore a highly difficult task in all unrecognized states, but for a number of these entities the task is near-impossible. Some territories such as the Taliban 'insurgent state' in Afghanistan have not – as yet – managed to gain the kind of territorial control and relative staying power that characterize unrecognized states,[7] while unrecognized states such as Chechnya and Republika Srpska Krajina were struggling to maintain a minimal degree of control and their existence was ultimately short-lived. These differences in outcome are, however, not explained solely by variations in access to resources, including the existence of an external patron. Another important factor is the internal dynamics in the entity, such as the degree of popular constraints and the extent to which the entity is characterized by infighting. These factors impact on state-building in recognized states as well, but they take on a specific form in the context of non-recognition, which acts both as an enabler and a constraint on state-building.

Unrecognized states are often described as havens for warlords, mercenaries, smugglers, and profiteers; as environments conducive to violence and crime. Thomas de Waal argues that the context of non-recognition and the accompanying 'outlaw' status is 'virtually an incentive to become a rogue state' (de Waal 2003: 246). I have argued elsewhere that the image of criminalized badlands is overplayed (Caspersen 2008), but this is not to say that such incentives and driving forces do not impact on internal developments. Even though these wars were frequently fought under the banner of ethno-nationalism, it would be erroneous to assume that the resulting entity can be seen as homogeneous or that collective interests will dominate. Ethnic groups are not homogeneous and ethnic conflicts are not solely, or even primarily, driven by a concern for collective interests. Gaspar Tamás argues that post-Cold War nationalism is anarchistic and indifferent to the 'raison d' état': 'ethno-anarchism destroys states ... and fails to replace them with anything' (1996: 172, 181), but it is rather the case that the self-proclaimed ethnic leaders are often more concerned with power and personal enrichment than with collective goals, and state-building is consequently not prioritized.

Elite greed clearly distracts resources and attention away from the needs of the entity, but even more damaging for any attempts at state-building is the infighting of warlords, which is frequently associated with a near-complete breakdown of central control and security.[8] Rivalling warlords most famously characterized the case of Chechnya, which gradually descended into something approaching pure anarchy (see Tishkov 2004; Hughes 2007). Chechnya was the ultimate 'failed' unrecognized state and the case has even given name to its own syndrome: the 'Chechen syndrome', which describes the infighting of warlords and the resulting collapse of statehood. This kind of fractionalization is typical of failed states, recognized or unrecognized, but the question is whether it is more likely in the context of non-recognition. It appears to be. In addition to the legacy of war, there is a lack of institutions and, therefore, of constraints on rivalling elites *and* the lack of recognition creates an opportune environment for shadow economies and hence provides elites with the resources needed to challenge rivals and ignore popular sentiments. Moreover, the reliance on an external patron, which is found in most unrecognized states, makes it more likely that the control of key resources is divided. External patrons are not necessarily motivated primarily by the need for unity and may make use of internal divisions to increase their influence in the entity. This happened, for example, in Republika Srpska Krajina, where the Serbian government used a divide-and-rule policy, and supplied rivalling leaders with both coercive and economic resources in order to maintain control in the entity (Caspersen 2010).

In some ways, unrecognized states are, therefore, predisposed to fractionalization and collapse, but in other respects they are actually in a good position to avoid dangerous infighting and succeed in state-building. Unrecognized states may lack the resources and institutions necessary to prevent criminalization, but they tend to be relatively homogeneous, which reduces the risk of dangerous fractionalization. Internal cohesion is furthermore strengthened by the persistence of an external threat and the leadership can make use of the internal legitimacy they have earned through their military success. Finally, the goal of recognition would appear to provide a powerful incentive for building effective entities. That these factors do not necessarily lead to a closing of ranks is, however, clearly illustrated by the cases of Chechnya and Republika Srpska Krajina. The external threat was, for example, very real in both cases but infighting nevertheless dominated. We cannot assume that collective interests are the main driving force or that popular cleavages are the only source of fractionalization – neither of these assumptions holds up to closer scrutiny. But the potential for internal cohesion can nevertheless be used to counteract infighting warlords and enable gradual state-building, and a number of cases have actually been successful in ensuring unity.

The unrecognized states that did not emerge from a full-blown war, such as Transnistria, are clearly at less risk of this kind of infighting, but also cases that have borne the full brunt of warfare have managed to overcome the damaging influence of rivalling warlords. Unlike cases such as Republika Srpska Krajina and Chechnya, Nagorno Karabakh was not plagued by infighting and this has had a significant impact on its ability to create effective statehood. A number of factors seem to account for the greater level of internal cohesion, but most notably, the army leadership had already managed to subsume various militias during the war. These efforts had been helped, in no small part, by support from Yerevan and from the Armenian Diaspora; unlike in the case of Republika

Srpska Krajina, the external backers did not support rivalling forces. The resulting army cohesiveness allowed one man to clearly emerge as Karabakh's strongman: the army commander and defence minister Samvel Babayan. Babayan's monolithic position was helped by the fact that a number of potentially powerful military leaders chose not to challenge his leadership,[9] and Babayan, in any case, made sure that serious rivals did not emerge from within his ranks. Thus, a feud with a military commander named 'Vacho' reportedly ended in an armed showdown and Vacho was forced to flee Karabakh (de Waal 2003: 242). Babayan's ability to avoid rivalry was further strengthened by his very substantial wealth, and his power rivalled, and at times even surpassed, that of the civilian leadership (ibid.: 241; Armenian News Network 2004). Interestingly, the civilian leadership actively promoted the cult of the army commander and war hero, most likely from the view that his dominance would be instrumental for the entity's survival, since it conveyed an image of Nagorno Karabakh as the embodiment of military victory and since the centralization of power allowed the entity to embark on a relatively speedy process of recovery. Importantly, Babayan's war-time credentials also helped confer legitimacy on the civilian leaders. The leaders, in this case, cared about the legitimacy of their position and this appears to have reduced the risk of fractionalization. This finding suggests that bottom-up conflicts are more likely to be associated with cohesiveness at the elite level, since they are exposed to some popular constraints and since we generally find a low level of heterogeneity in these cases.

Debilitating internal rivalry, therefore, may be more likely in unrecognized states than in recognized ones, due to the legacy of war, the weak institutions, and the external interference, but their specific situation may also make it easier to overcome this threat, due to internal cohesion, legitimacy of the victorious leadership, and external patrons. However, even if these initial, and very significant, obstacles are overcome, the unrecognized entities still face obstacles to statehood that set them apart from recognized states. And it is precisely the factors that matter for clearing the initial hurdle – such as centralization of resources, external support, internal cohesion, and lack of pluralism – that result in tensions and contradictions.

Creating democratic statehood: survival and recognition

The imitation of effective, democratic statehood constitutes a key strategy for unrecognized states, since it seemingly furthers their two primary goals: preserving their de facto independence and gaining international recognition.[10] These two driving forces share a lot of similarities and are both ultimately linked to the long-term survival of the entity, but they at times pull in different directions. The rule of Samvel Babayan in Nagorno Karabakh may, for example, have served the initial survival and recovery of the entity, but the commander's ruthless regime gradually became a liability for the civilian leaders. The cult of the war hero was difficult to control; they were mindful of Karabakh's international image and of the obstacle the army commander posed to the creation of effective statehood.[11] The problem of warlords is not over once they stop fighting each other, but lack of recognition – somewhat paradoxically – provides opportunities for undermining their hold on power. Yet tensions between the need for an effective defence, the need for popular legitimacy, and the struggle for international recognition persist. As a result, the internal developments in unrecognized states tend to mirror their international limbo; they remain torn between different forms of statehood, and unstable entities result.

Creating internationally acceptable entities

The aspiration for international recognition remains a defining characteristic of unrecognized states and a central part of the narrative employed by the political elites. Even entities such as Abkhazia and South Ossetia, which are partially recognized, still mention recognition as one of their key priorities. In an interview posted on the official Abkhaz website, the entity's president, for example, emphasizes 'the need to seek the recognition of an increasing number of countries, including from the Western community',[12] and the new Abkhaz foreign minister continues lobbying countries to recognize Abkhazia as an independent state (see, for example, RFE/RL 2010). This is despite Vladimir Putin's declaration that 'Abkhazia doesn't need to be recognized by any country other than Russia' (International Crisis Group 2010a: 11). More widespread recognition is needed for these entities to function as normal entities in the international system of sovereign states; partial recognition does not give them access to markets, loans, or the protection provided by norms of non-intervention. To further this goal of recognition, unrecognized states attempt to disassociate themselves from images of lawlessness, violence, and ethno-national radicalism, and instead convey an image of democratic, effective entities that are deemed acceptable by the international community and therefore – it is believed – 'worthy' of recognition. An analysis of the news reported on the (English language) official Somaliland website, for example, reveals a preoccupation with stability, a well-functioning state, democracy, and the entity's ability to function as a full member of the international system. Thus, the emphasis is on news related to the arrest of terrorist suspects, the capturing of pirates, elections, and meetings between the Somaliland government and international officials.[13]

That the creation of effective, democratic statehood is believed to increase the chance of recognition is clearly illustrated in statements made by the de facto authorities. For example, the foreign minister of Nagorno Karabakh emphasizes the importance of state-building when he argues that the decisive criterion for international recognition is viability,[14] while the then-president of Somaliland, Mohamed Egal, stressed the crucial importance of democratization when he publicly declared in 1999 that international recognition depended upon adopting a multi-party system of democracy (Bradbury 2008: 131). This interpretation of the politics of recognition appears to be based on a number of developments since the end of the Cold War, such as the conditions attached to the recognition of the former Yugoslav republics in the early 1990s: the international rhetorical emphasis on democratization;[15] the continued reference to the dangers posed by 'failed states';[16] the EU accession criteria, as set out in the so-called Copenhagen criteria from 1993 (European Commission 1993); and the conditions often attached to international aid. The dominance of such policies signal to the unrecognized states that, to be accepted into the exclusive group of acceptable, sovereign states, they have to create – at least a façade of – democracy and good governance.

The resulting rhetorical commitment to democratization and state-building has resulted in some significant internal changes, and in some not so significant ones. If we look at regime types, as classified by Freedom House, then we find that unrecognized states span the entire spectrum from 'non free' (South Ossetia and Transnistria), through 'partly free' (Abkhazia, Nagorno Karabakh, Somaliland) to 'free' (Northern Cyprus and Taiwan).[17] This represents a considerable difference from the 'anarchical badlands' of popular imagination and illustrates changes occurring since the cessation of warfare. However, if these changes are primarily externally driven, then one is invariably led to question the sustainability of the emerging statehood (see, for example, Zartman 1995a). A form of statehood that responds to the current international situation, or indeed to an interpretation of it, would not only lack a domestic basis, but also prove highly flexible and fluid. But this is not the whole picture: the entities are also the product of internal pressures and imperatives.

Creating strong entities capable of survival

One of the reasons why the recognition-through-democratization-and-state-building formula has proved so popular is that it actually overlaps with the main priority of these entities: to survive. The struggle for recognition will, after all, face a significant, if not irreversible, setback if the leaders lose control over the territory they lay claim to. No matter how much international favour Chechen leaders can manage to muster through tireless international lobbying, it all remains hypothetical as long as Moscow is in firm control of the region. The same is now true for the former leaders of Tamil Eelam. The leaders of these entities are of course aware of this. More than any other entities, they exist in a situation of international anarchy; the external threat is very real and, unlike their recognized counterparts, there is no norm of non-intervention to protect their de facto independence.[18] The precarious position of the entities pushes them towards de facto statehood and forces upon them an interest in state-building. Charles Tilly (1985) argued that modern statehood was based on the need for effective 'war machines', and this need is felt even more acutely in these self-proclaimed states.

Resources permitting, this need most obviously fosters the creation of a well-equipped and well-organized army that is able to defend the entity's de facto independence. But strong statehood, and an enhanced chance of survival, entails more than this. It also refers to the entity's ability to feed its population, raise taxes, and build effective governing institutions. Finally, the entity's chance of survival would appear to be enhanced if the leadership enjoys popular legitimacy. The leaders of unrecognized states are, in some ways, in an opportune position for ensuring popular legitimacy, due to the military victory and due to the importance of ethno-nationalism, which at least in some cases has a popular basis. And it could be argued that internal legitimacy is not a significant problem for the leaders of unrecognized states, since they can always play the 'external threat card'. There is arguably a low threshold for internal legitimacy if the authorities can portray themselves as embodying the nation's mission and argue that the withdrawal of popular support would lead to the only possible alternative: reintegration into the parent state. But although the external threat is clearly an important governing tool, which offers the leaders of unrecognized states some insulation against popular dissatisfaction and limits the threat it poses, a reduction in popular support carries the risk of apathy and the possibility that people might choose to vote with their feet. Unrecognized states generally depend on being able to mobilize a highly motivated and well-disciplined army and are, moreover, extremely vulnerable to emigration. Such considerations are clearly present when the prime minister of Nagorno Karabakh emphasizes the need for the entity to be self-sufficient and also stresses the need for reversing the demographic decline experienced by the entity since the onset of war.[19] The experience of war and the deliberate homogenization of territory through ethnic cleansing have often left these entities under-populated, and the parent states are often deliberately trying to make life in the entities unliveable in the hope that this will lead to further depopulation and weaker entities. Unrecognized states may have territory, but they also need people to populate it. Abkhazia is, for example, now estimated to have a population of just over 200,000, whereas its pre-war population was 525,061 (International Crisis Group 2010a: 8). A potential strategy for maintaining the population numbers would be for the authorities to make it hard for people to leave. However, this tends to lead to apathy, if not outright resistance, and will ultimately weaken the entity. People in Republika Srpska Krajina had few places to go to, but the authorities were still worried about emigration and, towards the end of the entity's existence, permission from the military was required for anyone to leave the territory, even if only for a short trip.[20] The army also began to forcibly mobilize people,[21] but morale was rapidly declining. One soldier recalls how he almost felt relieved when the Croatian army finally launched its military offensive.[22] This kind of attitude clearly does not provide a basis for a strong fighting force. Therefore, it is crucial for the entity's leaders to keep the population content or at least be able to justify current shortcomings and thereby maintain a level of popular legitimacy.

Leaders of unrecognized states are not protected from popular dissatisfaction, especially once it becomes clear that the promised international recognition is unlikely to materialize. Not even war heroes can count on unconditional support and Abkhazia's first president, Vladislav Ardzinba, was, for example, increasingly criticized (including for corruption) before he finally stepped down in 2005. If they have the resources for it, the authorities can attempt to 'buy' popular support. The Karabakh government has, for example, increased the level of social benefits and promises incentives for young people to remain in the entity and have children.[23] But if this is not an option, or if it proves insufficient, then another strategy for beleaguered war heroes is to introduce political reforms.[24] Democratization may well stave off popular discontent and the associated risk of severe fractionalization is, in most cases, not significant, due to the high level of homogeneity that tends to characterize these entities and due to the persistence of an external threat.[25]

Democracy can, therefore, be a way of ensuring continued popular support, even when times are hard. But pressure for political reform is also found in entities that are able to provide their populations with basic public services and a powerful narrative of future recognition. Many of these entities were created by movements that used democracy or popular sovereignty as a powerful mobilizing force and this is likely to constrain their ability to stray too far towards authoritarian rule. The Somali National Movement, which still dominates Somaliland, was, for example, formed in 1981 with the stated goal of establishing a devolved and democratic form of government, and this goal of democracy was maintained even when other demands radicalized (Bradbury 2008: 61ff.). In the case of Nagorno Karabakh, the stated goal was national self-determination, but it was from the beginning closely linked to a demand for democracy, and the advisor to the Karabakh president therefore argues that 'without democracy, the Karabakh independence movement makes no sense'.[26]

If the leaders of these entities are driven by collective interests, it consequently makes sense for them to emphasize state-building and democratization. It may reflect a somewhat naive view of world politics but it also furthers the goal of preserving their de facto independence. Moreover, the belief in 'earned sovereignty' has been cleverly instrumentalized in some cases and the civilian authorities in Nagorno Karabakh, for example, used it to great effect when they tried to rid themselves of the powerful military commander. This struggle could be portrayed as a fight of democracy versus authoritarianism and as a necessary step in the struggle for international recognition.[27] Thus, the perception of an external pressure to create a certain kind of entity can be used to promote state-building in the sense of ensuring central, civilian command over armed forces, even if this means ridding the entity of a popular war hero. It, moreover, also clearly serves narrower elite interests and the argument, therefore, does not have to rest on simplified assumptions of collective goals. External legitimacy may therefore have been *the* issue for unrecognized states, which is something that sets them apart from recognized states, but the need for internal legitimacy as well as internal power struggles have also been crucial in developing these states without sovereignty.

But if all these factors point towards the creation of effective, democratic entities, why does the title of this chapter suggest that unrecognized states are *imitating* democratic statehood? Why are they not able to create the 'real deal'? There are two reasons for this: first, they cannot do it on their own, but these entities are, once recognition is formally declared, likely to face international isolation and will consequently have to rely on an external patron. Second, they face a seemingly inescapable tension between creating a strong defence, ensuring popular legitimacy, and presenting themselves as democratic and inclusive entities. These tensions define the specific nature of statehood without sovereignty.

Independent states or puppet regimes?

A key obstacle to the creation of effective statehood in unrecognized states is a lack of resources. The starting point for a number of these entities was anything but promising: they had little or no infrastructure, no functioning economy, and their state-building ambitions therefore brought with them an undeniable need for external resources. Such resources are, however, hard to come by for these entities. Their lack of recognition and precarious position make them highly unattractive to foreign investors and they are, in most cases, also blocked from receiving international assistance and loans. As a consequence, most of these entities have to rely almost entirely on a patron state: Armenia in the case of Nagorno Karabakh; Turkey in the case of Northern Cyprus; Russia in the case of Abkhazia, South Ossetia and Transnistria. These patron states provide the entities with military, economic, and political support, thereby creating a situation that has aptly been described as states 'on the dole' (Kolstø and Blakkisrud 2008: 494). The patron states, for example, supply military personnel and equipment, they pay local pensions, and they provide the inhabitants with passports and the governments with loans and grant. In the case of Abkhazia, an official states 'we have two main concerns: security and our economy. Our relationship with Russia meets our needs in both areas' (International Crisis Group 2010a: 11). This kind of support is vital for the unrecognized states, but it also creates a dilemma for the entities: the external dependence enables their de facto independence, but at the same time subtracts from its substance. The Abkhaz official declares that Abkhazia has 'the amount of independence that we require' (ibid.), but other entities are less nonchalant about the prospect of diminished independence and, despite the Abkhaz official's rhetoric, there are 'muffled grumblings and apprehension regarding the danger of over-reliance on Moscow' (ibid.) and divisions are appearing below the surface (Khashig 2009). External dependence undermines the independence of unrecognized states, it undercuts their strategy for gaining international recognition by undermining their claim to independent viability and making them seem like 'puppet states', and it reduces the power of the authorities. The reliance on an external patron, therefore, potentially affects both the external and internal legitimacy of unrecognized states.

Even when this dependence is largely desired and, for example, based on kinship ties, it is associated with significant tensions. The relationship is frequently conflictual and not as straightforward as the popular image of 'puppets' would have us believe. Continued dependence is, as a consequence, often combined with an insistence on separateness and this is not merely meant for international consumption. As the advisor to the president of Nagorno Karabakh confidently puts it, the question is 'who depends on whom?'.[28] Unrecognized states could argue that recognized states also depend on external support for their survival, but recognized states often rely on a variety of links and do, moreover, not have to justify their independence. Unrecognized states will, in most cases, face international isolation and, although they can draw on support from various transnational (or rather trans-state) networks, including diaspora support, this is rarely enough, and significant dependence on a patron state almost seems to be a condition of non-recognition.

There are exceptions, however, in unrecognized states such as Taiwan, Kurdistan, and pre-independence Montenegro. These entities have not formally declared independence and have not been created – directly – through warfare, and, therefore, they do not face the same level of international isolation.[29] The same is true for a case like Somaliland, which, despite its formal declaration of independence, is allowed limited international engagement, which can be explained by its strategically important position and the lack of a functioning parent state. We should, however, not overlook the fact that the US functions as a form of patron state in all four cases. This support helps account for their lack of isolation and also results in more direct support. During Slobodan Milošević's rule, Montenegro was, for example, the second largest per capita recipient of US aid. This is, in any case, a difficult strategy for other unrecognized states to emulate; they cannot scale back their demand for independence unless this forms part of an overall settlement. Moreover, the entities that have not formally declared independence are not exempt from the tensions of unrecognized statehood. Their proclaimed viability may be less open to attack, but the authorities are likely to face significant internal pressures to formally declare independence, and until they do so, they cannot rely on the internal legitimacy that comes from promising future recognition and explaining away current shortcomings as a painful but necessary transitional step. They consequently also face the problems of building an entity that is capable of self-defence, meets with popular approval, and lives up to international norms.

Model-democracy or ethnic sparta?

The precarious situation in which these entities find themselves may be a powerful incentive for state-building, but the resulting entity will very much be dominated by the need for a strong defence. The military takes priority and other areas in need of support are starved of resources. This form of militarized state-building hampers the creation of an effective state, and it also undermines the other stated goal of the self-proclaimed states: the creation of a democratic entity. Nagorno Karabakh, for example, still operates under martial law and, even though the authorities claim that its importance is largely symbolic[30] and some of the provisions are no longer in place, its mere existence restricts the development of genuine political pluralism. The dominant position of the military, also in the political sphere, is often characterized as a post-war syndrome and is by no means unique to unrecognized states, but this tendency is reinforced by the context of non-recognition and the persistence of an external threat. Recognized states may of course also face external threats, but they are still protected by the norms of non-intervention and also have the option of joining military alliances. Unrecognized states are, as argued above, limited to the protection offered by a patron state and such protection frequently undermines their de facto independence; Abkhazia and South Ossetia may, for example, be more secure now that Russia guards their borders but they have also become less independent (see, for example, International Crisis Group 2010a). Militarization and/or external dependence therefore appears to be an inescapable characteristic, as long as these entities exist in an international limbo.

The problem, moreover, goes deeper than just a strong role for the military. Militarization, and the lack of criticism of this trend, is symptomatic of a strong emphasis on unity, which makes it difficult for these entities to move towards genuine democratization. Tilly's war machines are not necessarily the most likely candidates for successful democratization, and the goal of building a strong entity seemingly undermines the goal of being a democratic one. Amitai Etzioni (1993) has argued that breakaway territories do not allow for the level of pluralism that is needed for genuine democratization. Unrecognized states are based on the deliberate fostering of homogeneity, they frequently exclude minorities, and they seek to impose intra-communal unity. Democratization in the context of a claim to national self-determination tends to involve a narrow and ethnic definition of the people (Popescu 2006a: 19), and this tendency is reinforced by the context of non-recognition, since the uncertain future status of these entities makes preserving a majority position even more delicate. Identity and demography are at the heart of many of these conflicts and, coupled with persistent uncertainty, this makes it less likely that unrecognized states will extend democratic rights to minorities, especially if they share ethnicity with the majority in the 'parent state'. Refugees and internally displaced persons (IDPs) are the biggest victims of this tendency. Unrecognized states may proclaim their adherence to democratic values, but they clearly separate this from the right of return. The authorities of Nagorno Karabakh, for example, proudly proclaim that they even have an Azeri radio station and point to the cultural and religious rights guaranteed in their constitution, but these remain symbolic as long as the Azeri IDPs are not allowed to return. The authorities deny that this contradicts their democratic rhetoric, since they argue that returns will be allowed eventually, but just not until the status of the entity is decided (i.e. until independence is granted).[31] Again, we see how the status of non-recognition means that the authorities are imitating rather than realizing democratic statehood. The case of Abkhazia, moreover, demonstrates that partial recognition does not solve the problem; Abkhazia has allowed Georgian returns to the Gali district on the Georgian border, but conditions remain trying, the issue of 'citizenship' has proved very controversial, and the authorities now explicitly refuse to consider returns to other parts of Abkhazia (International Crisis Group 2010a: 2). Lack of recognition and uncertainty over status reinforces the tendency to define the entity in ethnic terms and undercuts the proclaimed adherence to liberal democracy.

The context of non-recognition and the perceived need for unity even present obstacles when it comes to democratization for the majority. Internal cohesion is part of their strength (Kolstø 2006), so why would they risk jeopardizing this by encouraging political divisions? There is a pronounced fear that any divisions will weaken the entities and people are worried about discussing internal problems 'when we have an enemy on the other side' who 'is listening'.[32] Unity should, therefore, be presented to the outside world and this means that some issues are not open to debate. If anyone, for example, dares to question the goal of independence, then they are likely to be accused of being a traitor. This perception provides a powerful argument against internal criticism. In Somaliland, for example, the authorities fear the apparent fragility of political consensus and have, therefore, on more than one occasion, restricted freedom of expression. Thus, in 2004, the minister of the interior banned all organized debates on the potential impact of the Somalia National Reconciliation Conference, which was seen as a potential threat to Somaliland's existence (Bradbury 2008). Resulting from this is an ambiguous political scene in which competition and debate is simultaneously encouraged and constrained. As the director of Apsnypress in Abkhazia argues, unity is 'unfortunately ... often understood as agreement of opinion' (Gurgulia 2004). Such unity is imposed not necessarily through direct suppression of dissent, but rather through the dominant political discourses and framing of debates. The opposition imposes self-restraint and curbs its activities. For example, the leader of the Transnistrian opposition did not run against the incumbent president in the 2006 presidential elections, arguing that it would risk destabilizing the state and '[f]or us the main priority is to resist external threats and to preserve Pridnestrovie as a state' (Isachenko 2009: 98). Similarly, when all opposition parties in the 2007 Nagorno Karabakh presidential election backed the regime candidate, they justified it by pointing to the need for national unity (Owen 2007). The prevalent siege mentality makes it easier for the authorities to constrain and limit the process of democratization, and makes it more likely that the opposition will voluntarily curb its activities. The persistence of an external threat will, in any case, make it easier for the authorities to avoid demands for political reform; the population might be prepared to accept stagnated democratization, if they can be convinced that untimely demands for genuine democratization would weaken the entity and increase the risk of military defeat.

There are, however, significant factors pulling in a different direction and this is what produces the ambiguity and instability of unrecognized statehood. Most of these entities are, as previously noted, very concerned with their international image, and the image of an ethnically exclusive, militarized entity is not what they are hoping to convey. The hope for recognition, therefore, offers a possible catalyst for change. The gradual process of state-building has provided opportunities for an opposition to emerge and these forces can, in their struggle for further reform, make use of the rhetorical commitment to democracy and the linking of democratic reforms with the prospect of international recognition. Allegations of corruption, abuse of power, and incompetence thereby cease to be merely political issues, since the opposition can argue that such misrule endangers the very existence of the entity. For example, the Nagorno Karabakh opposition coalition ARF-Movement88 in its manifesto for the 2005 parliamentary elections asserted that 'our country's future is endangered' and it accused the government of wanting to prolong an atmosphere of 'acquiescence … corruption, bribery…'.[33] Unrecognized states need a measure of popular legitimacy to avoid depopulation and convince people to stay and fight, so the authorities cannot just ignore such sentiments without weakening the entity, and they may find it hard to put the lid back on the promise of political reforms. Thus, lack of recognition can be a powerful force for change and some notable developments have in fact been seen in the years of 'no war, no peace'. If we look, for example, at the first elections in the unrecognized states in the Caucasus, then there was little or no political competition,[34] but the political debate is now livelier and pluralism is, contrary to Etzioni's claim, gradually emerging.

A similar combination of internal and external pressures could even serve to make the process of democratization less ethnically exclusive. This is illustrated in the Abkhaz leadership's attempts to construct a more inclusive national identity and hence a more inclusive form of statehood. The Abkhaz authorities were keen to reject accusations that the entity is ethnically exclusive and that Abkhazia's Georgian population, which constituted a majority prior to the outbreak of war, has been disenfranchized. Sergei Shamba, then Abkhazia's foreign minister, consequently claimed that the entity was doing everything it could to integrate the Georgian population into Abkhaz society (Rimple 2007). Although tensions between an ethnic and a civic understanding of the nation remained – for example, in the Abkhaz constitution (Clogg 2008: 311) – the beginning attempts to forge a new form of Abkhaz identity were not without importance. It was not just the perception of external pressure that pulled in another direction. For Abkhazia's long-term survival, it actually makes sense to construct a more inclusive entity; the entity suffers from an acute population shortage, especially in the Gali district, and a more inclusive identity would, furthermore, help overcome its weak claim to majority support for independence. It nevertheless remains a balancing act, since the authorities cannot afford to alienate their core support and since they also gain support from internal cohesion. Interestingly, since Abkhazia was recognized by Russia and three other states, these hesitant efforts to create a more inclusive entity appear to have met an impasse and the Abkhaz president appears to be taking a tougher line on the issue of Georgian returnees, stating that returns are 'problematic' due to the risk of renewed warfare, while other officials say that returns cannot be considered at this time 'because they could become a fifth column' (International Crisis Group 2010a: 9). Since the security risks have in fact diminished due to Russia's effective control, this seems to indicate that the declining interest in reforms springs from a less pressing need for international acceptance. Once international acceptance is not coveted as much as before, the regimes will be tempted to scale back reforms that do not directly affect the internal sustainability of the regime and that might even undermine it.

In this case, we therefore see stagnation and this is not unique to Abkhazia or to other partially recognized entities. When recognition is not forthcoming after more than a decade of de facto independence, these entities tend to run out of steam; why pursue difficult reforms if they do not bring the desired international acceptability and bring isolation to an end? Moreover, the domestic pressure for reforms may be satisfied at a relatively low level. There are, after all, few alternatives and the 'external threat card' remains powerful. The entities therefore tend to end up imitating rather than realizing effective, democratic statehood. The tendency to run out of steam as far as internal reforms are concerned seems to have been reinforced by the recognition or partial recognition of Kosovo, Abkhazia, and South Ossetia. These recognitions appeared to demonstrate that, in the current international system, what really matters for international recognition is having powerful friends, rather than abiding by international norms.

Conclusion: unstable states without sovereignty

Statehood without sovereignty is therefore characterized by a tension between the need for survival, the attempt to demonstrate viability as an independent state, and the struggle for international acceptance. What tends to dominate of these three driving forces? To a great extent, this depends on the situation in which the entities find themselves; how severe is the external threat?; does the entity have access to resources that do not originate with the patron state?; how dependent are the leaders on domestic support? The less significant popular support is, the more likely we are to see merely a façade democracy. But the international environment is also a significant factor; in particular, what are the international responses to the entity and its emerging statehood? Has support, and possible recognition, from the external patron made the entity less interested in international acceptance? Factors such as these would seem to affect the relative weight given to the different driving forces, but there is nevertheless a tendency for the regimes to try to square the circle, to try to do everything at once, and the result is an imitation of democratic statehood. This does not mean that it is completely absent, but it differs in important respects from what we can find in recognized states. In order to ensure the long-term survival of the entity, and also of their own careers, the leaders of unrecognized states cannot afford to veer too far in one direction. It might be tempting to give up on the goal of recognition. The leaders of Nagorno Karabakh have, for example, recently suggested that *de jure* recognition is no longer their primary goal; they instead argue that their unrecognized status is sustainable and can fulfil their goals of security and independence.[35] But the problem is that they lack the imagination, or the models, to imagine, statehood without recognition as anything other than a temporary state of affairs. Moreover, their legitimacy remains tied up with the promise of international recognition, especially since the population is not convinced that their security is guaranteed in a context of non-recognition.[36] Similarly, Abkhazia and South Ossetia may now have found that by moving, or being forced to move, too close to their external patron, they risk undermining their de facto independence. What results is therefore a highly unstable and conflictual form of statehood, which is both constrained and enabled by the lack of recognition, and shaped by the need for both external and internal legitimacy.

Effective statehood can therefore be achieved without external sovereignty, but it takes on a specific form. Unrecognized statehood is strongly affected by international structures due to the goal of recognition and the imperative of survival in the face of a persistent external threat, but these two goals frequently pull in different directions and this creates tensions. Although we find great variation between unrecognized states, they face similar conditions in an international system based on sovereign states. Unrecognized states may therefore span the spectrum from effective, democratic statehood to collapsing statehood, but this spectrum differs from that of their recognized counterparts. Some may argue that this is not a new form of statehood or sovereignty; it is not a permanent status, but rather a transitional status, which will eventually result in either independent statehood or, more likely, reintegration with the parent state. The tensions and contradictions explored in this chapter affect the sustainability of these entities; they find themselves in a limbo and this is also reflected in their internal developments and results in a high degree of instability. Yet these entities have shown themselves capable of surviving for several decades. Their statehood may be under strain, but if no palatable alternatives are put on the table and if the entity receives enough external support to sustain itself, then they can have considerable staying power, especially if the leaders manage to find the right balance between the competing goals and if they learn to manoeuvre in the globalized international system. These entities may therefore not be permanent, but they are not completely transient either.

Notes

1 Research for this chapter was funded by a grant from the Economic and Social Research Council (RES-000–22–2728). Parts of the chapter draw on previously published articles (Caspersen 2008 and Caspersen 2009), as well as a forthcoming publication (Caspersen 2011).
2 Quote taken from http://pridnestrovie.net/government.html.
3 Author's interview with Natella Akaba (via email, 30 August 2006).
4 See also Chorev's chapter in this volume.
5 Data from 2006: www.gio.gov.tw/ct.asp?xItem=35644&ctNode=2589.
6 Reliable macroeconomic indicators for unrecognized states are hard to obtain and this figure is actually an estimate for Somalia as a whole and therefore likely underestimates Somaliland's economic performance. It is, however, not exceptionally low for unrecognized states. Thus, Abkhazia's GDP per capita was in 2001 estimated at $350 (International Alert 2004: 123).
7 For 'insurgent states', see McColl (1969).
8 See also Bakke's chapter in this volume.
9 Author's interview with Karine Ohanyan, journalist (Stepanakert, 3 November 2008).
10 See also Closson's chapter in this volume, which includes an examination of how unrecognized states 'simulate sovereignty'.
11 Author's interview with Arkady Ghukasyan, former NKR president, 1997–2007 (Stepanakert, 3 November 2008).
12 www.therepublicofabkhazia.org/pages/issues-points-interview/sergei-bagapsh.shtml.
13 www.somalilandgov.com.

14 NKR Foreign Minister Georgy Petrossian's Interview to 'Demo' Newspaper, 4 February 2008: www.armtown.com/news/en/aza/20071122/2372/.
15 As it reads on the website of the US State Department, 'democracy is the one national interest that helps to secure all the others': www.state.gov/g/drl/democ/.
16 The 2002 National Security Strategy famously declared, 'America is now threatened less by conquering states than we are by failing ones': http://georgewbush-whitehouse.archives.gov/nsc/nss/2002/.
17 See Freedom House Index, country reports from 2009: www.freedomhouse.org.
18 They are, thus, in a very different situation than Jackson's 'quasi-states' that are 'exempted from the power contest at least in part' (1990: 23).
19 Author's interview with Araik Harutyunian, prime minister of NKR (Stepanakert, 30 October 2008).
20 Author's interview with Dragan Đević, deputy mayor of Donji Lapac (Donji Lapac, 2 April 2009).
21 Author's interviews with Ninko Mirić (Karlovac, 27 March 2009) and with Nikola Sužnjevic (Glina, 27 March 2009). Both were judges in Republika Srpska Krajina.
22 Author's interview with Stanko Momčilović, mayor of Udbina (Zagreb, 1 April 2009).
23 Author's interview with Araik Harutyunian (Stepanakert, 30 October 2008).
24 For the link between democratization and lack of resources, see Popescu (2006a).
25 For the risk of fractionalization and fragmentation if democratization is introduced in weak states, see Ottoway (1995).
26 Author's interview with David Babayan (Stepanakert, 28 October 2008).
27 The civilian leader was presented as 'a political leader legitimized by democratic elections with an ambitious agenda of combating corruption and controlling the power of the military' (Giragosian 2000).
28 Author's interview with David Babayan (Stepanakert, 13 September 2006).
29 Abkhazia did not formally declare independence until 1999 but was nevertheless faced with international isolation following the end of the war with Georgia in 1993.
30 Author's interview with David Babayan (Stepanakert, 28 October 2008).
31 Author's interview with David Babayan (Stepanakert, 28 October 2008).
32 Author's interview with Karine Ohanyan (Stepanakert, 3 November 2008).
33 'ARF – Movement88 issues address to people,' 14 June 2005: www.armeniandiaspora.com/showthread.php?30023-ARF-Movement-88-issues-address-to-people.
34 The main opposition party in Nagorno Karabakh, the Dashnaks, refrained from running in the first elections after the ceasefire, reportedly to avoid weakening the entity. Author's interview with Artur Mosiyan, president of the Dashnaks (Stepanakert, 13 September 2006).
35 Author's interviews with David Babayan (Stepanakert, 28 October 2008) and Hrachya Arzoumanyan, expert in the NKR foreign ministry (Stepanakert, 1 November 2008).
36 Author's interview with Naira Ayrumyan, journalist/editor (Stepanakert, 5 November 2008).

6 After the war ends

Violence and viability of post-Soviet unrecognized states

Kristin M. Bakke

The most common types of conflict in the world today are conflicts within, rather than between, states, often between central governments and ethnic groups in pursuit of greater autonomy or independence – self-determination, or separatist, conflicts (Marshall and Gurr 2005). This chapter focuses on the *aftermath* of such struggles. While much research has addressed why violent self-determination struggles emerge (see, for example, Gurr 2000; Hechter 2000; Horowitz 1981; Hale 2008; Toft 2003), we know less about the conditions that bring about peace and stability after the fighting officially ends. Indeed, in many cases, the post-war era is far from peaceful. Peace settlements are assumed to bring an end to the war, but they are, in some cases, followed by high levels of criminal violence and civilian victimization and, in other cases, they are followed by political violence among former enemies – even among former allies (see, for example, Keen 2001; Zinecker 2006; Boyle 2009; Atlas and Licklider 1999). Why?

The consequences of continued violence in states that have just emerged from an armed conflict can be dire. In the worst case, continued violence can lead to a recurrence of the war or even state failure, which has destabilizing effects both regionally and internationally (see, for example, Collier *et al.* 2003; Rotberg 2004). Short of that, continued violence has grave effects for the well-being of the population, as well as the capacity of the post-war society to recover from the war. While a growing body of research has examined features of post-conflict societies (see, for example, Tishkov 2004; Suhrke 2007; Bakke *et al.* 2009; O'Loughlin and Toal 2009), there is a need for both theoretical and systematic empirical investigation of the dynamics that foster stability and peace following war. The issue at stake is not only the recurrence of civil war between former enemies, but also low-level violence among both former enemies and allies.[1]

Among the self-determination conflicts of the last decades, only a handful has resulted in the creation of sovereign states. A more common outcome has been unrecognized or de facto sovereign states, while in most cases, the separatist groups have stayed put, sometimes appeased with regional autonomy within decentralized states (Seymour 2008). None of these outcomes do necessarily produce peaceful post-war societies, but we know the least about the unrecognized states. While questions about the reasons and consequences of continued violence apply to every post-war society, they are particularly important in unrecognized states, whose lack of external legitimacy has made claims to *internal* legitimacy integral to their quest for recognition (Caspersen 2008). Continued violence may jeopardize the post-war state's public goods provision or democracy, both of which can hurt its internal legitimacy. Indeed, citizens of an unrecognized state plagued by post-war violence may cease to support a regime that cannot provide for their security. Lack of public support is problematic for any regime, but it is especially problematic for unrecognized states, whose survival as state-like entities is vulnerable from the outset.

As a first step towards theorizing post-war violence in unrecognized states, in this chapter, I outline the consequences of continued violence for unrecognized states' viability, discuss and describe types of violence observed in post-conflict societies, and provide explanations for the causes of post-war violence. I argue that a fruitful avenue for further research pays attention to the ways in which post-war violence may follow from the organization and nature of violence during the war itself

Viability and violence

While unrecognized states have been features on the international scene for decades (think about Taiwan), the post-Cold War era has seen a proliferation of such "statelets." The collapse of the Soviet Union and conflicts in Russia, Azerbaijan, Georgia, and Moldova were followed by the emergence of a number of unrecognized states – Chechnya, Nagorno Karabakh, Abkhazia, South Ossetia, and Transnistria (see Table 6.1).[2] While Nagorno Karabakh, Abkhazia, South Ossetia, and Transnistria still exist as state-like entities, others, like Chechnya, have had relatively short lives. Chechnya functioned as an unrecognized state from 1996 until 1999, but it was recaptured by the Russian Federation.

A growing literature has suggested reasons why unrecognized states manage to survive as units in the international system, despite their lack of international recognition. Less work has studied violence within them. While understanding the possible determinants for post-war violence by itself is an important research objective, post-war violence may also help further our understanding of the viability of these entities. In particular, violence within unrecognized states may adversely affect their viability, most importantly by diminishing these state-like entities' internal legitimacy.

The literature suggests at least four explanations for why some unrecognized states endure as unrecognized states in the international system – are viable entities, that is – while others do not. First, viability may rest with the benefits that the unrecognized states' elites reap from positions of power and illicit economies (King 2001; Roper 2001; Lynch 2002). As long as an unrecognized state provides people with political and economic benefits, they have few incentives to change the *status quo*. Second, unrecognized states may endure due to their

Table 6.1 Post-Soviet unrecognized states

Separatist group	*Parent state*	*Conflict begins*	*Ceasefire/"birth" of unrecognized state*	*Unrecognized state*	*Endurance of unrecognized state*
Armenians	USSR/Azerbaijan	1988	1994	Nagorno Karabakh	Still existing
Dniester Slavs	Moldova	1990	1992	Transnistria	Still existing
Chechens	Russia	1994	1996	Chechen Republic of Ichkeria[1]	Recaptured by Moscow in 1999
Ossetians	Georgia	1991	1992	South Ossetia	Still existing
Abkhaz		1992	1994	Abkhazia	Still existing

Source: Based on Seymour (2008).

Note
1 We can also consider Chechnya between 1992 and 1994 an unrecognized state, but I do not consider it here as I am primarily interested in these entities as post-conflict states, and Chechnya between 1992 and 1994 was not a post-conflict state.

military defense and the relative weakness of the parent state they officially belong to (Kolstø 2006). In the post-Soviet world, besides Russia, which can be considered a strong state, Azerbaijan, Georgia, and Moldova are relatively weak parent states, unable to defeat the unrecognized states within their borders or offer incentives for them to return (Lynch 2002) – although this changed in Georgia with the "rose revolution" and Mikheil Saakashvili's reforms (Stanislawski 2008). Third, while unrecognized states are, by definition, not recognized by the international community, some nonetheless have a certain degree of external support (Lapidus 2002; Lynch 2002; Kolstø 2006; Stanislawski 2008). One can think of Russia's backing of South Ossetia and Abkhazia. Unrecognized states often make claims for international recognition (external legitimacy) based on the principle of self-determination, but as Caspersen (2008) argues, some also claim that they deserve to become sovereign states because they have proved they are viable democracies and have internal legitimacy. Fourth, unrecognized states endure due to internal legitimacy. While the internal legitimacy of states often rests with their ability to provide citizens with public goods, such as welfare and defense, unrecognized states may gain legitimacy through nation-building efforts, highlighting the population's shared war experiences and common enemy to create in-group solidarity (Lynch 2002; Kolstø 2006). Yet researchers have little systematic knowledge of the sources of internal legitimacy in unrecognized states (O'Loughlin *et al.* 2008). Internal legitimacy may be based on ethnic group solidarity, but also provision of public goods, democracy, and, as this chapter emphasizes, security. Indeed, if an unrecognized state is characterized by a lack of individual security, internal legitimacy is likely to suffer both directly and indirectly.

Directly, unrecognized states unable to provide for their citizens' security may be less likely to be perceived as legitimate than peaceful ones. One of the key challenges facing any war-torn society is the (re)building of social capital, including trust in other citizens and trust in the government. Trust in government, which is one indicator of a legitimate state, has been found to influence attitudes, such as volunteerism, that are crucial ingredients of post-war reconciliation and reconstruction (Widner 2004). A civic culture, including inter-personal trust, has long been considered a crucial determinant for democracy (Almond and Verba 1963). Others have found that, reversely, it is experiences of democracy that cause inter-personal trust (Muller and Seligson 1994). Embracing the endogenous nature of the relationship between trust in government and trust in people, Brehm and Rahn (1997) suggest that among the exogenous factors influencing trust is individuals' experiences of victimization (fear of crime).[3] It is reasonable to expect that continued violence will have a similarly negative effect on trust in both fellow citizens and the regime. Precisely because unrecognized states are unrecognized and lack external legitimacy, citizen trust in the government may be critical to the viability of these entities.

Indirectly, continued violence in a post-war society may jeopardize public goods provision, democracy, and in-group solidarity, thus diminishing internal legitimacy. Indeed, to the degree that the post-war era is characterized by empowered warlords, crime, and corruption, public goods provision may suffer as the governing elites may be inclined to spend the state's resources on attracting support from loyal "strongmen," rather than providing public goods (Reno 2002). Moreover, post-war societies face material destruction and disrupted, often diminished, economic growth (see, for example, Collier 2006; Kang and Meernik 2009). This problem is likely to be exaggerated by foreign investments remaining low. Because unrecognized states are unrecognized, they are particularly hard pressed to attract foreign investors. Indeed, for investors, these state-like entities may represent a legal vacuum. As such, post-war violence in unrecognized states may be highly damaging for economic growth, which will affect public goods provision. In terms of continued violence's effect on democracy, without a clear break from the violent past (in the form of demilitarization, for example), post-war elections are likely to be dominated by questions related to security, which can stem or prevent the transition to democracy (Lyons 2004). Finally, it is also reasonable to expect that any in-group solidarity that has been formed during the violent conflict may deteriorate in the post-war society if that society is characterized by violence among members of that very in-group.

Thus, questions about violence and viability of unrecognized states are likely to be closely linked. Understanding post-war violence in unrecognized states may help shed light on these entities' viability in the international system.

Violence in post-war states

In the unrecognized states in the post-Soviet world, many of the violent conflicts from which these entities emerged have not formally come to an end through a fully fledged peace settlement, but rather a military victory followed by a ceasefire.[4]

While the post-Soviet unrecognized states defeated their parent states on the battleground, often after iterations of broken ceasefires, the authorities in Abkhazia, Nagorno Karabakh, South Ossetia, and Transnistria consider their victories and status in the international system fragile. The example of Chechnya, which was forced back into the Russian Federation when the second Chechen war broke out in 1999, looms large as a warning (Lynch 2004a: 56). Because there is no peace agreement, these conflicts are sometimes referred to as "frozen" conflicts – not officially resolved, yet no longer violent enough to register as a civil war.[5] Such an in-between status also characterizes a number of conflicts that are "resolved" through a peace agreement.[6] Indeed, a growing body of research is pointing out that so-called post-conflict societies are not so *post*-conflict after all, as they continue to be plagued by violence.[7] One can think about post-war violence along different dimensions (cf. Boyle 2009). For example, is the violence strategic or not? Are the targets civilians or elites? Is the violence directed at former adversaries or former allies?

Strategic violence is politically motivated violent acts with the purpose of "transforming the balance of power and resources in a contested area" (Boyle 2009: 211). These acts may be aimed at individuals, often elites (assassinations), or groups, including civilians (riots or pogroms, reprisal attacks), or property (attacks on religious shrines and government buildings). Non-strategic violence would include personally motivated revenge attacks and criminal violence. While we often assume that violence in intrastate conflicts is of a strategic or political character, revolving around a master narrative of what the struggle is about and who the opposing parties are, a growing body of research is suggesting that the motives among those fighting may be more mixed (see, for example, Kalyvas 2003, 2006). The same goes for post-war violence. Whether or not the violence is strategic, it can be directed either at former enemies (the out-group) *or* former allies (the in-group). While studies of the recurrence of civil war tend to be concerned about conflicts among former enemies, this chapter also examines violence among former allies. Indeed, while one might expect to see occasional flares in violence between long-time former adversaries despite a peace agreement, it is far more puzzling why former allies would be fighting one another in the post-war era.

In the conflicts giving birth to the unrecognized states in the post-Soviet states, ethnic minorities were fighting for independence from their parent states – the Chechens from Russia, the Abkhaz and South Ossetians from Georgia, the Karabakh Armenians from Azerbaijan, and the Dniester Slavs from Moldova. While the Chechens, Karabakh Armenians, and South Ossetians constituted the majority of the population in their republics, the Abkhaz formed only a minority in Abkhazia, and the Dniester Slavs (mainly Russians and Ukrainians) formed about half of the population in Transnistria.[8] After the armed conflicts "froze" through ceasefires, some of the resulting unrecognized states have experienced inter-ethnic violence between the war-time enemies, while some have also experienced intra-ethnic violence among the war-time allies. Others again have experienced no significant post-war violence.

Violence between war-time enemies

In each of the post-Soviet unrecognized states, the war they fought against their parent states in the early 1990s had lasting legacies, and some have seen continued violence between the war-time enemies. The violence has been both strategic and criminal, fought between armed groups but also directed against civilians.

With the exception of Chechnya, where the armed struggle against the Russian federal forces resumed in the fall of 1999, the ceasefires that marked an end to the armed conflicts held until 2008 in Abkhazia and South Ossetia, and still hold in Nagorno Karabakh and Transnistria. In August 2008, Georgian forces attacked South Ossetia, which led to a short-lived but deadly interstate conflict as Russian forces sided with South Ossetia to counter Georgian troops.[9] Abkhaz forces, with the help of Russian air power, used the opportunity to establish control over the upper Kodori Valley, which the Abkhaz authorities consider part of Abkhazia but which had been under the control of Georgia. Prior to the August 2008 war, the only ceasefire that had been broken was between Chechnya and the Russian authorities in Moscow, but the ceasefires in both Abkhazia and Nagorno Karabakh had been challenged by border skirmishes and clashes between armed forces and civilians or paramilitary forces. The resumption of war, ceasefire violations, and border clashes can be considered strategic violence, aimed at establishing control over a contested territory, although the line between strategic and non-strategic violence may be blurred, as criminal violence may emerge in the shadow of strategic violence.

Ceasefire violations and border clashes have often followed from the return of displaced/refugee populations to their pre-war homes. In Chechnya, Abkhazia, and Nagorno-Karabakh, the war led to a massive out-migration, both voluntary and forced, of members of the out-group – Russians from Chechnya, Georgians from Abkhazia, and Azeris from Nagorno Karabakh (Lynch 2004a: 91–5). In South Ossetia and Transnistria, smaller numbers of Georgians and Moldovans, respectively, fled or were forced to flee (Socor 2006).

Within Georgia, as many as 260,000 people (249,000 from Abkhazia) were, by January 2003, still displaced following the conflicts in Abkhazia and South Ossetia (Norwegian Refugee Council 2003). In Abkhazia, the spontaneous return of thousands of Georgians who were forced to leave their homes during the war led to border clashes in 1997–1998, in the Gali district in the south, resulting in the expulsion of 30,000–40,000 of the returnees (International Crisis Group 2006d: 11). The clashes were between the Abkhaz militia and a Georgian paramilitary group known as the White Legion (Lynch 2004a: 29–30), but they were also directed at civilians:

> Returned Georgian villagers were harassed by the Abkhaz militia, who undertook frequent patrols into Gali to demonstrate Abkhaz sovereignty over the district. The often unruly Abkhaz militiamen conducted document checks and forced villagers to "register" with the Abkhaz government and pay "taxes." (…) To defend themselves, Georgian villagers took to placing anti-personnel mines around their villages, which helped to deter Abkhaz raids but also constituted a substantial hazard to neighboring villagers as well as to PKF and UNOMIG personnel.
>
> (Walker 1998: 12)

While the Abkhaz constituted only a minority in Abkhazia prior to the war (95,000 out of 525,000), one estimate is that about half of the post-war population is Abkhaz, although the number is disputed (International Crisis Group 2006d: 9). Despite inter-ethnic clashes, about 40,000–45,000 Georgians had returned to the Gali district a decade after the conflict came to an end (Lynch 2004a: 52–4; International Crisis Group 2006d: 10). A key motivation for the separatist quest in Abkhazia in the early 1990s was a fear that the Abkhaz language and culture would disappear if the region remained part of Georgia. The Abkhaz considered an independent Abkhaz state necessary to their survival (International Crisis Group 2006d). As such, in post-war Abkhazia, "'citizens' of the self-declared Abkhaz state cannot be allowed to include the displaced

Georgian population, as this would leave the Abkhaz as a small minority once again" (Lynch 2004a: 53). The result has been continued tension in areas of refugee return. Indeed, the Gali district, where 96 percent of the pre-war population was Georgian, has continued to see clashes between ethnic groups that each claim allegiance to the territory. As I turn to below, the region has also been the scene of criminal violence: shootings, abductions, killings, and armed robberies.

In contrast to Abkhazia, South Ossetia experienced less out-migration during the war and less ensuing inter-ethnic violence, at least between 1993 and 2001.[10] From 2001, the situation grew tense, and the ceasefire was challenged in 2004. Following the Georgian government's attempt at shutting down smuggling between Russia and Georgia via South Ossetia, armed clashes between Georgian forces and South Ossetian militias left dozens dead in August 2004 (Tuathail 2008: 679–80). Since then, until the August 2008 war, the ceasefire remained fragile. According to an International Crisis Group report, "crimes, detentions, shootings and exchanges of fire have become routine. Killings, kidnappings, shelling, mine explosions and other ceasefire violations occur, as do direct confrontations between armed personnel, especially in the warmer months" (2007b: 14). Violence in South Ossetia illustrates the intertwined relationship between strategic and criminal violence: The violence is strategic in the sense that it is motivated by a wish on the part of both South Ossetians and Georgians to control the territory, but for certain groups within South Ossetia, control over the territory also implies access to lucrative smuggling routes.

The conflict over Nagorno Karabakh, fought between Azerbaijan and Armenians from Nagorno Karabakh (and from Armenia), led to massive displacements and ethnic cleansing, of Azeris from Nagorno Karabakh and Armenia, as well as Armenians from Azerbaijan. While numbers are disputed, it is estimated that 413,000 Armenians left Azerbaijan and 724,000 Azeris (and Kurds) left Armenia and Nagorno Karabakh. With a pre-war population of nearly 190,000, about 120,000 inhabitants remain in Nagorno Karabakh, mainly Armenians (98 percent) (International Crisis Group 2005: 2–5). Low-level violence still characterizes Nagorno Karabakh – shootings and prisoner takings – and civilians and soldiers who accidentally cross the front line, which is not monitored by international forces, have been captured. Displaced Azeris who have tried to move home have been blown up by mines on the front line (ibid.: 27). Due to attacks in the border areas in the south of Azerbaijan and across the Armenian–Azerbaijan border, observers considered 2003 the most violent year since 1996 (de Waal 2003). In the spring of 2005, a number of ceasefire violations made the peace look fragile (International Crisis Group 2005: 27), and both in the spring and fall of 2008, serious gunfights between Armenian and Azerbaijani forces in Azerbaijani districts north and south of Nagorno Karabakh took place (Ohanian *et al.* 2008; Ahmedbeyli and Beglarian 2008). While the boundary between strategic and criminal violence also in this case is not clear-cut, clashes between Azeris and Armenians appear to primarily be motivated by a quest to control the territory considered to be home for either group.

Transnistria has not seen any serious threats to the ceasefire, and there have been no major inter-ethnic clashes concerning control over the territory. The conflict itself was the least violent among the struggles preceding the formation of the unrecognized post-Soviet states, and it was not accompanied by large-scale population displacements. Because there was (and is) no single majority ethnic group in the region – and the out-group, the Moldovans, still constitute a significant share of the population – the elites in Transnistria attempted to fashion a civic, rather than ethnic, nationalism (O'Loughlin *et al.* 1998). Yet in recent years there has been concern about "linguistic cleansing" and forced closing of Moldovan Latin language schools within Transnistria (United States Mission to the OSCE 2004; Amnesty International 2004), and the government in Tiraspol has been criticized for minority group discrimination, such as interfering with Moldovans' right to vote (United States Department of State 2000). Thus, while Transnistria, in contrast to the other unrecognized post-Soviet states, has experienced "negative peace," in the sense that there is an absence of direct violence between the former war-time enemies, it has not reached what Galtung (1969) calls "positive peace" – the absence of structural violence and social injustice.

The most serious ceasefire breach among the post-Soviet unrecognized states took place in Chechnya, leading to a recurrence of civil war in the fall of 1999. Two incidents in August and September 1999 proved critical in spurring Moscow's renewed full-scale invasion of Chechnya. In August, two of the Chechen warlords opposed to then-Chechen President Aslan Maskhadov, Shamil Basayev and Ibn-ul-Khattab, carried out unsanctioned attacks into Chechnya's neighbor region Dagestan. In September, a series of apartment buildings in Moscow were bombed, and Moscow blamed Basayev and Khattab (although this accusation has never been corroborated). Subsequent negotiations with Moscow failed.[11] Since the beginning of the second war in 1999, the Russian government has several times declared the war to be over. Since 2001, and especially since 2005, violence has dwindled and the war has taken on more of an intra-Chechen character, but there are still frequent reports of violent attacks between Chechen rebels and Russian forces, both sides seeking territorial control over the small mountainous republic.

Prior to the first Chechen war, which led to the de facto Chechen state (1996–1999), then-Chechen President Dzhokhar Dudayev, who was married to a Russian woman, appears to have wanted the Chechen nationalist movement not to alienate the ethnic Russian population (Sheehy 1991). Once Dudayev came to power, however, he set out to establish a state where the focus was on Chechens. Per the 1989 census, about 70 percent of the republic's 1.27 million inhabitants belonged to the two titular nationalities, the Chechens (735,000) and the Ingush (163,700).[12] Between the summer of 1990 and the summer of 1992, about 70,000 ethnic Russians or Russian speakers left the republic, more than three times as many as in the previous decade (20,000 left between 1979 and 1989) (Dunlop 1998: 134–7). Other observers have noted that the Chechen nationalists did little to appeal to the sentiments of Chechnya's other minority group, the Ingush

(Lieven 1998: 70). Both the first and second wars led to massive population losses, displacements, and human rights violations.[13] As noted above, a large share of the republic's ethnic Russian population left even prior to the first war, which reduced the chances of inter-ethnic clashes in Chechnya following the first war. However, as I discuss further below, the de facto independent Chechen state that existed between 1997 and 1999 saw the development of a hostage industry inside and outside the republic, where both rebel groups and criminals took Russian, Chechen, and Western hostages for ransom, including journalists (Tishkov 2004: 107–26).

In sum, the post-Soviet unrecognized states exhibit significant variation in terms of continued violence between members of the war-time opposing groups. As the following section shows, they also demonstrate variation in terms of intra-group conflict and violence.

Violence between war-time allies

The domestic politics of the unrecognized states emerging after the fall of the USSR have all been marked by the armed struggles from which they emerged. In most, the commanders that led the armed struggle have continued to play a key role after the fighting officially ended, in many cases resulting in elite-level struggles over political power. In the Chechen case, elite-level struggles between former field commanders (former allies) were key to the outbreak of the second Chechen war, between the former war-time enemies. Some of the unrecognized states have also been plagued by a turn to criminal violence.

The commanders that led the unrecognized states to battlefield victories entered the post-war era as heroes. One of these heroes was General Samvel Babayan in Nagorno Karabakh, who came to dominate the statelet's (and also Armenia's) politics, serving a dual role as defense minister and commander of the republic's armed forces from 1994 to 1999 (de Waal 2004: 241–50, 256–8). He used his position to exploit and reinforce corruption, and came to control a number of factories, as well as the import of cigarettes and oil to both Armenia and Nagorno Karabakh. De Waal observes that,

> Anyone who got in Babayan's way risked ending up in Shusha jail and being ordered a large bribe to secure his or her release. One father was asked to play a much higher bribe: the delivery of either of his teenage daughters to Babayan.
>
> (2004: 242)

While Babayan was feared and known to be corrupt, he was powerful enough to be beyond critique. Moreover, because of Nagorno Karabakh's unrecognized status, the governing elites may have wanted to keep up an appearance of unity. Some observers also note that, while there may have been disagreement about how best to improve the economy, there was widespread unity with respect to the question of Karabakh's status (Tchilingirian 1999: 449). While a political opposition slowly developed, the government did not allow much criticism (Panossian 2001: 149–50). By the end of 1999, however, elite struggles over control of the army – Babayan against the civilian leadership under President Arkady Ghukasian and Prime Minister Anushavan Danielian – resulted in Babayan's dismissal. A few months later, in March 2000, President Ghukasian was victim of an assassination attempt. In Stepanakert, Nagorno Karabakh's capital, the rumor was that Babayan was behind the plot (de Waal 2004: 243), and many of Babayan's supporters and members of the opposition were arrested. Also Babayan himself was arrested and was sentenced to 14 years in jail for the assassination plot (but was released in 2004).[14] Thus, while there has been an absence of deadly collective intra-group violence, post-war Nagorno Karabakh has faced both corruption and strategic elite-level struggles.

In Abkhazia, too, civilian and former military elites have struggled for power. The Abkhaz independence movement's leader and first president, Vladislav Ardzinba, whose health in the early 2000s was failing, was in 2003–2004 increasingly challenged by the large war veterans group Amtsakhara, whose members considered him unfit to rule (Khashig 2003). Founded in 1999, Amtsakhara had quickly become a political force, and in the spring of 2003 it was instrumental in bringing down the government of Prime Minister Gennady Gagulia, against President's Ardzinba's will. In June 2004, Amtsakhara's political secretary, Gary Aiba, was assassinated. The assassination, which took place prior to scheduled presidential elections, undermined the government's reputation, and the opposition used the opportunity to call for the government's resignation (Anjaparidze 2004). The outcome of the October elections was disputed and followed by mass protests, with as many as 10,000 people in the streets. The opposition party Unified Abkhazia, allied with Amtsakhara, seized the presidential palace, the government building, and parliament in Sukhumi, the capital, resulting in several wounded and one death (Khashig 2004). Then-opposition leader Sergei Bagapsh eventually emerged as the victor and is today Abkhazia's president.

In addition to strategic violence in the form of elite-level struggles over political control, Abkhazia has also been the scene of criminal violence, especially in the Gali district, where the activities of both Abkhaz and Georgian criminal networks, which can easily operate across the porous border, suggests that the Abkhaz authorities have little control over their territory (Lynch 2004a: 44–5). While Abkhazia has a relatively small standing army, it has a large group of reserves and a well-armed population (International Crisis Group 2006d: 11–14), which possibly contributes to the authorities' lack of monopoly on the use of violence.

The post-Soviet unrecognized state most plagued by internal violence was the Chechen republic under President Maskhadov, the former Chechen field commander who had led the Chechens to their victory in 1996. In January 1997, Maskhadov was elected president of Chechnya. With the support of more than 60 percent of the population and eager to accommodate his potential opponents within Chechnya by including them in his cabinet, Maskhadov initially achieved what his predecessors had failed to do: In 1997, he met with President Boris

Yeltsin of the Russian Federation and signed a peace settlement concerning relations between Chechnya and Russia. Increasingly, however, Maskhadov was challenged by Chechen opponents who found him to be a Moscow sell-out and had a different vision of what an independent Chechnya would look like, including the rebel forces loyal to the field commanders Shamil Basayev and Salman Raduyev, or some who appeared to have mere criminal motives, most notably Arbi Barayev and his Islamic Regiment. The result was an increasingly volatile and lawless situation within Chechnya, including a growing kidnapping-for-ransom industry. As described by Tishkov (2004: 105–6):

> The end of the war was followed by apathy and internal division, rather than the expected enthusiasm and solidarity. The split could be seen in several directions: between the commanders and the rank and file, the war veterans and the new recruits, the highland (red-haired) and lowland (city) Chechens. The entry of the *boyeviki* into towns instituted a change in Chechen society. Instead of showing generosity, the victors began violently to persecute other Chechens, particularly those who did not cooperate with them. A scramble for posts, awards, and property followed, particularly on the part of those who had not yet acquired an apartment in Grozny.

The recurrence of the war with Moscow in many ways followed from the internal struggles in Chechnya, as Maskhadov was unable to control Basayev, who, along with the Arab fighter Khattab, orchestrated the attack into Dagestan in 1999, which spurred Moscow to again intervene.

Neither in South Ossetia nor in Transnistria has the post-war era featured elite-level struggles as in the other post-Soviet unrecognized states, yet both entities have been challenged with criminal violence. In South Ossetia, the brothers Albert and Jambulat of the Tedeyev clan, who controlled private militias, came to control the security forces and, with that, gained control over politics as well as the black market. In 2001, the Tedeyev clan helped Eduard Kokoyev come to power, but in 2003 Kokoyev, allegedly in an attempt to cut the link between the government and organized crime, broke off ties with the Tedeyev clan (Devdariani 2003). South Ossetia has come to be considered a North Caucasus smuggling route (Lynch 2004a: 61, 98). According to an International Crisis Group report (2007b: 15–16), criminal activities on both the Georgian and South Ossetian side of the border have been intertwined with kidnappings and killings, although the government in Tskhinvali claims that accusations of crime, corruption, smuggling, and counterfeiting are meant to give the entity a bad reputation and excuse for intervention. Indeed, the Georgian government's campaign into South Ossetia in 2004, discussed above, was justified as an anti-smuggling effort (Tuathail 2008: 680). In sum, internal post-war violence in South Ossetia has primarily been linked to crime, especially smuggling between Russia and Georgia.

Similarly, Transnistria has seen neither elite-level struggles as in Nagorno-Karabakh nor on-the-ground violence as in Abkhazia, but it is close to an example of what William Reno (2002) calls shadow-state, with widespread corruption and porous borders that allow smuggling of drugs, weapons (some of them rumored to also be produced in Transnistria), and people. The financial-industrial group Sheriff, run by a former police member, controls much of the entity's economic activities. In return for President Igor Smirnov allowing these activities (and exempting the company from taxes), Sheriff provides the state with social services (Lynch 2004a: 66–7). Some of the accusations of Transnistria as a free-for-all zone for aggravated crime, such as drug smuggling, may be exaggerated or poorly backed up, but smuggling of "normal" goods (such as frozen chickens) is key to the entity's economy.[15]

Thus, just like the unrecognized states exhibit variation in violence between former enemies, they also show variation in violent struggles among former allies – from armed clashes between rebel groups in Chechnya, to elite-level struggles in Nagorno Karabakh and Abkhazia, and criminal violence in nearly all of the statelets.

Explaining post-war violence

Peace agreements or ceasefires are not clear-cut cures for lasting peace. About 40 percent of all peace settlements signed between 1989 and 2005, including both ceasefires and agreements, were followed by a recurrence of armed conflict within five years, while a third of all settlements were not fully implemented (UCDP Peace Agreement Dataset 2005). Indeed, it has been argued that the best solution for lasting peace is a military victory of one of the warring parties, as the defeated party will have lost its capacity to organize and carry out a violent struggle. In conflicts where the issue at stake is identity, Licklider (1995) finds that military victories are more likely to "stick" than negotiated peace settlements, although a serious drawback is that military victories are more likely to be followed by genocide – a different, but equally serious, form of political violence. The unrecognized states in the former Soviet Union have all emerged out of ceasefires following their military successes against the parent states that they are officially part of, yet the authorities in the unrecognized states are doubtful of the "stickiness" of their victories – and rightly so. Military victory has not been a guarantee for post-war peace.

Existing scholarship points to several routes through which peace settlements fail to establish lasting peace, notably the failure of negotiations to resolve the conflict's underlying reasons and the inability of the warring parties to credibly enforce a settlement. I review these explanations in the post-Soviet context and argue that a fruitful avenue for further research builds on the emerging scholarship on the internal dynamics of armed conflicts, which emphasizes the organization and nature of violence and can thus shed light on post-war violence both between former enemies *and* among former allies.

Failure to resolve the conflict

Perhaps the most obvious reason why peace would fail is that the parties cannot reach a settlement, or the settlement itself does not adequately address the reasons that caused the conflict in the first place (cf. Burton 1993). Indeed, from a grievance-based perspective, why would either of the warring parties respect a post-war peace that has not resolved the issues that made them pick up arms in the first place? In such a scenario, the party that considers the agreement insufficient may decide that the potential benefits of picking up arms again may be worth the costs.

There are several reasons why a peace settlement may fail to address the issues that motivated the conflict. First, some issues do no lend themselves to compromise solutions. Conflicts over so-called indivisible stakes, which are often tied to the actors' identity rather than resources, are particularly hard to resolve. One such indivisible stake is struggles where an ethnic group wants control over a territory that it considers to be its homeland, and the central government considers the territory integral to the state (Toft 2003). This is precisely the kind of conflict that has given birth to the post-Soviet unrecognized states, which helps explain why an agreement is so hard to reach. In Nagorno Karabakh, for example, both Armenians and Azerbaijanis consider the territory integral to their history (Tchilingirian 1999; de Waal 2004).[16] Indeed, the conflicts that gave birth to the post-Soviet unrecognized states all ended through a military victory followed by a ceasefire or only partial agreement, as in the Chechen case, where the republic's status was left to be decided in five years' time.

Second, peace negotiations that involve external mediators may be more likely to resolve the underlying issues than conflicts where the warring parties are left to themselves, as the mediators can encourage dialogue and help the parties consider each other's views (Zartman 1995b). This explanation, however, does not seem to explain the lack of peace agreements in the post-Soviet unrecognized states. Foreign governments and international organizations have acted as mediators in each of these "frozen" conflicts, but to no or little avail.[17] In Transnistria, the Organization for Security and Cooperation in Europe (OSCE) tried to mediate in the early 1990s, but the Transnistrian authorities considered the organization to be too pro-Moldovan (Roper 2001: 111), hence had little faith in the mediators.

Third, if some of the warring parties are excluded from the bargaining table, their views and grievances may not be represented, and they may, therefore, become "outside spoilers" that seek to challenge the implementation of the agreement (Stedman 1997; Nilsson 2008). Unless the reason for a partial agreement is the exclusion of weaker voices and certain actors from the bargaining table, it is hard to explain the presence of such an agreement in the first place. One would not expect the warring parties to have signed an agreement that somehow failed to address their grievances – or, if they did, it suggests that they may be content with a partial agreement, and the explanation for failure must rest elsewhere (Werner 1999).[18] Indeed, in the unrecognized states, the main problem is that the parties have not even reached an agreement on the key issue at stake (Walker 1998). Lacking international recognition, the unrecognized states' involvement in the negotiation processes has been problematic, as including an unrecognized state in negotiations implicitly recognizes it.[19] Thus Azerbaijan has refused to recognize Nagorno Karabakh as a negotiation partner, and OSCE-mediated negotiations have taken place between Armenia and Azerbaijan, while representatives from Karabakh have not been considered a formal party to the negotiations (Panossian 2001: 158). Yet the degree to which the unrecognized states have been excluded or included in the negotiations does not seem to explain the lack of fully fledged settlements. In Transnistria, the leadership was part of the negotiations, but refused to sign ceasefires reached in 1992 (Roper 2001: 109), and later negotiations have also not succeeded in reaching an agreement as the parties cannot agree on the status of the region. Similarly, in the Chechen case, after the Chechens defeated the Russian forces in the summer of 1996, they negotiated the Khasavyurt accord, but the accord left Chechnya's status – the main issue at stake – undecided until 2001.

Civil wars often take on a life of their own, creating new motivations and even vested interests in continued warfare or dysfunctional states (e.g. Reno 2002; Collier *et al.* 2003; Weinstein 2007), which means that it is not a given that somehow resolving the conflict's initial causes will do the trick. Similarly, even if the agreement does resolve the conflict's underlying reasons, the warring parties are still asked to do something almost unthinkable: to put down their weapons and, somehow, trust that the opposing party will do the same.

Credible commitment problem

Even after reaching a settlement, parties who have spent months, even years, fighting one another find themselves in a very vulnerable situation. How can they trust that their former enemies will stick to the agreed terms? And if no such trust exists, is it not an enormous risk to begin disarming? Because the parties find themselves in such a vulnerable situation, the dynamics of a reverse security dilemma makes the return to violence and failure to implement a peace agreement very probable, as there is no credible commitment to peace. Walter (1999: 43) argues that, "As groups begin to disarm, they create an increasingly tense situation. The fewer arms they have, the more vulnerable they feel. The more vulnerable they feel, the more sensitive they become to possible violations." The solution is for third parties to step in and guarantee – by monitoring and enforcing – the terms of the settlement, as well as for the settlement to include clear provisions of power-sharing among the former warring parties (Walter 1999, 2002).[20]

The lack of credible commitments can help shed light on why former combatants may or may not adhere to a peace agreement, and why ceasefires, which are agreements about cessation of violence but do not include power-sharing plans (or any plans at all) for the future, are unlikely to bring about lasting peace. Given that most unrecognized states have emerged after mere ceasefires, the second component of the credible commitment strategy, a power-sharing agreement, is missing. In that respect, it is perhaps surprising that there has not been a resumption of armed conflict in more of the unrecognized states. Yet because many of the unrecognized states have seen an out-migration, both voluntary and forced, of members of the war-time opposing group, the security dilemma in the post-war era should no longer be as pertinent, except in areas of refugee return, as in the Gali district in Abkhazia, or on the border with the parent state, as in the case of ceasefire breaches in Nagorno Karabakh. The credible commitment theory is not, however, aimed at explaining why former allies may be fighting one another following the "official" end to an armed conflict. To do so, it would have to emphasize the potential divisions within the warring parties.

Spoilers and factional struggles

A number of scholars have pointed to the role of the kind of actors Stedman (1997) calls "inside spoilers," suggesting that different actors within the same camp may have different goals. In contrast to outside spoilers, who never agreed to a peace settlement, inside spoilers are groups or factions who sign or concede to a settlement, then proceed to jeopardize its implementation, as they may have agreed to the settlement simply to stall for time and regroup or, due to enhanced capabilities or new interests, they believe they can reach a better deal (Werner 1999; Greenhill and Major 2006/2007). Spoiler arguments typically focus on the struggle between the war-time adversaries, assuming that the spoilers' goal is to put pressure on their opponents. Yet, as Pearlman (2009) argues, spoiler behavior may just as well stem from struggles *internal* to their own group – in the case of separatist struggles, internal to the ethnic group.

Indeed, while scholars often think about the warring parties in a conflict as relatively unitary actors, non-state actors who have found themselves in an armed struggle against the state are often fraught with divisions (Pearlman forthcoming; Cunningham 2008; Cunningham *et al.* 2010; Lawrence 2010) – as is often the state itself (Lapidus 1998). Different factions of the group may find themselves in a power struggle over which faction shall legitimately represent the group as a whole. In such a setting, peace negotiations and settlements "can heighten contestation over the terms of legitimate representation because it favors some factions and disfavors others" (Pearlman 2009: 84). Thus factions may seek to derail a peace settlement because it empowers other factions within the group. Such intra-group competition can explain why the post-war era may be plagued by violence not just between former enemies, but also between former allies. Moreover, over the course of a conflict, new cleavages, organizations, and motives may emerge (Kalyvas 2008), likely to have implications for the post-war era. Indeed, even if the war-time aim of a self-determination struggle is relatively unified – say, independence – the post-war era may bring out competing views of the future (Suhrke 2007).[21]

Building on these insights, I suggest that the organization of violence *during* the conflict affects violence in the unrecognized states born out of the struggle: War-time fragmented separatist groups increase the likelihood of internal violence in the post-war era. Separatist groups that are relatively cohesive are less likely to experience internal fighting over political relevance or dominance (Cunningham *et al.* 2010). Similarly, separatist groups that have a relatively institutionalized system of representation are less likely to experience internal fighting over who has the right to represent the group than groups without such institutionalization (Pearlman 2009; Boyle 2009). By itself, war-time competition over political domination or representation among the separatists makes violence a likely feature of the post-war order. If anything, one might expect that once the struggle against their common enemy, the parent state, disappears, the struggle among them rises to the forefront. Such fragmentation and intra-group competition also gives the parent state the opportunity to use split-and-rule strategies to destabilize the unrecognized states, playing different factions against each other. Thus, the organization of the war-time group – specifically, whether it is fragmented or not – is likely to influence post-war peace.

In Chechnya, the nationalist leadership under President Dudayev was already, from 1992, challenged by internal opposition groups and attempted coup attempts (Bakke 2010). In the summer of 1993, the Chechen parliament called for Dudayev's resignation, upon which violent clashes between Dudayev's opponents and supporters broke out in the center of Grozny. In turn, Dudayev dismissed the "treacherous" parliament, effectively ending any institutionalized and legitimate system of representation.[22] The outbreak of war with Moscow in December 1994 temporarily put a lid on such intra-group struggles within Chechnya, but even the organization of the Chechen forces that fought the Russian army in 1994–1996 showed signs of these divisions. The National Guard, for example, consisted of a number of units under the control of field commanders, including the forces of Beslan Gantemirov, who as late as October 1994 had sought to topple Dudayev. In addition, the fighting was carried out by occasional fighters organized along family (clan) or neighborhood lines, village self-defense units, and a relatively small contingent of foreign fighters (Dunlop 1998; Lieven 1998; Avioutskii and Mili 2003; German 2003; Zürcher 2007). The troubles of the unrecognized Chechen state between 1997 and 1999 were largely caused by President Maskhadov's inability to rein in the former field commanders, despite winning the elections. The former field commanders' opposition to Maskhadov was amplified by the fact that the peace agreement he brokered with Moscow in 1997 left Chechnya's status undecided – and promised reconstruction funds from Moscow never materialized.

While none of the self-determination movements fighting their post-Soviet parent states – in Abkhazia, South Ossetia, Nagorno Karabakh, Transnistria, and Chechnya – may have had a highly institutionalized system of legitimate representation, only in Chechnya was the movement's leadership, almost from the outset, challenged by violent internal opposition. While the causal chain from war-time to post-war violence will have to be more systematically investigated across cases, it is suggestive that Chechnya was the unrecognized state most characterized by internal violence between former war-time allies.

The nature of violence

It is also possible that the organization of the war-time group – whether it is fragmented or not, or institutionalized or not – is intertwined with the nature of violence, which in turn may affect the post-war peace. In particular, it is not unreasonable to expect that war-time targeting of civilians makes for a tense post-war era, in particular if the group fighting in the name of an ethnic group targets civilians of that very ethnic group – now at the core of the group's state-building effort.

While civilians have always been victims in wars, researchers have recently begun to systematically examine why warring parties – be they states or non-state groups – intentionally target civilians (see, for example, Downes 2006; Kalyvas 2006, 2008; Weinstein 2007). Weinstein (2007), for example, argues that, depending on whether rebel groups attract opportunistic recruits or true believers, they are more or less likely, respectively, to use indiscriminate violence against innocent civilians. Cunningham *et al.* (2010) find that, in self-determination conflicts with a large number of factions fighting the state in the name of an ethnic group, civilians *of that group* are more likely to be targeted than in conflicts with more cohesive challengers. The rationale is that a large number of factions representing the same group increases intra-group competition, and violence against co-ethnic civilians becomes a means to control the population and punish those who support other factions. While all wars are likely to end with bad feelings against the war-time enemy, one might expect that following self-determination conflicts where separatists targeted civilians of their own ethnic group, the post-war society is filled with revenge motives not only among the war-time enemy population (the out-group), but also among the war-time allies (the in-group) – hence a higher chance of post-war violence.

In the Chechen case, Tishkov (2004: 91) notes on the pre-war days:

> The facts of the Dudayev regime's brutal assaults and the killings it inflicted on Chechens who did not share his ultraradical platform of militant secession are not mentioned often enough. Yavus Akhmadov and Dzhabrail [...] witnessed Dudayev's death squads shoot people on the square, kill members of parliament inside the parliament building, and, finally, shoot a dozen disloyal policemen at the city's police headquarters.

Similarly, during the final days of the first war, "Chechen combatants retook Grozny from the federal troops and hunted for all those who had collaborated with pro-Russian authorities" (ibid.). Not surprisingly, the post-war era, too, was characterized by revenge-motivated violence (ibid.: 106). Again, further research is needed to establish if and how the nature of war-time violence affects post-war violence by systematically examining evidence across cases. To the degree that we are interested in explaining violence both between former enemies and between former allies, it may be instructive to look at intra-group dynamics as well as dynamics between the former adversaries.

Conclusion

Perhaps somewhat misleadingly, both scholars and policymakers often talk about "post-conflict" societies, using a term that denotes an order that is more stable and peaceful than it really is. My goal in this chapter has been to describe and provide hypotheses for explaining different forms of violence in a special kind of post-conflict state – unrecognized states born out of self-determination struggles. While continued violence is a challenge for any post-war society, it may be particularly so for unrecognized states, whose lack of external legitimacy may make internal legitimacy crucial to their endurance. Continued violence is likely to pose an obstacle to internal legitimacy. This chapter suggests that post-war violence may follow from the organization and nature of war-time violence. By doing so, it builds on a growing body of research in pointing to the intra-group dynamics of violent struggles. Because the actors engaged in self-determination struggles are simultaneously seeking to break and build an existing order, the struggle is taking place not only between the state and the wannabe state-makers but also among the wannabe state-makers. Taking this dual struggle seriously helps us understand why post-war societies are prone to violence not only between the war-time enemies, but also among the war-time allies.

Notes

1 Civil wars, or intrastate armed conflicts, include both conflicts over control of the central government or conflicts over control of a certain territory. Self-determination (also called separatist or secessionist) struggles typically fall under the last category, as one of the issues at stake may include control over the territory that an ethnic group inhabits and/or considers to be home (cf. Horowitz 1981). In the Uppsala Conflict Data, an intrastate conflict is not considered an armed conflict until it reaches 25 battle-related deaths per year (Gleditsch *et al.* 2002); per the Correlates of War data, the threshold is 1,000 (Sarkees *et al.* 2003). In this article, I conceptualize peace as the absence of personal or direct violence (be that criminal or political) – in Galtung's (1969) term, "negative peace."

2 Unrecognized states have caught both scholarly and popular attention. See, for example, the 2005 BBC documentary "Holidays in the Danger Zone: Places that Don't Exist" (online at www.bbc.co.uk/bbcfour/documentaries/features/places-that-dont-exist.shtml).

3 Research based on survey data in the conflict-ridden North Caucasus shows that individuals who perceive that they live in communities disproportionally targeted by the Russian military and its allied paramilitary forces, as well as individuals who feel that their lives have been significantly changed by violence, are less likely to forgive perpetrators of violence than people without such experiences (Bakke *et al.* 2009). Forgiveness is a key ingredient of conflict reconciliation in a war-torn society (e.g. Nadler *et al.* 2008).

4 A ceasefire is a settlement where the warring parties agree to lay down their weapons. It can be formal or informal. A peace agreement is a formal settlement between the warring parties, where they agree to lay down their weapons and also take significant steps towards a political solution of the conflict.

5 Lynch (2004a: 42) notes that the term "frozen" is somewhat misleading, as the dynamics "on the ground today are very different from the context that gave rise to these conflicts in the late 1980s."

6 Lake and Rothchild (1996) note that it is very difficult to *resolve* the underlying reasons for ethnic conflicts; at best, policymakers can hope to manage or contain such conflicts.

7 For an ongoing project on post-conflict violence, see Suhrke *et al.* (2006).
8 Some of the conflicts represented both intrastate and interstate struggles: In the case of Nagorno Karabakh, the Armenians fought on the side of the Karabakh Armenians against Azerbaijan (see, for example, de Waal 2004). In Transnistria, soldiers from the Russian 14th Army supported the Transnistrian paramilitaries against Moldovan forces (see, for example, Roper 2001).
9 On the competing storylines of the Georgian and Russian governments with respect to the war, see Tuathail (2008).
10 The 1991–1992 war in South Ossetia led to 30,000 displaced Georgians (to Georgia) and 37,000 displaced South Ossetians (to North Ossetia in Russia). Facilitated by OSCE and UNHCR, an agreement on return was reached in 1997; by January 2003, 12,000 remained displaced (Norwegian Refugee Council 2003). Pre-conflict South Ossetia was characterized by high inter-marriage rates, and the Ossetian forces claimed that they were attacking only those perceived as their *political*, not ethnic, enemies – although ethnicized violence did take place (Tuathail 2008: 678).
11 Notably, Maskhadov's calls for negotiations with Moscow following the acts of Basayev and Khattab failed, as Moscow opted to meet with representatives of an anti-Maskhadov Chechen government in exile instead (Bohlen 1999; BBC 1999).
12 From 1934 until 1992, Chechnya was part of the Chechen-Ingush ASSR, consisting of two titular national groups, the Chechens and the Ingush. The two formally separated in June 1992, as the Ingush did not want to join the Chechen nationalists' struggle for independence.
13 The two wars have been characterized by massive civilian suffering and human rights violations. While both the Chechen rebels and Russian forces have committed atrocities, most of the violations have been at the hands of Russian forces. For first-hand accounts of violence in Chechnya, see Politkovskaya (2001, 2003) and Nivat (2001).
14 See also Caspersen's chapter in this volume.
15 See Kolstø and Blakkisrud's chapter in this volume.
16 For strategies for reintegrating unrecognized states, see Anderson's chapter in this volume.
17 In Transnistria, mediation efforts were carried out by Russia, Ukraine, and the Organization for Security and Cooperation in Europe (OSCE). In Chechnya, the OSCE tried to initiate negotiations in the fall of 1996. In Nagorno Karabakh, both Russia and the OSCE Minsk Group have been mediators. In Abkhazia, the lead mediator was Russia. In South Ossetia, Russia, the OSCE, and the EU have been involved.
18 For an overview of peace settlements from 1989 to 2005, see Harbom *et al.* (2006).
19 See also Herrberg's chapter in this volume.
20 Building on Lijphart (e.g. Lijphart 1990), both scholars and policymakers have considered power-sharing one of the means best suited for ending civil wars, although a number of scholars have begun to question its merits (e.g. Spears 2002; Roeder and Rothchild 2005).
21 Even in the case of the peaceful sovereignty movement in Québec, the movement has, in recent years, seen deep divides when it come to the question of what an independent Québec, if it were to come about, would indeed look like (Bakke 2009).
22 The November 1991 elections that brought Dudayev to power in Chechnya can hardly be considered free and fair, but survey data suggest that, at the time, 60–70 percent of Chechen voters actually did vote for Dudayev (Dunlop 1998: 114).

7 'Separatism is the mother of terrorism'

Internationalizing the security discourse on unrecognized states

Pål Kolstø and Helge Blakkisrud[1]

Since unrecognized states are denied membership in virtually all international organizations, they are not bound by the conflict-reducing mechanisms that these organizations provide. No international conventions can be applied on their territory and no effective monitoring is possible (Kolstø 2006). This creates a lack of transparency, which may prove extremely attractive for criminal and other shady businesses. As Thomas de Waal (2003: 246) has remarked with regard to Nagorno Karabakh, 'None of its laws or institutions were valid outside its own borders, and no foreign diplomats, apart from peace negotiators, set foot there. That was virtually an invitation to become a rogue state.' Not only may the unregulated status of the unrecognized states affect the lives of their citizens, it may also represent a danger to the outside world, in particular – but not limited to – their immediate neighbours.

At least theoretically, however, the logic of non-recognition may also work in the opposite direction. As Nina Caspersen (2008) has pointed out, since the unrecognized states are keenly interested in achieving recognition, they may be prompted to try to prove that they can live up to the standards of democracy, rule of law, and functional statehood no worse and perhaps even better than many recognized states.[2] Thus, we cannot make any a priori assumptions about the threat emanating from unrecognized states. Each case must be studied empirically.

This chapter discusses how the perceived threats emanating from unrecognized states have been securitized by their respective parent states. The two cases selected for study here are Transnistria (officially known as the Pridnestrovian Moldavian Republic) and the Nagorno Karabakh Republic, with their parent states, Moldova and Azerbaijan. The political class in the parent states is in one respect uniquely placed to monitor developments in the breakaway statelets. It often has much more thorough knowledge about its former province, both its history and current development, than do outside observers, and may be able to provide a corrective to the overly rosy picture that the secessionist regimes are prone to present of themselves. On the other hand, parent-state observers cannot be regarded as unbiased witnesses. They have a direct interest in the elimination of the unrecognized political entity and its re-absorption into the parent state, and that may tempt them to exaggerate the security risk posed by such unrecognized states, in order to attract international support.

Securitization

In our analysis of the debates unfolding within the parent states, we draw on the insights of the Copenhagen school of security studies and the concept of 'securitization' introduced by the three foremost representatives of this school – Barry Buzan, Ole Wæver and Jaap de Wilde (see Buzan *et al.* 1998; Wæver 1995). This concept is intended to capture the constructed nature of 'security'. Traditional security studies start with the assumption that states are confronted with specific objective threats and see it as the task of the security analysts to identify these threats. Wæver and his colleagues do not deny the existence of 'real' threats, but they bracket this ontological issue and treat security as the intersubjective establishment of something as an existential threat

Securitization, as they define it, is a special kind of *politization.* Any public issue may, in principle, be presented by the actors as either non-political or political. In the latter case, once an issue is politicized, it becomes part of public policy, requiring government decision and resource allocation. Securitization means that the issue is not only politicized, but presented as *an existential threat* to the community ('the referent object'): as a matter of survival that requires emergency measures outside the normal bounds of political procedure (Buzan *et al.* 1998: 24). Thus, public issues may be moved in and out of the field of 'vital' security concerns by deliberate acts of securitization and desecuritization.

Securitization is a speech-act, in the sense of the term as used by John Austin (2001). This means that a potential threat to the community *becomes* a security issue by being pronounced as such. However, 'security' – and related words such as 'danger' and 'threat' – are not magic wands to be brandished at will: 'Successful securitization is not decided by the securitizer but by the audience of the security speech act: does the audience accept that something is an existential threat to a shared value?' (Buzan *et al.* 1998: 31).

Who is the securitizer and who is the audience in the Moldovan and Azerbaijani security debates? As Buzan *et al.* emphasize, anyone can in principle fill the role of the securitizer. No-one is guaranteed the ability to make people accept a claim for a necessary security action, nor is anyone excluded from attempting to present their own threat perceptions. Even so, some figures are clearly better placed to make an impact on the security debate, and among them are state leaders and professional security analysts. Thus, we focus on how the unrecognized states are represented as threats by these groups.

Concerning the audience, we believe it would be a mistake to narrow it down to the local, internal audience in Moldova and Azerbaijan. As small and relatively weak states that have lost a civil war against the secessionists, these countries must try to harness strong outside actors like the USA and the major European countries to their cause in order to attain their objective: recapturing the lost territory. Hence, they seek to secure endorsement of the unrecognized state as an existential threat to a shared value. Buzan *et al.* note that during the Cold War 'local powers appealed to the superpowers for support by trying to locate their own security concerns within the context of superpower rivalry' (Buzan *et al.* 1998: 64). These attempts were often successful since the superpowers saw many local conflicts as extensions of their own rivalry (ibid.). After the Cold War these local–global dynamics have become much weaker, according to Buzan *et al.* This, we believe, is no doubt true with regard to attitudes and priorities in the great powers – but not in the securitization discourse in weak states. Weak states are still keen to sell their own concerns as a part of a larger threat picture that includes the great powers as well.

The parent states of unrecognized states can easily frame the security threats associated with the unrecognized states, but they lack the resources necessary for acting on these threats. Although the local audience endorses the measures, to overcome this stalemate, we argue, the security actors in the parent states will seek to redefine the referent object (the object of the perceived threat) away from the state itself, to a wider category that can encompass major external powers. In this process, security threats are reframed as regional (or even global) in the hope of attracting the attention of important external actors. As an extension of securitization theory, we call this the *internationalization* of security. Just as securitization is a special kind of politization, internationalization is a variety of securitization.

Background

Transnistria and the Nagorno Karabakh Republic were both established in the early 1990s during the collapse of the Soviet Union, and both experienced a war with the parent state after proclaiming their independence. Moreover, both have achieved a reasonably high degree of statehood and functional institutions, at least when compared with the other post-Soviet unrecognized states – Abkhazia, South Ossetia, and the now-defunct Chechnya (Ichkeria) (Kolstø and Blakkisrud 2008, Tishkov 2004). In many other respects, however, Transnistria and the Nagorno Karabakh Republic represent rather different cases. The 1992 civil war in Moldova was brief and limited; the total number of casualties is estimated at less than one thousand.[3] By contrast, the civil war in Azerbaijan lasted for six years, claimed close to 30,000 lives, and caused a large numbers of IDPs (de Waal 2003: 285). Furthermore, while neither conflict is settled in the sense that no peace agreement has been signed in either, the Transnistrian conflict is today much better regulated. Here, the parties have agreed on a regime of peacekeepers, consisting of Russian troops in addition to contingents from both sides. In Azerbaijan, there are no peacekeepers or demilitarized zone, and the parties face each other directly. Incidents and skirmishes are frequent, claiming several thousand lives since the conclusion of ceasefire in 1994 (International Crisis Group 2007a: 1).

Also in other respects, relations between the parent state and the unrecognized state differ greatly. In Azerbaijan, the border is hermetically sealed, with no civilian or commercial traffic going either way, while in Moldova thousands of trucks, cars, and share taxis pass the various crossing points each day. Many

Transnistrian firms are registered in Chisinau and operate with Moldovan licenses. Transnistrian newspapers may be bought in Chisinau kiosks, and Transnistrian citizens with dual Transnistrian–Moldovan citizenship may travel abroad on Moldovan passports. By contrast, anyone with a passport bearing a Nagorno Karabakh stamp is automatically denied entry into Azerbaijan.

Obviously, under such disparate circumstances, threat perceptions and 'enemy images' are very different. Even so, the unrecognized state issue is securitized in both Moldova and Azerbaijan in sometimes strikingly similar ways, while there are also marked differences.

Below, we present the evolving security discourse in each country as identified in articles, reports, and booklets written by political scientists and other putative security experts throughout the last decade. To limit the sample, we focus on the period between the onset of the international 'War on Terror', which opened up new possibilities for the parent states to reinterpret domestic security threats and engage the international community, and the 2008 war in Georgia, which again shifted the direction of the discourse on unrecognized states.[4] Since we are primarily interested in the messages which the political class in these two countries want to send to the outside world we have collected material written in English and Russian only. When Azerbaijani and Moldovan scholars write in English, it is first and foremost a Western audience they want to sway; Russian-language texts address the entire post-Soviet readership, since Russian remains a lingua franca in most Soviet successor states. While these texts are primarily meant for export, they can also be read by domestic audiences.

Types of danger

The various types of threat perceptions we have identified in the security discourse in our two cases may, for the sake of simplicity, be organized into four categories. We start with more clear-cut economic threats, crossing over to political security in categories 2 and 3, gradually moving towards more 'traditional' military security:

1 *General criminality*: This category includes the production of and smuggling of innocuous, 'civilian' goods that could have been exported legally if tolls and taxes had been paid. Such activities may harm the economy of the parent state as well as that of other states.
2 *Aggravated criminality*: By this we mean involvement in activities that would be illegal under all circumstances and in all countries, such as the production and smuggling of narcotic substances or weapons, trafficking of women, sale of body parts for transplantation on the black market, and so on. Such activities harm not only the economy but also the societal fabric in the countries that are the end destination of these commodities and people.
3 *Terrorism*: This includes targeted attacks by non-military actors on the territory of the parent state in order to terrorize the population and destabilize

the political situation there, as well as turning the unrecognized state into a safe haven for international networks of terrorism.

4 *Armed conflict*: Here we mean not only the threat of a new civil war, but also the process of military build-up (import, production, and stockpiling of weapons) as well as military provocations along the ceasefire line, and other acts of military posturing.

Charges that the unrecognized states represent all four threat types can be found in the securitization discourse in both Moldova and Azerbaijan, but in different mixtures. The security threats may be ordered in a hierarchy, from relatively low danger in the case of general criminality, to high in the case of military build-up and the threat of renewed hostilities (see Table 7.1). Of course, this categorization is a schematic simplification; the boundaries between the various types will often be blurred. Thus, for instance, one author may, in the same article, claim that the unrecognized state is selling narcotics (2) in order to buy weapons, which could either go to strengthen military capabilities (4) or to supply a terrorist group (3).

Moldova

A clear example of the Moldovan discourse on the security threats associated with the continued existence of Transnistria as an unrecognized state is a report presented by the executive director of the think-tank IDIS Viitorul, Igor Munteanu, at a 2004 roundtable discussion organized by the Euro-Atlantic Council Romania–Casa NATO and the Norwegian Atlantic Committee. In his presentation, Munteanu referred to all four types of security threats listed above:

1 *General criminality*: After more than ten years of isolation, the Transnistrian regime had converted its statelet into a kind of ‘duty-free shop’, a haven for smugglers. ‘Every year, Moldova loses nearly 900 million lei, as a result of smuggling operated through the area.’[5]

2 *Aggravated criminality*: The list of smuggled goods included drugs and arms, and human trafficking was also widespread.

3 *Terrorism*: ‘These outlaw areas … not only provide centers for criminal activity, such as money laundering, which supports organized crime in Europe and the US, but they can also be breeding grounds and staging points for local and international terrorism.’

Table 7.1 Typology of threat perceptions in parent states

	Type of security threatened	*Strength/potency of threat*
General criminality	Economic	Low
Aggravated criminality	Economic/political	↕
Terrorism	Political/military	
Armed conflict	Military	High

4 *Armed conflict*: Finally, the Transnistrian regime exports instability by meddling in other local conflicts. 'Participation of mercenaries from Transnistria in the Abkhaz war, and recently, in the hostilities provoked in South Ossetia against Georgian Government proves the expanding geography of their active involvement' (Munteanu 2004: 2–3).

Munteanu's message is clear, albeit stated indirectly: the only way to combat these extremely disturbing tendencies is to include Moldova in the NATO family: 'Many of Europe's major concerns, such as drug, arms, and human trafficking, illegal immigration, terrorism, and possible nuclear proliferation can only be addressed by including the Black Sea region within the NATO framework' (ibid.: 3).

In another article, published in 2007, Igor Munteanu and co-author Angela Munteanu repeat most of the charges made in the roundtable discussion three years earlier:

> Transnistria has served for a decade and a half as a shipping point for weapons and drugs, and the smuggling of the latter; taking leadership of the 'club of unrecognized secessions'; and even supplying other warfare zones with arms and military.
>
> (Munteanu and Munteanu 2007: 58)

The link between Transnistria and terrorism has now been upgraded from a possibility to reality. Transnistria, the Munteanus claim, 'fell under the label of transnational organized crime and terrorism many years before the "war against terrorism" was launched' (Munteanu and Munteanu 2007: 59).

Although there are several similar examples of attempts at internationalizing the Transnistrian issue by linking the activities of the unrecognized state to the discourse on international terror (see also below), Moldovan pundits seem more hesitant to play up traditional security threats (i.e. the threat of renewed hostilities) in their securitizing moves. The main exception here is the Russian factor. Whereas the Transnistrian forces as such are hard to sell as a credible threat to regional security, the prospect of Transnistria serving as a bridgehead for projecting Russian power in the wider region is more likely to set off the alarm in Western capitals. An example of such an attempt to play the Russian card is a 2006 report by Mihai Gribincea of the Institute of Political and Military Studies, on the presence of Russian troops and the security threat they represent. Gribincea claims that 'more and more observers' believe that Russia sustains Transnistrian separatism and keeps troops in the region in order to turn Transnistria into a second Kaliningrad (Gribincea 2006). He sees the Russian initiative for conflict resolution in 2003 – the 'Kozak Memorandum' – as an attempt to establish a permanent Russian military presence 'on the new eastern border of NATO'.

However, the credibility of this threat has been questioned by a group of researchers in an analytical paper published by the Institute for Public Policy after the August 2008 war in Georgia (Barbarosie *et al.* 2008). These researchers hold that the events in Georgia prove that 'tough scenarios' may materialize in Russia's zone of interest; and in their reading of Russian foreign policy statements, Moldova clearly falls within that zone. Moreover, the capacity of Moldova to defend herself militarily, they believe, is 'extremely low'. Even so, they conclude: 'in the short term, the repetition of events like those in Georgia is less possible in the case of the Republic of Moldova' (ibid.: 5). As reasons for this guarded optimism they point out that Moldova, unlike Georgia, is a neighbour to a NATO and EU member state, and Transnistria is less easy for Moscow to use as a bridgehead for aggression than South Ossetia or Abkhazia.

A similar conclusion is reached by Nicu Popescu in an analysis published by the Open Society Institute (Budapest) in 2006. Popescu adopts a somewhat different approach to the unrecognized state-problem, focusing on the internal political system of Transnistria and its democratic qualities. He compares Transnistria to Abkhazia, which he finds has a much higher level of genuine political pluralism. This Popescu regards as counterintuitive, since Abkhazia is a much poorer and more war-torn society, with scarcely any functioning state institutions and with high criminality. By contrast, Transnistria is highly authoritarian, even though it is

> industrialized, urban, relatively developed, almost half of its trade is with the EU and the US, *war with Moldova does not seem to be even a theoretical possibility*, foreigners can travel easily there and it has the biggest population of the secessionist entities in the former Soviet Union (emphasis added).
>
> (Popescu 2006a: 4–5)

Thus, in an analysis primarily devoted to levels of democracy in unrecognized states, this Moldovan scholar opines that the Transnistrian regime does not represent any military danger – not to Moldova, nor, by implication, to the region at large.

Instead, the thrust of the securitization moves seems centred on the destabilizing role Transnistria plays as a criminal hub. One example is the executive summary of the '3D' (demilitarization, decriminalization, and democratization) strategy, a conflict resolution initiative instigated by the Institute for Public Policy and supported by several Moldovan think-tanks, NGOs, and security analysts (including Igor Munteanu, who is credited as one of the co-authors of the strategy). 'Transnistria … has become a lawless territory for criminal activities, arms, goods and drugs smuggling, human trafficking to Western Europe and Middle East.… These conflicts become a real security problem at the EU and NATO's South-eastern border.' (Moldova's Transnistrian conflict 2004) Although the executive summary does not go into detail, the gist is clear: the criminal activity evolving under the protection of the Transnistrian regime is not only a local problem, it is a pan-European problem that affects EU and NATO members as well.

The same message is a key point for Oazu Nantoi, an analyst of the Institute for Public Policy (and a co-author of the 3D strategy). 'If Moldova until just recently was alone with her problems, then now a whole range of new actors (the EU, USA, Ukraine, and Romania) are increasingly impatient in their attitude towards the Transnistrian regime' (Nantoi 2005). He claims that Transnistrian President Igor Smirnov is a Russian marionette, who gives criminal cover to an international network of organized crime. 'Smirnov's "hobby" [i.e. the Transnistrian unrecognized state] has over the last decade and a half developed into a hearth of criminality in the region' (ibid.).[6]

A major problem with much of the analysis provided by Moldovan experts on the Transnistrian issue is the lack of references to sources of information. This is in many respects understandable. Breakaway regimes will hardly publish statistics on the revenues from drug sales, trafficking, weapon smuggling, etc., to the extent that they are involved in such. Scholarly discussions on these topics are necessarily conjectural, or perhaps – but less likely – based on intelligence sources that cannot be disclosed.

Some Moldovan researchers are somewhat more scrupulous than others about citing their sources. Ceslav Ciobanu, former Moldovan ambassador to the USA and later senior fellow at the United States Institute of Peace, has equipped his USIP report from 2004 with numerous footnotes. To be sure, some of the information provided by Ciobanu remains undocumented – including the claim that 40 per cent of the prostitutes in Moscow come from Transnistria, and the estimate that the criminal activities of the Smirnov regime generate $2 billion a year (as against the skimpy $85 million Transnistrian state budget) (Ciobanu 2004: 29–30). On the other hand, Ciobanu's claim that Transnistria is 'a key link in the arms-smuggling network that peddles the Soviet Union's former military hardware on the international market' (ibid.: 5) is taken from an article in *The Christian Science Monitor* by Daniel Twining, former foreign policy adviser to John McCain. Twining (2004) also surmises – with Ciobanu's approval – that 'if Al Qaeda has not gone shopping yet [in Transnistria], it is only a matter of time'. Also, the claim that Transnistria has modified at least thirty-eight Alazan rockets to carry radioactive warheads, 'effectively creating the world's first surface-to-surface dirty bomb', is seemingly documented, this time with a reference to an article in *The Washington Post* (Ciobanu 2004: 5). However, that documentation is partially circular, since one of the sources of *The Washington Post* article is precisely Ciobanu himself (Warrick 2003).

In a later work, Ciobanu modifies his threat assessment somewhat. When he, in 2008, returns to a discussion of the political economy of post-Soviet unrecognized states, he points out that some observers – *in casu* William Hill, former head of the OSCE mission in Moldova – regard as 'overstated' the concern that Transnistrian weapons may fall into terrorist hands (Ciobanu 2008: 161). The EU Border Assistance Mission (EUBAM), established in December 2005 to monitor the border between Moldova and Ukraine, had in any case not produced much evidence of this. Ciobanu continues to insist that the unofficial shadow economy in Transnistria amounts to at least 50 per cent of the officially calculated GDP, but the composition of this economy, as he presents it, has changed somewhat. It now consists of 'alcohol, cigarettes, groceries, and most importantly – until recently – illegal trafficking of small arms, light weapons and related ammunition; drugs; and human beings' (Ciobanu 2008: 165). The qualifier 'until recently' is significant, as is the omission of any references to heavy weapons, nuclear substances, and terrorism. With international presence at the border crossings making the previous alarmist discourse difficult to sustain, Ciobanu moderates his image of the Transnistrian threat.

Turning from the academic to the political input in the unrecognized state-debate in Moldova, we find a remarkable degree of concurrence. In particular, Moldovan President Vladimir Voronin (2001–2009) has on several occasions lashed out against the criminalized Transnistrian regime. The accession to power in 2001 of Voronin, a pro-Russian Communist, had originally raised high hopes for resolution of the stalemated conflict, and the first year of his incumbency indeed saw a flurry of negotiation initiatives. With the Transnistrian leaders proving unexpectedly intransigent, however, relations between Chisinau and Tiraspol soon soured. Already in 2002, Voronin at a NATO summit in Prague called Transnistria 'a black offshore state' in which, he claimed, contraband weapons, including dual-purpose material, were produced. 'PMR is not only a case of political separatism. To our great disappointment, the criminal component of the Transnistrian problem outweighs its political side by far' (*Nezavisimaya Moldova* 2002). Voronin emphasized that Transnistria was not only a Moldovan problem, but represented a threat against all of southeastern Europe (ibid.).

Voronin later adhered to this assessment with great consistency (see, for example, *Nezavisimaya Moldova* 2003; *NEWSru.com* 2006). In an interview with the Russian news agency *RIA Novosti* in May 2007, he explained that the main obstacle to resolution of the Transnistrian conflict was 'organized criminal groups who want to exploit this territory as a "black hole" for the smuggling and production of weapons'. In addition to weapons, the illegal border business included 'trafficking, pharmaceuticals, drugs, and other goods', he claimed (*Nezavisimaya Moldova* 2007). Voronin never directly accused the Tiraspol regime of terrorism, but complained that among the most serious problems his government had to deal with were 'terrorism and aggressive, implacable separatism' (*Infotag* 2005).

Azerbaijan

In the Moldovan discourse, although the topic of terrorism is occasionally broached, it has not been a major issue. By contrast, in Azerbaijan, the theme occupies centre stage. This is in one sense natural, since Armenian nationalists were indeed engaged in terrorist activities throughout most of the twentieth century. In particular, the Armenian Revolutionary Federation, the Dashnaktsutiun, has been involved in several assassinations and bomb attacks in Europe and America. These attacks, however, have been directed against either Turkish officials as revenge for the 1915 massacre or members of rival Armenian groups, and have not been linked to the Nagorno Karabakh issue. Even so, in current Azerbaijani optics, the past history of Armenian political violence and the activities of the contemporary leadership in Nagorno Karabakh are woven together into a seamless pattern. The documentable international ramifications of violent Armenian activism also mean that the danger stemming from Nagorno Karabakh through this link may be presented as a threat not only to Azerbaijan, but also to Europe and indeed to the entire world.

A typical collection of articles and documentation in this debate was published by Rovshan Mustafayev, Director of the Institute on Human Rights of the Azerbaijani Academy of Sciences, in 2002. In *Crimes of Armenian Terrorist and Bandit Formations against the Humanity (19th–21st centuries)*, Mustafayev explains the direct link between the Nagorno Karabakh Republic Defence Army and the Dashnaktsutiun:

> The aims, forms and means by which the [Defence Army] carries out its terrorist acts give reason to think it is an ethno-terrorist organization. Today, the struggle against ethnic terrorist organizations has become a global problem and is no longer confined to the decisions of each state domestically.
>
> (Mustafayev 2002: 330)

Mustafayev points out that various international treaties have been adopted to combat terrorism. As practical policy advice, Mustafayev therefore recommends that Azerbaijan should address international organizations and parliaments in other states in order to have Armenia outlawed as a country engaged in covert state terrorism. Another recommendation is to re-establish the constitutional and public order in Nagorno Karabakh by employing 'the domestic law-enforcement organs of the Republic of Azerbaijan'. That amounts to a plea for a direct military attack on the unrecognized state.

In a book on international terrorism, another researcher from the Institute on Human Rights of the Azerbaijani Academy of Sciences, Ramiz Sevdimaliev, discusses terrorism in various parts of the world in a comparative perspective (Sevdimaliev 2004). A common feature in most terrorist situations, Sevdimaliev explains, is that the boundary between international and domestic terror has faded away, as has the distinction between terrorists and other organized criminal groups. Furthermore, he points out, illegal territories outside state control are ideal for the establishment of infrastructures for money laundering and other kinds of illegal business needed for international terrorism. Proof of this Sevdimaliev finds, *inter alia*, in Transnistria, which allegedly exports weapons to al-Qaeda, Hamas, Hezbollah, PKK, and terrorist groups in the territory of the former Yugoslavia (ibid.: 45). With Nagorno Karabakh, Sevdimaliev believes that the criminal economic activity has come full circle:

> Nagorno Karabakh, which finds itself outside the control of both Azerbaijan and the international community, is under the control of international terrorism and other kinds of transnational criminal activity, while also fulfilling the role as a satellite of Armenia in the realization of this state's policy of state terrorism
>
> (ibid.: 44)

A less alarmist approach is taken by Azerbaijani scholar Anar Valiyev, a post-doctoral fellow at the Masaryk University in Brno, the Czech Republic. In the 2008 article 'Foreign terrorist groups and the rise of home-grown radicalism in Azerbaijan', he notes that, after 11 September, it became fashionable to look for traces of al-Qaeda in various parts of the world, and 'Azerbaijan did not become an exception' (Valiyev 2008: 100). According to Valiyev, however, it is highly unlikely that al-Qaeda should target Azerbaijan, but this does not mean that there are no threats to this country's national security. If we shift the focus away from the spectre of al-Qaeda, we will be able to see whence the real threat emanates: it is the oft-overlooked Karabakh problem (ibid.: 96). This ungoverned territory poses a threat also to the United States and its interests in the Caspian Basin:

> Lack of an effective state presence in Karabakh also have additional factors that can make it an actual or potential terrorist sanctuary, including a remote geography, opportunities for illegal activities to fund terrorism, and even the support from the native population through cultural ties.
>
> (ibid.)

Thus, the theme of Armenian terrorism is reintroduced by Valiyev as an aspect of the Nagorno Karabakh conflict.

The researcher in Azerbaijan who has written most extensively on Nagorno Karabakh and whose writings apparently have also had the greatest impact among policymakers is Rovshan Novruzoglu. In addition to several articles and short reports, he has written a 125-page treatise, *Karabakh: A Black Market for International Terrorism* (Novruzoglu 2003). Here he gives detailed information about various clandestine international umbrella organizations for terrorist groups around the world. One of these, allegedly established in Nagorno Karabakh only ten weeks after the attack on the Twin Towers in New York, unites three terrorist groups: al-Qaeda, Hamas, and the Armenian Secret Army for the Liberation of Armenia (ASALA). The latter is a Marxist–Leninist organization active in the Middle East and Western Europe in the 1970s and 1980s, but according to most sources it ceased operations in 1986 (Chiclet 2004: 170). Novruzoglu insists that it is still active and as sinister as ever. The aim of the new umbrella organization is to carry out 'diversionary projects against diplomatic corps, embassies and chambers of commerce, oil companies, charity centers and humanitarian aid throughout the CIS space' (Novruzoglu 2003: 8).

What makes the activities of ASALA and its terrorist partners particularly ominous is that they have access to nuclear technology, Novruzoglu claims. He has found that several technicians at the Russian nuclear research centre in Dubna outside Moscow are ethnic Armenians and believes he can document links between these scientists, the ASALA terrorists, and Tehran. Even if the Armenian terrorists lack the technology to produce real nuclear weapons they are able – and willing – to produce small 'dirty bombs': rockets supplied with radioactive nuclear waste.

Novruzoglu meticulously details the conspiracies he has discovered with exact names, dates, places, and so on. Thus, for instance, he provides full names, professions, and other details about nine Armenians who have adopted Islam and work for al-Qaeda, receiving from 5,000 to 6,500 USD per month (Novruzoglu 2003: 32). Unfortunately, the sources of his information are usually given as 'our research has shown', or 'according to the facts'. Novruzoglu might perhaps have been dismissed as a nutty conspiracy theorist, were it not for the fact that official Azerbaijani sources cite him as an authority on the Nagorno Karabakh conflict, as seen, for example, on the official websites of several Azerbaijani embassies.

These websites feature identical undated texts on global terrorism, in which it is declared that, since Azerbaijan is the target of Armenian terrorism, 'we deem it necessary to touch upon this issue as a contribution to the joint fight' (Embassy of the Republic of Azerbaijan in Poland n.d.). The text emphasizes the allegedly heavy involvement of Armenian terrorists in the drug business as well as their connections to Islamic fundamentalism. It is admitted that the close ties between Armenian terrorism and radical Islamic terrorist organizations 'can cause astonishment and raise questions' – Armenians are, after all, Christians – but at the same time it is stressed that the links between Osama bin Laden and Armenian groups like ASALA have been studied by Rovshan Novruzoglu (ibid.).

The ties between the analytic community and the politicians in Azerbaijan seem very close: not only the same claims and viewpoints but also the exact same phrases and paragraphs may sometimes be found in both analytical and political texts. Thus, for instance, texts with the identical heading 'The illegal activity of Armenia on the occupied territories of Azerbaijan', although with slightly differing content, may be found on several Azerbaijani websites. One of these websites, analitika.az, belongs to the research centre Southern Caucasus, which presents itself as an independent think-tank that 'belongs to none of political camps'.[7] A slightly longer version of the same text has been published by the Azerbaijani Ministry of National Security (Ministerstvo 2005), while a third version is posted on the website of the Coordinating Council of Azerbaijani Youth (KSAM 2005).[8] The document relates that, between 1989 and 1994, Armenian separatists and terrorists provoked 373 terrorist acts on the territory of Azerbaijan, as a result of which 1,568 people died and 1,808 were injured.[9] It also asserts that Armenia deals in the trade of human beings: 'In order to make a profit Armenian state organs have turned Azerbaijani prisoners, hostages, and missing persons into objects of trade, and have in that connection contacted various criminal groups.' To this, the Ministry of National Security has added in its version of the text that the Armenians have established training camps for international terrorists on the occupied territories (Ministerstvo 2005).

The terrorism theme thus runs deep also in the official Azerbaijani discourse. After 9/11, Azerbaijani authorities wasted no time but, in their own words, 'unconditionally and without hesitation' joined the antiterrorist coalition (*Mnogostoronnaya* 2002: 6). Already in October 2001, the Academy of Sciences in Baku organized a lecture series under the heading 'Armenian terrorism is a global danger for human rights'. Conference participants recommended that Azerbaijani 'should appeal to international organizations and the world countries and declare that Armenia is a country pursuing a secret terror policy' (Akhmedli 2001).

These initiatives were followed up in various forums, albeit with mixed success at best. The Commonwealth of Independent States (CIS) has established a special CIS Antiterrorist Centre, but Azerbaijan found little practical solidarity in this organization; as a member of the CIS, Armenia could veto any anti-Armenian resolutions (Mustafayeva 2003). In a 2002 position paper to the Council of Europe, Azerbaijan demanded that the members of this organization should relinquish their policy of 'double standards' in their attitude towards terrorism, extremism, and separatism. 'It is impossible to combat effectively these phenomena on your own territory and fail to react (and sometimes even support) analogous processes in other states' (*Mnogostoronnaya* 2002: 5). The struggle against terror must be carried out 'on a broad front':

> Separatist regimes in the newly independent states, including Nagorno-Karabakh, use the territory under their control in the interest of narco-business, illegal trade of arms and people, money laundering, and other illegal activity, the profit of which is channelled into the financing of terror.
>
> (ibid.: 2)

This anti-terror rhetoric has been strong also in the speeches and statements of the two Aliyevs, father and son (the former and current presidents of Azerbaijan). In a meeting with the American head of the Minsk group – the OSCE-sponsored group charged with negotiating a peaceful settlement of the Nagorno Karabakh conflict – Heydar Aliyev in October 2001 complained that:

> so far the USA and the OSCE had 'not been sufficiently active' in the regulation of the Karabakh conflict. At the same time [Aliyev] expressed the hope that after the events of 11 September the international community would better understand the threat stemming from terrorism and separatism and fight more actively against such phenomena. Aliyev emphasized in particular that one should not distinguish between separatism and terrorism, since 'separatism is the mother of terrorism'.
>
> (Turan Information Agency 2001)

In September 2001, Aliyev junior headed an Azerbaijani delegation to the Parliamentary Assembly of Council of Europe (PACE) in Strasbourg, and took the opportunity to urge the PACE members to take a stand on the Nagorno-Karabakh conflict:

> The international community must unite in its struggle against all forms of terrorism all over the world. Now is the moment of truth. It is not possible for some countries to sit on two chairs trying to have good relations with both the victims of terror and its organizers.
>
> (Aliyev 2001b)

This clearly echoed George W. Bush's challenge: 'You are either with us or against us.' In Ilham Aliyev's mind, there was no doubt: 'In the battle with terrorism Azerbaijan is in one alliance with the United States' (Aliyev 2001b).

Azerbaijan had become a member of the Council of Europe only nine months prior to Ilham Aliyev's speech at the PACE meeting, and the very first Azerbaijani delegation to this organization had been headed by President Heydar Aliyev himself in January 2001. Interestingly, the tone of Aliyev senior's speech to the assembly was markedly different from that of his son's post-9/11 speech. True, also Aliyev senior underscored that Azerbaijan had become 'the victim of a full-scaled military aggression from neighbouring Armenia' and 'it is unfortunate that the international community is silently observing this continuing tragedy' (Aliyev 2001). The word 'terrorism', however, later to become a mantra in official Azerbaijani statements on this issue,[10] was conspicuously absent. Instead, Aliyev latched his speech onto the discourse of democracy. He averred that Azerbaijan had already ensured the full freedom of the media and the unimpeded development of NGOs, and sought to stand as a paragon of democracy in the world. In particular, he saw 'a special role and responsibility' for Azerbaijan in the spreading of 'advanced democratic ideas' to neighbouring countries and the export of the spirit of democracy to states that were 'inflamed by the ideology of aggressive nationalism, national superiority, and territorial claims on neighbouring states' (ibid.).

Another example of pre-9/11 Azerbaijani official discourse is Ilham Aliyev's address to the PACE in April 2001. This PACE session was devoted to the fight against economic and transnational organized crime. In his intervention, Aliyev claimed that 'the so-called Nagorno-Karabakh republic' had developed into 'one of the center of the organized crime in Europe'; in particular he accused it of producing and smuggling narcotic substances (Aliyev 2001a). Although Aliyev briefly referred to international conventions on the fight against terrorism, Armenian state-sponsored terrorism was not an issue.

These statements demonstrate how the struggle to gain international sympathy for the Azerbaijani side in the Nagorno Karabakh conflict can take various shapes and can be adapted to changing audiences and circumstances. Returning to our threat categories: Ilham Aliyev before 9/11 placed the security concerns associated with the continued existence of the Nagorno Karabakh Republic squarely within 'aggravated criminality'; afterwards, 'terrorism' unquestionably plays the lead – alone, or fused with the 'aggravated criminality' category.

Successful internationalization?

A superpower like the United States may perhaps single-mindedly pursue its goals in world politics without regard for the interests and viewpoints of the outside world, but that is hardly an option for smaller, weaker states. For them, it is vital to engage members of the international community and strike alliances to counter threats to their security.

Regaining control over their lost territory is top priority for the parent states from which today's unrecognized states have seceded. The international community accepts in theory that this is their right under international law: no group of people may unilaterally decide to secede from another state. Weak parent states, however, have found it extremely difficult to secure active support from strong actors. In Western capitals, such secessionist conflicts are usually dismissed as involving 'far-away places of which we know nothing'. Before they will act, the leaders of other states must become convinced that the unrecognized states represent a source of instability and disorder, not only in relation to the parent state, but for the wider region as well. Hence, the securitization moves in both parent states studied here not only focus consistently on the threat to the country itself, but strenuously try to internationalize the issue. This is true with regard to all the four categories of threat identified above as standard elements in the security discourses.

1 *General criminality*: The unrecognized states are accused of engaging in the production of and trade in goods that would have been legal business if Transnistria and Nagorno Karabakh had been recognized by the international community. This charge is heard frequently in Moldova but is usually not highlighted in the Azerbaijani discourse. The charge is no doubt true; indeed, the unrecognized states could hardly survive without such economic activity. For the purpose of securitizing the existence of unrecognized states, however, references to general criminality are not very effective beyond the borders of the parent state, at least for the process we have referred to as internationalization. Third-party countries generally do not see this as a threat to their own immediate survival – otherwise, the unrecognized states would have had far greater difficulty finding business partners around the world.
2 *Aggravated criminality*: Accusations of the unrecognized states engaging in trafficking, the production and sale of narcotic substances and military hardware represent a more potent securitizing move. Regularly and insistently, the political class in Moldova and in Azerbaijan accuse Transnistria and Nagorno Karabakh, respectively, of extensive weapons smuggling. These claims, however, have not been accepted at face value in the West. The International Crisis Group, whose reports enjoy high credibility among Western policymakers, hardly mentions this in any of their many reports on these two conflicts. On the contrary, one ICG report on the Transnistrian conflict maintains that 'Transnistria has often been described as an arms trafficking hub, but there is little evidence of this.... Although illegal

trafficking of arms … cannot be ruled out, it is unlikely to account for a significant proportion of GDP' (International Crisis Group 2006c: 5).

Indeed, a common feature of most of the charges related to aggravated criminality is that they are backed up by very little hard evidence. Although several researchers note the high level of criminality in unrecognized states (Kolossov and O'Loughlin 1999; King 2001; Lynch 2004a), the examples they give are almost invariably taken from what we have here called 'general' rather than 'aggravated' criminality. According to a Radio Free Europe article, 'Western diplomats in Moldova and Ukraine say reports of massive arms and drug smuggling emanating from Moldova's breakaway Transdniester region appear to be wildly exaggerated' (Lobjakas 2005). An ICG report thinks that one of the most important goods transported by Transnistrian smugglers is frozen chickens (International Crisis Group 2006c: 4). Once again, Moldovan and Azerbaijani securitizing moves seem to have fallen largely on rocky ground.

3 *Terrorism*: One of the gravest accusations levelled against the unrecognized states by politicians and political analysts in the parent states is that these are involved in state-sponsored terrorism. This is also potentially one of the most forceful attempts to internationalize the security concern; hardly any other issue can conjure up as much horror among the public and politicians in Western countries, particularly in the aftermath of 9/11.

In Moldova, charges of terrorism in Transnistria crop up only occasionally and do not really belong to the hegemonic security discourse. The reason is perhaps that the security situation here is too transparent. Contacts between Transnistria and right-bank Moldova are multifarious; too many people have a reasonably good idea of what can and cannot be done in Transnistria, and this kind of demonization would simply ring hollow. In Azerbaijan, the situation is radically different. Here, 'Armenian terrorism' is a stable ingredient in the security discourse among politicians and analysts alike. In one sense, this charge is more credible than any talk about 'Transnistrian terrorism', since Armenian nationalists have indeed indulged in terror in the past. That, however, was under very different circumstances and directed against other countries and groups than Azerbaijan. Establishing direct links between historical Armenian terrorism and Nagorno Karabakh separatism has proven difficult.[11] Sometimes Azerbaijani politicians have fallen back on general statements such as 'separatism is the mother of terrorism'. To ratchet up fears in the West to top pitch, Azerbaijani commentators occasionally conjure forth pictures of Armenian separatists equipped with nuclear bombs.

4 *Armed conflict*: On the other hand, the chances that the unrecognized states will restart the war are slim. They won the previous war and have no further objectives that can be achieved by military means. As a result, Transnistria and Nagorno Karabakh are clearly status quo-oriented players. The only scenario in which hostilities will be renewed in the conflict is if the parent state should attempt to retake the breakaway region by force. Outside observers are therefore likely to shrug off as not credible any attempt to

present the unrecognized states as aggressors bent on capturing more land. In any case, such a military threat, even if it were real, would represent a danger to the parent states only, and not to the major security actors in world politics whom they need to enlist for their cause. (See Table 7.2 for a summary of these points.)

In actual fact, the securitization discourse in both Moldova and Azerbaijan is only to a very limited degree focused on the danger of renewed hostilities. In Moldova, as we saw, one analyst admitted that a new war was 'not even a theoretical possibility'. When the issue is broached in Azerbaijan, it usually takes the form of calls for an Azerbaijani military attack on Nagorno Karabakh and discussions on how the world may best be persuaded to accept such an attack.[12]

The high degree of overlap between arguments and claims presented in the scholarly and semi-scholarly debates and in political statements in both countries indicates that the securitization moves have been successful in their national constituencies. Both Moldova and Azerbaijan have, however, experienced problems when it comes to internationalizing their security concerns. In order to engage major Western actors, Moldovan and Azerbaijani authorities have sought to reframe the 'referent object' of their discourse: the security threats emanating from the unrecognized states represent a danger not only to the parent state, but to Europe as such, or even to the whole world. Moreover, as shown by the upsurge in the terrorist theme after 9/11, they have sought to hitch their own threat perceptions onto existing international discourses.

Their campaigns to gain sympathy for their predicament in the outside world have generally proven an up-hill struggle. In Western capitals, the stalemated post-Soviet secessionist conflicts are usually referred to as 'frozen conflicts' (Halbach 2007; Meurs 2007; Blank 2008), and the securitizing moves initiated by the parent states have not managed to supplant this discourse. The only (partially) successful securitizing move within the period examined here comes in the field of 'aggravated criminality': the establishment of the EUBAM, the EU's

Table 7.2 Typology of threat perceptions in parent states – findings

	Moldova		*Azerbaijan*	
	Local threat	*Internationalized threat*	*Local threat*	*Internationalized threat*
General criminality	X	X		
Aggravated criminality	X	X	X	X
Terrorism		X	X	X
Armed conflict		x	x	x

Notes
X = strongly present in the discourse.
x = weakly present in the discourse.

border assistance mission to Moldova, can be interpreted as a response to Moldova's insistence that Transnistria as a criminal hub. Moldovan and even more Azerbaijani politicians and analysts have thus often felt tempted to exaggerate the threat emanating from the breakaway units. One would perhaps think that, if nothing else works, the image of terrorists with nukes ought to sound the alarm in Western capitals, but emotions remain unperturbed. Raising the stakes with a weak hand often produces the opposite result of what was hoped for.

Notes

1 We would like to thank Dumitru Minzarari and Rail Safiyev for their assistance in identifying relevant Moldovan, respectively Azerbaijani, texts on the securitization of unrecognized states.
2 See also Caspersen's chapter in this volume.
3 An official PMR publication lists 626 deaths from the entire period of armed confrontations, all fronts. See *Kniga* ... (1995).
4 The texts that we analyse have been compiled by a local scholar in each country. The sample has been selected on the criterion of security discourse and threat perceptions. Texts that do not thematize security issues have been ignored – these include discussions of the negotiating process, conflict resolution, and the economy and political system in the unrecognized states.
5 All English-language quotes are rendered verbatim; Russian-language quotes have been translated by the authors.
6 In this activity, Smirnov has not only been abetted but actively supported by influential people from Moldova proper, Nantoi maintains. 'Igor Smirnov has a long list of sidekicks in his pocket, former "patriots" from the right bank, who together with him have robbed the country under the cover of the "negotiation process"' (Nantoi 2005).
7 For the above-mentioned text, see Yuzhnyi Kavkaz (2005).
8 Here, the text is attributed to the Ministry of National Security.
9 These exact figures do not, however, square with a claim made by Ilham Aliyev in 2001 that, since the beginning of Armenian aggression, 32 acts of terrorism had been committed in Azerbaijan, as a result of which '2,000 people were killed, tens of thousands injured' (Aliyev 2001b).
10 One Azerbaijani author who has taken this cue is Nuraddin Ibragimov, who has accused Armenia of 'ideological terrorism'. This variety of terrorism, Ibragimov explains, consists in the attempts of Armenian ideologues to 'press upon the world its view that their fight for Karabakh is a just cause' (Ibragimov n.d.).
11 Admittedly, some former Armenian terrorists did fight in the Nagorno Karabakh war, the most famous of whom is Monte Melkonian. See, for example, de Waal (2003).
12 For instance, in 2007, some Azerbaijan journalists claimed that the Kurdish militant separatist organization PKK had established bases in Nagorno Karabakh. They saw this as a golden opportunity for Azerbaijan to launch an attack:

> If PKK should start any kind of activity, we must be prepared for it. And actually, such activity could even play into our hands. We are bound by our commitment to resolve the Nagorno-Karabakh problem exclusively by peaceful means, but what if some foreign organization starts operating on the uncontrolled territory of Nagorno-Karabakh and this organization is not bound to the Armenian terrorists by ethnic ties or in any other way? In that case, naturally, Azerbaijan would get a carte blanche, in accordance with international legal norms, to start real military operations to quench such a threat.
>
> (*Day.Az* 2007)

8 The foreign policies of unrecognized states

Francis Owtram

Despite the growing literature on unrecognized states, up to now there has been relatively little systematic analysis undertaken on the foreign policy component. Yet unrecognized states invest a considerable amount of those resources available to them in conducting foreign policy: establishing a Ministry of Foreign Affairs or similarly named department offices in countries identified as significant. How can we explain and understand this phenomenon in global politics and what is its significance in terms of the possible outcomes for unrecognized states? The purpose of this chapter is to advance some initial lines of inquiry to the following research question: why do unrecognized states engage in foreign policy and what is the significance of this foreign policy as an explanatory factor in terms of movement of the unrecognized state towards recognition? It should be noted at this point that recognition is a matter of degree in quantitative terms of the number of states and international organizations extending recognition. The argument advanced, building on the existing literature (Pegg 1998; King 2001; Bahcheli *et al.* 2004; Kolstø 2006), is that unrecognized states engage in foreign policy for a number of reasons but that ultimately, in terms of outcomes, it is not the key factor in explaining whether they are initially reintegrated into another state either in a federal or confederal arrangement, or whether it gains significant recognition, durability, and admission as a member of international organizations, the ultimate recognition being admitted as a full member of the United Nations. The key factors identified in this initial process, building on commentaries by Halliday (2008) and Keating (2008), are the international system, great power politics, and political geography (Hill 2003: 171). However, the passage of time is an important factor, of particular significance in international law, and so in that part of the process I term consolidation, having achieved some kind of recognition that enables the entity to survive, the practice of foreign policy will be a significant factor both as indication that it fulfils the criteria for a state and also in practical terms in ensuring survival, militarily, politically, and economically. This chapter first reviews some key literature on unrecognized states and foreign policy to place the phenomenon in the relevant empirical and theoretical context. It then proceeds to examine examples and case studies of the foreign policy of unrecognized states in different parts of the world with regard to key characteristics. These case studies give 'snapshots' of recent foreign policy activity, as well as paying particular consideration as to how these unrecognized states represent themselves to the world in terms of foreign policy aims and activity. It then engages in analysis and commentary to support the argument advanced. The chapter concludes with a consideration of the phenomena of foreign policies of unrecognized states in global politics.

Unrecognized states and foreign policy

In terms of the object of enquiry there has been a variety of nomenclature deployed in the literature: *quasi-state*, de facto state, and unrecognized state are just some of the terms used, seemingly interchangeably, and it will be useful to briefly review these terms. The term *quasi-state* is often associated, in recent times, with Jackson's (1990) classic work *Quasi-States: Sovereignty, International Relations and the Third World* and its definitional reworking by Kolstø (2006). As Jackson's title suggests, we must also be cognisant of the term sovereignty. Sovereignty can be conveniently divided into internal sovereignty and external sovereignty (recognition by other states).[1] Much of the discussion of the phenomenon of quasi-states has been clouded by assuming that the notion of state sovereignty, which is the referent in the term *quasi-state* and de facto state, is the sovereignty of a unitary state. This conflation obscures the different possibilities of sovereign power and forms of government that are the potential of federal systems of government. For analytical clarity, it may also be useful to briefly remind ourselves of the underlying notion of certain key terms attached to the word 'state' in this discussion.

The Cambridge Dictionary Online (2010) defines the prefix *quasi* as being used to show that something is almost, but not completely, the thing described.[2] De facto is used to denote that something exists in fact, although not necessarily intended, legal or accepted. *De jure* indicates having the right or existence as stated by law. The key reason as to why an entity remains in a de facto or *quasi* status relates to its external sovereignty – that is, it is not recognized externally; hence the utility of the term 'unrecognized states'.

We should emphasize, however, as previously noted, that in connection with recognition there is a spectrum of degrees of recognition. We can categorize these degrees of recognition in summary form with relevant examples at time of writing in May 2010. In descending decrees of recognition, there are: a state which is recognized by all other states and is a member of the United Nations (United States of America, United Kingdom of Great Britain and Northern Ireland, Federal Republic of Germany, and so on); a state which is a member of the United Nations but not recognized by some other members (State of Israel); a state which was a member of the United Nations but which was replaced by a competing state (Republic of China, commonly known as Taiwan); an entity which is recognized by key great powers (Republic of Kosovo); a state which is recognized by one state (Turkish Republic of North Cyprus); and finally a state entity which is recognized by no other state (Republic of Somaliland). In terms of empirical analysis, this chapter will exclude foreign policy behaviour of states now admitted as full members to the UN, although potentially it includes their foreign policy phenomena before that point.

In order to engage with the phenomenon of the foreign policies of unrecognized states, I would first like to make two definitional points concerning recognition and criteria for qualifying as a state – how can we know a state is recognized? As we will see on this issue, it is, to an extent, a matter of degree but, in Keating's (2008) phrase, the 'gold standard' consists of admission as a member to the United Nations. The actual mechanism of achieving this seems, bearing in mind the significance, remarkably mundane – it consists of writing a letter to the Secretary-General requesting membership. The Security Council will refer the letter to the General Assembly, which must vote by a two-thirds majority that the entity can carry out the duties of the UN Charter (Keating 2008). For empirical accuracy, we should bear in mind, however, that there are states, notably Israel, which have been admitted as members to the United Nations but which remain unrecognized by a sizeable number (20) of other members of the United Nations.

From a social science perspective, the state can be analysed theoretically in a number of ways – the Westphalian state, Weberian approach, or in terms of historical sociology, to mention just a few. I will return briefly to these perspectives later, but at this point I would merely like to highlight the classic requirements of statehood from the perspective of international law, set out succinctly in article 1 of the 1933 Montevideo Declaration (Radan 2008: 19) and of which practitioners of international politics, including leaders of unrecognized states, are most likely to be cognizant. As Lynch (2002: 835) notes, the 1933 Montevideo Declaration on Rights and Duties of States holds that 'to qualify as a state the entity must have (1) a permanent population; (2) a defined territory; (3) a government; and (4) the capacity to enter into relations with other states'. This fourth criterion is not required by declarative theories of statehood but deemed necessary by constitutive theory, which holds that a state is a person in international law only if it is recognized by other states (ibid.: 837). This external recognition constitutes external sovereignty – that is, recognition by the group of states as a person in international law. Under declarative theory, Somaliland is a state, whilst under constitutive theory Somalia is a state – albeit a failed one – as it has external recognition.

Formation of unrecognized states

In an insightful work, Fabry (2008) argues that the qualification as a sovereign independent state lies in the international rather than the domestic sphere. He notes that:

> It is foreign acknowledgement that gives the community the standing of a sovereign state in international relations and law; to be denied that acknowledgement is to exist as an outcast in a precarious, life-threatening condition of international illegitimacy.

He goes on to identify how international society has shifted its practice in the last two hundred years from self-determination as a negative right to a positive right. It is this, he argues, in relation to qualification as a sovereign independent state that explains why 'Croatia, Bosnia and Herzegovina, Eritrea, Slovakia, Georgia, East Timor and Montenegro have achieved this status, but Somaliland, Krajina, Abkhazia, Republic Srpska, Chechenya, Tamil Eelam, and Bougainville have not?' (Fabry 2008: 51)

Since 1945, there have been three main contexts in which unrecognized states have come into being. All unrecognized states are created in the process of a civil war. These civil wars have come about as a result of circumstances of European decolonization, collapse of the communist states of the USSR and Yugoslavia, or civil war resulting from ideological conflict. It can be argued that the collapse of the Soviet Union was actually part of the process of European decolonization, just one in which the imperial power was not separated from the colonies by salt water.

A further necessary and useful distinction is made between recognition of states and recognition of governments (Talmon 1998). Thus, whilst the Taliban government went unrecognized, no-one interpreted this as the state of Afghanistan ceasing to exist (Sloane 2002: 114). A key aspect of unrecognized states is that we need to be aware that the degree of non-recognition varies in quantitative (number) terms across a spectrum. To this can be added a qualitative aspect – recognition by a great power or a power in close proximity is of greater utility than recognition by a less powerful, distant state.

Notwithstanding the case of Somaliland, which presently remains unrecognized by any state, we should recognize that the issue often is of partial recognition – that is, that the unrecognized state only has recognition from one or a handful of states.

The significance of the declaration of independence

In a seminal article, which adopted a comparative approach drawing evidence from all regions of the world, Kolstø (2006) provided a useful definition of unrecognized quasi-states and an analysis of factors influencing the outcomes or 'sustainability' for such entities. He notes that 'unrecognized quasi-states' (he argues that Jackson's use of quasi-state would now be termed a 'failed state') must fulfil three criteria: 'its leadership must be in control of (most of) the territory it lays claim to, and it must have sought but not achieved international recognition as an independent state...' The third criterion is that, for practical purposes, he only considers entities that have been unrecognized for at least two years. In terms of the sustainability of unrecognized states, he identifies the roles of the weak parent state, external patron, and international community. Thus a key definitional issue is that there must have been a declaration of independence, which then goes unrecognized.

Whilst Kolstø considers the Kurdish-populated area of Northern Iraq between the first and second Gulf Wars a borderline case, I prefer to adhere to his key definitional criteria of declaration of independence and thus exclude it from the list of historical unrecognized states as it never declared independence.[3] In this case, whilst there was a great desire for independence, due to the external constraints of being surrounded by hostile states and lacking an external patron supportive of independence, the elites perceived it not to be feasible or realistic to declare independence. Therefore, since 2005, it is has been in the process of being integrated on a federal basis within Iraq (on the role of perception of the costs of secession, see Bartkus 1999). The foreign relations of the Kurdistan Regional Government since 2005 can now be placed in the category of paradiplomacy of non-central governments, alongside the likes of Catalan and Quebec analysed by Keating and Aldecoa (1999). Further exclusions from our units of analysis can be stipulated: as Zahar's (2004) account describes, the reintegration of entities into the parent state on a formalized federal or confederal basis supported by international aid removes from our consideration certain entities, such as the Republika Srpska in Bosnia.

Based on a review of the empirical data, Kolstø (2006: 734–738) lists a number of possible outcomes for the unrecognized state: inclusion into the external patron state; full independence; reabsorption in the parent states; or inclusion in the parent state as a separate entity. He concludes:

> a negotiated federal settlement nevertheless is the solution that creates the lowest number of people who are so disgruntled that they will work actively to overturn it. In addition the factors that militate against the alternative outcomes are clearly stronger. On balance, therefore this compromise solution must be regarded as the most likely end to most unrecognized quasi-states.
> (2006: 738)[4]

To this can be added that the 'international community' prefers such compromise solutions and conversely has an aversion to secession, due to the fear that an unbridled right of secession could lead to the bloody break-up of the large federal post-colonial states of Nigeria, India, and indeed Russia. It thus seeks to avoid setting any such precedence in overt terms.

Foreign policy

Having considered the meaning of state, and appropriate prefix or adjective, and the context of their formation, we can now briefly consider some key aspects of the term 'foreign policy'. Literature on foreign policy has generally not sought to engage in any way with the phenomenon of unrecognized states and their foreign policies (Smith *et al.* 2007; Webber and Smith 2002). A notable exception is that of Hill (2003) in *The Changing Politics of Foreign Policy*. For the purposes of our discussion, it is worth considering two key passages in full as he provides both a definition of foreign policy open to a wider range of actors and specifically engages with the notion of foreign policies of unrecognized states:

> A brief definition of foreign policy can be given as follows: the sum of official external relations conducted by an independent actor (usually a state) in international relations. The phrase 'an independent actor' enables the inclusion of phenomena such as the European Union; external relations are 'official' to allow the inclusion of outputs from all parts of the governing mechanisms of the state or enterprise while also maintaining parsimony with respect to the vast number of international transactions now being conducted; policy is the 'sum' of these official relations because otherwise every particular action could be seen as a separate foreign policy – whereas actors usually seek some degree of coherence towards the outside world. Lastly, the policy is 'foreign' because the world is still more separated into distinctive communities than it is a single, homogenizing entity. These communities therefore need strategies for coping with foreigners (or strangers) in their various aspects (it should be noted that the word 'foreign' derives from the Latin 'foris' meaning 'outside').
>
> (2003: 3)

Hill's definition, as already noted, allows consideration of a range of phenomena not just states, including the European Union and unrecognized states. Indeed, Hill explicitly addresses the extension of his analysis to the foreign policy of unrecognized states.

> States and foreign policies are nearly Siamese twins, but not quite. There are other actors which generate activities resembling foreign policies and this complicates the conventional domestic/foreign divide further. It is not always clear who is representing whom in international relations. Some unrecognized states effectively conduct independent external strategies, even if the lack of normal representative facilities and/or dependence on what is often an overbearing supports make them difficult to implement. Taiwan and Northern Cyprus since 1974 are prominent examples. Hong Kong has maintained extensive external relations in the sphere of political economy since becoming a Special Administrative Region of the People's Republic of China in 1997, including becoming a member of the WTO before China itself. It does not assert a profile on traditional foreign policy issues, but civil society's views on human rights and democratic governance seep out into the world through the still relatively free media. It thus has something like a partial foreign policy, even if it would never dare to use the term. There are also cases of disposed peoples without any clear-cut territorial base. Such as the Palestinians before 1994 and the African National Congress, representing most black South Africans, between 1961–91. Most of these cases are relatively straightforward, since they represent actors wanting to be states and trying to emulate state foreign policies.
>
> (2003: 40)

This last sentence of Hill's suggests the question as to what, if anything, is distinctive about the foreign policies of unrecognized states. The answer given here is that a distinctive feature will be the maintenance and management of the relationship with the parent and patron state and the interaction with the international community and international organizations on the issues of recognition and aid. Given that the maintenance of relationships with key states is the same for most states of the world it can be argued that the only difference is the issue of recognition and the level of capability. As Hill notes:

> The formal possession of sovereignty makes it highly likely that a state will have a foreign policy. Conversely, where sovereignty is denied or the capacity to exercise it severely impeded, foreign policy becomes particularly difficult, but not impossible. Ultimately foreign policy rests on the effectiveness of the state at home and abroad, which is more a matter of political sociology than law.
>
> (2003: 31)

If, as Kolstø argues, the prospect for most unrecognized states is to be reabsorbed into the parent state in some form of federal or confederal arrangement, strategies for pursuing economic and political interests will still be required as the practice of paradiplomacy indicates.

A further point that needs to be drawn from the literature on foreign policy is that foreign policy 'looks two ways'. It looks inward to the domestic base and is outward looking to the external environment (Hill 2003). As Hinnebusch notes in his analysis of states in the Middle East, 'foreign policy making elites are "Janus faced", looking both inward and outward, attempting to reconcile demands from domestic actors with threats or constraints from external powers' (2003: 93). For Halliday, this involves the 'partial reconciliation of two distinct analytical approaches, those of historical sociology and of foreign policy analysis' (2005: 43) in explaining the degree of state autonomy in the conduct of foreign policy – that is, the room for manoeuvre limited by both internal and external forces. This contrasts with explanations that explain foreign policy only by recourse to some internal factor, be it class or ethnicity. This is of considerable significance in assessing the important observations that have been made on the political economy of unrecognized states by Kolstø and King. They note that unrecognized states encourage certain kinds of illicit economic activity and that key actors have an interest in this, thus resisting a resolution of the underlying dispute that sustains the existence of the unrecognized state (Kolstø 2006; King 2001). Furthermore, in relation to this, all unrecognized states need to be availing themselves of resources, either in aid, trade, or investment, which will enable them to sustain their legitimacy in the eyes of their population by providing employment, patronage, and services.[5] The role of foreign policy in achieving this is an important focus for unrecognized states, constituting, as it does, the nexus between the international system and domestic politics. Thus, foreign policy, as foreign economic policy much as for recognized states, will be critical.

A difference can be identified in that, although unrecognized states seek to attract foreign direct investment from transnational companies, the role of diaspora and aid from individual states or international organizations will be significant.

The international system and power politics

Hill notes that the international system is 'not only in flux but that it can move a very long way in a mere half century, at no-one particular's behest', citing examples of the Cold War division of Europe and collapse in 1989 and post-World War II decolonization (2003: 186). This theme was taken further by the late Fred Halliday in a brief online article written in 2008, in which he postulated, in connection with the impact of the international system on political and ethnic disputes, 'the syndrome of post-colonial sequestration'. On this, he elaborates:

> the cases where countries or peoples have – at a decisive moment of international change, amid the retreat of imperial or hegemonic powers – failed (through bad timing and/or bad leadership) to establish their independence ... An essential element in understanding this syndrome – both from 'within' (the people or country concerned) and 'outside' (the international order) – is to abandon the idea that the division of the world into today's 'nation states' corresponds to any fundamental principles. The map of the world, now containing around close to 200 independent entities, is not drawn according to ideas of natural justice, divine or even historic entitlement, nor even of the democratic and liberal self-realisation of 'nations'. It is, rather – as scholars of nationalism, from Ernest Gellner to Tom Nairn, have pointed out – also arbitrary and contingent – a result of power politics; accidents; wars; state crises; and hegemonic, colonial, or (in the case of the central Asian republics of the former Soviet Union) ideology ... In this haphazard context, the chances of failure or success in achieving international recognition can be equally contingent. The arbitrary nature of states and frontiers in Africa, the Middle East, central Asia and Latin America testifies to this, as do the examples of Belgium, Switzerland, and most recently Kosovo in Europe. Some entities gain established existence and recognition, others do not: there is no natural order in deciding their fate, even if larger political trends and dynamics may in some areas offer a more propitious context.
>
> (2008: 1–2)

Furthermore, Halliday argues that in every individual case 'it is usually international politics that plays the decisive role. In particular, the key moment of possibility – and danger – is the convulsive change that occurs when wars end or colonial powers prepare to withdraw.' This chapter explores Halliday's outline in further detail.

The foreign policies of unrecognized states: aims, capabilities, and key relations

Following from this review of selected literature on unrecognized states, foreign policy, and global politics, it is possible to set out the argument of this chapter in more detail in terms of the aims, capabilities, and key relations in the foreign policies of unrecognized states.

Aims of foreign policy

The first aim of these unrecognized states is survival – militarily, politically, and economically – in the form of promotion of trade, investment, or aid. Underlying all this is the search for recognition or engagement. Any kind of recognition assists the unrecognized state politically or economically. Even though at a certain point in their development some sectors and individuals may have an interest in persisting in a frozen state of conflict, it is contended that these unrecognized states wish to continue as states and become recognized. As King notes in the context of the limited ability of the parent states to exert any attraction: 'Why be a mayor of a small city if you can be president of a country? Why be a lieutenant in someone else's army if you can be a general of your own?' (2001: 551). Just as in the Arab world after the collapse of Ottoman rule, once a territory is divided, politics and opportunities tend to revolve around the political centres created, which militates against unifying to a larger territory. These new political centres enable politicians to enhance their chances of surviving politically and assist them in the accumulation of wealth and resources. Connected with this aim of securing recognition, the unrecognized state engages in foreign policy behaviour for two further interrelated aims.

The second aim is to acquire material resources in the form of aid and foreign investment. The third aim is to engage in foreign policy to demonstrate the apparatus and behaviour of a state (point four of the Montevideo Declaration) by demonstrating the capability to engage in relations with other states. Underlying all this is a fourth aim, which is to increase the degree of recognition by recognized states, either of a de facto or of a formal kind.

The only difference with recognized states then is that a major foreign policy aim is to increase its recognition and consolidation as a state, even of a de facto kind, through economic engagement. Although the resources it has to pursue these goals will often be less than many recognized states, in many cases – even if we exclude Taiwan – unrecognized states, through their economy or external patron, will have more resources in the form of a greater GDP than the micro-states of Oceania, such as Nauru, Tuvalu, Palau, and Kiribati. Hill's assessment of the challenge of diplomacy for weak states can just as well be applied to most unrecognized states: 'As a means of implementing policy, diplomacy is particularly important to weak states. With few resources they have little choice but to play a poor hand as skilfully as possible' (2003: 139).

Capabilities to conduct and implement foreign policy

Unrecognized states create governmental institutions to conduct foreign policy, which typically consists of relations with a variety of categories of states. Generally this will be the creation of a Ministry of Foreign Affairs with representative offices or missions abroad, alongside other government departments to emphasize this aspect of its stateness. These offices generate income through issuance of visas, promote interaction and trade and investment, and seek recognition. They do not have formal diplomatic status under the provisions of the Vienna Declaration on Diplomatic Conventions.

1 Relations with patron state.
   To survive in a situation of existential conflict, as Kolstø notes, unrecognized states will generally have to have an external supporter in the form of an external patron, which can be listed as: Taiwan (United States); Northern Cyprus (Turkey), South Ossetia (Russia), Abkhazia (Russia), Nagorno-Karabakh (Armenia). Maintaining its relationship with the patron state will generally be accorded a high priority. This should not be portrayed as a willingness to comply with all demands of the patron state – the unrecognized state will try and manage the tension between its interest and possible divergence in interests and policy of the patron state.
2 Relations with great powers.
   The attitude of great powers will have a fundamental bearing on the prospects for the unrecognized state. In this connection, any bilateral contact, either directly or with associated organizations such as USAID, will be pursued.
3 Relations with international organizations.
   These can include the United Nations, European Union, International Monetary Fund, World Trade Organization and Unrepresented Nations People's Organization.

Case studies

We now proceed to examine, through the rubric of the type of foreign relations identified, a number of 'snapshots' of cases, selected to represent different points on the spectrum of recognition and consolidation: Taiwan, Palestinian National Authority, Northern Cyprus, South Ossetia, and Somaliland.

Republic of China (Taiwan)

The case of Taiwan is at one end of our spectrum and sets the others in sharp relief. During the course of the Chinese civil war (1945–1949), the government of the Republic of China (Taiwan) fled to the island of Formosa. The Republic of China (RoC) had a permanent seat on the Security Council but was evicted from all UN organs and replaced by the People's Republic of China (PRC) in 1971 due to Nixon's consideration of US interests. Since then, the number of states recognizing the RoC has steadily declined to 23, as the PRC makes the severing of ties with the RoC and recognition of the PRC as the sole legitimate government of China, including Taiwan, a precondition for establishment of diplomatic relations. It also uses aid as an instrument of policy – for example, the Republic of Macedonia recognized the RoC in 1999 but switched its position after the PRC imposed economic sanctions and used its veto on the UN Security Council.

Taiwan is one of the largest economies in Asia. The website of the Ministry of Foreign Affairs, which is responsible for Taiwan's foreign policy, states that (Article 141 of its constitution):

> the foreign policy of the Republic of China shall, in a spirit of independence and initiative and on the basis of the principles of equality and reciprocity, cultivate good-neighborliness with other nations, and respect treaties and the Charter of the United Nations, in order to protect the rights and interests of Chinese citizens residing abroad, promote international cooperation, advance international justice and ensure world peace. The ultimate goal of foreign policy is to ensure a favorable environment for a nation's preservation and sustainable development.
>
> One of the most important tasks of the Ministry of Foreign Affairs is to create a favorable environment for economic development. We have to compete with other countries as we try to cooperate with them in this age of globalization.
>
> (Ministry of Foreign Affairs 2010)

Relationship with patron state

Whilst the RoC has official bilateral relations with 23 states, this number does not include the United States, which switched its recognition to the PRC in 1979. The United States, however, can be seen as the patron state of RoC – without its support, it is unlikely Taiwan would have sustained its existence militarily, and thus politically would have been absorbed into the PRC. The Republic of China is represented on the International Monetary Fund and the World Bank with the designation Chinese Taipei.[6]

The Palestinian National Authority

A state of Palestine was declared in 1988. Robinson (2007: 396) notes that 'the Palestine Authority had an active foreign policy during the Oslo period of limited autonomy'. He specifies the different audiences of the Palestinian Authority (PA) foreign policy.

> The United States was a key partner, as only the United States had the leverage over Israel to deliver central Palestinian goals. The EU was likewise an important foreign policy partner, both because it contributed the most aid to

> the PA and because European powers, especially Britain, could (it was thought) influence Washington on key final status issues. The Arab states constituted a third target audience because they could help deliver regional support and legitimacy to the Oslo process and Palestinian goals. Finally, there was Israel, the foreign power that firmly held control over all Palestinian lands and must be convinced to relinquish that control.

He goes on to the note that the PA had three main foreign policy goals: (1) to obtain sufficient financial resources to perform a patronage function in distributing jobs and money to key supporters; (2) that the interim period generated sufficient advance in Palestinian sovereignty over the occupied territories; and (3) to garner enough international support to be able to deliver a good final status agreement. Foreign donors gave a total of US$3 billion (1994–2000).

Turkish Republic of Northern Cyprus

Following independence from the UK of the Republic of Cyprus in 1960 and the Turkish invasion of 1974, the Turkish Republic of Northern Cyprus (TRNC) declared its independence in 1983 (Bahcheli 2004). It is recognized only by Turkey, which has a formal embassy in the TNRC. The TNRC has an embassy and consulates in Turkey and representative offices in London, Washington, New York, Brussels, Rome, Baku, Pakistan, Abu Dhabi, Doha, Muscat, and Tel Aviv. Germany and the USA, and Australia maintain Northern Cyprus offices in Lefkasa. The British High Commission is situated in Lefkasa, as is the EU support office.[7]

In 2002, UN Secretary-General Kofi Annan presented a reunification plan, suggesting a two-part federation with a rotating presidency. Accession of the Republic of Cyprus to the EU has been the most significant development for the TRNC in recent times. In a referendum in April 2004, the Greek Cypriots rejected and the Turkish Cypriots approved the UN-sponsored unity plan known as the Annan Plan. The Republic of Cyprus joined the EU on 1 May 2004 as a divided island. Legally, the entire territory of Cyprus is part of the EU, in spite of the fact that the government in Nicosia cannot control the northern part of the island. The Greek Cypriot rejection of the Annan plan disappointed EU officials, who had agreed to allow Cyprus to join that year, partly in the hope that doing so would encourage a solution to the Cyprus problem.[8]

Republic of South Ossetia

Following a war of Soviet succession, a ceasefire agreement in July 1992 led to a cessation of hostilities and negotiations for final status under OSCE auspices (King 2001: 534). A South Ossetian constitution was adopted by referendum on 8 April 2001. The people of South Ossetia voted overwhelmingly for full independence in a referendum held on 12 November 2006. Georgia's reckless president, Mikhail Saakashvili, emboldened by perceptions of US and NATO support, blundered into a war in August 2008, in which the country lost heavily to a Russian response. Following this war, Russia conferred recognition to the Republic of South Ossetia on 26 August 2008. The Russian permanent envoy to the OSCE, Anvar Asimov, stated that the decision to recognize the sovereignty and independence of Abkhazia and South Ossetia, made in accordance with the decree by the Russian president, dated 26 August 2008, was 'irrevocable and irreversible' and pledged to strengthen ties with the two republics with bilateral accords on cooperation in transport, communications, and the military sphere. It encouraged other states in the OSCE to recognize the independence of Abkhazia and South Ossetia, as sovereign, independent states, reflecting the new political and legal reality in the Caucasus.

The president of South Ossetia is Eduard Kokoity, and Murat Kuzmich Dzhioev is the Minister of Foreign Affairs. South Ossetia states its foreign policy goals as 'a final settlement of the conflict with Georgia, expanded international trade, and good relations with all nations based on friendship and mutual respect'.[9] In April 2010, Russia signed a forty-nine-year renewable agreement with South Ossetia on stationing a permanent Russian military base on its territory and adopted joint border protection agreements with South Ossetia and Abkhazia, assuming authority to secure their borders (International Crisis Group 2010b). In the area of foreign economic policy, it seeks to rehabilitate its post-war economy by concentrating on the establishment of factories for producing building materials, airport development, and modernization of the agricultural sector. It perceives that it offers investment opportunities in tourism, food processing, light industry, and linking transport networks between South Ossetia and North Ossetia in Russia.[10]

Somaliland

Somaliland declared independence in 1991 and has the dubious distinction, with Transnistria and Nagorno Karabakh, of being completely unrecognized by any state. Since 2006, the Minister of Foreign Affairs has been Abdillahi Mohamed Duale. Somaliland maintains a mission office in the United Kingdom. It has representatives in the Federal Republic of Ethiopia, USA, Djibouti, and Italy. To some extent, Ethiopia plays the role of a patron state for Somaliland. In June 2007, the Ethiopian prime minister, Meles Zenawi, referred to Somaliland's president, Dahir Rayale Kahin, in an official communiqué as president of Somaliland. Given Ethiopia's difficult relationship with Eritrea, access to the Red Sea via the Somaliland port of Berbera is of great importance.

Relations with great powers

In March 2010, a delegation from the Republic of Somaliland visited the United States. The Somaliland delegation, which included the deputy speaker of the Somaliland parliament, the deputy chair of the Somaliland House of Elders, and the ministers of foreign affairs, planning, home affairs and natural resources, discussed with the USAID officials areas of mutual interest, including current USAID assistance to Somaliland and the possibility of further projects in Somaliland to be funded by USAID (Unrepresented Nations People's Organization 2010a). According to Dr Sa'ad Sh. Osman Nur, the Somaliland representative in the United States of America, the Somaliland delegation also met with members of the National Security Council at the White House in Washington. Dr Osman Nur stated that the discussions between the delegation and the Security Council staff focused on the security and stability in the Horn of Africa and the efforts to combat terrorism and piracy in the region.

The Somaliland delegation has also met with senior officials from the State Department in Washington, at the State Department's request, to discuss matters of common concern. The Somaliland Press Online commented: 'Given the significant role Somaliland plays in safeguarding its coastal waters and checking the spread of Islamism with its meager resources, it is clear that Somaliland can be a vital geopolitical partner for the United States and the EU' (Unrepresented Nations People's Organization 2010b). Also, in March 2010, President Kahin met with a delegation from Russia, who expressed an interest in exploring the possibility of cooperation on future projects in Somaliland. The Soviet Union helped develop the port of Berbera and Berbera International Airport in connection with its relationship with Somalia. In February 2010, it was reported that Israel was ready to recognize Somaliland, as it had done in February 1960 when British Somaliland came to an end due to its growing strategic interest in the Red Sea. President Kahin has, however, been wary of damaging his relationship with the Islamic world as their import of livestock is the mainstay of the Somaliland economy (Unrepresented Nations People's Organization 2010c).

Relations with international organizations

In February 2010, Somaliland's President Kahin met with representatives from the international agencies, including Mr Mark Bowden from the UNDP's Somaliland/Somalia office, and officials from the World Bank, the European Union, and several other departments from the United Nations.

Analysis of case studies

Three points can be made in terms of the analysis, regarding periodization, the most significant factor, and the overall context of the foreign policies of unrecognized states.

In terms of Kolstø's possible outcome of attainment of independence, I have suggested a two-part periodization: an initial stage and then consolidation stage. If the unrecognized state has an external patron who will recognize and support them and prevent them from being swallowed up by the parent state until they can develop away from the political economy of conflict, then in time they may be able to develop sufficient economic resources to survive on their own, even if the patron state changes its position. The longer de facto sovereignty is maintained the better, from the perspective of international law. As Keating (2008) notes, 'the 900 year old Sovereign Order of Malta has diplomatic relations with 100 countries and observer status at the United Nations even though its entire territory is contained in a few buildings in Rome'. Let us turn to a prognosis of prospects for the cases we have considered.

The Republic of China was removed from the UN due to the change in view of the Nixon administration. It demonstrates that international power politics takes precedence over international law. That the Republic of China has continued to endure and prosper this long bodes well for its continued existence. The final denouement may take some time. Either final recognition will have to wait for the day that the Communist Party in China ceases to rule, in which case a way forward for recognition of two Chinese states may become a possibility, or Chinese power increases and US power declines to the point where it will be traded off and some special status with the PRC, like Hong Kong, will be negotiated. The resolution of the status of the Republic of China will probably have to wait some time.

What about the arguably essential core of our group: those states that have either no or very limited recognition as constituting a fully sovereign state? The United States and the United Nations have become involved in the Cyprus issue mainly because of concerns that it could lead to violent warfare between two NATO members, Greece and Turkey. If change were to take place in Cyprus, it would most likely be due to a change in the relationship between Greece, Turkey, and the European Union. The TRNC could not survive without the support of Turkey, and it is Turkish pressure that could lead it to reintegrate in confederal or federal form with the Republic of Cyprus.

If an unrecognized state can be of strategic use to a great power, this will considerably enhance its prospects of durability. In this regard, Somalia makes Somaliland look good. Somaliland may have potential as an ally against al-Qaeda in the 'War on Terror'. The endurance of the Republic of South Ossetia has weakened Georgia and lessened the possibility of NATO encroachment on Moscow's near abroad. Russia extended recognition to South Ossetia in the immediate aftermath of the conflict of August 2008, which most likely will ensure its existence, rather than reintegration into Georgia.

In all of the cases, the ability of significant regional or international powers and the reality of the international system to overcome the constraints imposed by international legal principles when needed is clear. International law will not, as the invasion of Iraq demonstrates, constrain a hegemonic power, and the resources of the most able international lawyers will be brought to bear to argue that international law was, indeed, not broken. International law, created by states, has a default aversion to secession due to the fear that an unbridled right could lead to the bloody break-up of the large federal post-colonial states of Nigeria, India, and Russia, and thus seeks to avoid setting any such precedence in overt terms. Where such instances occur due to great power consideration, as in Kosovo, the endless caveats, qualifications, and complexities deployed by international lawyers can be used to attempt to obscure that this was the case – although not always to convincing effect (Armstrong *et al.* 2007: 117–31).

Conclusion

This chapter has reviewed literature on unrecognized states and foreign policy in global politics and noted that, whilst it is a neglected area in foreign policy studies, there are instances in the foreign policy literature cognizant of the existence and possibility of unrecognized states to conduct foreign policy along with other transnational actors. Its approach has been that we should not restrict our consideration of this matter to those states that have entirely no recognition from sovereign states, which would only constitute a few cases, such as Somaliland, Nagorno Karabakh, and Transnistria. Rather, we need to be aware that there is a continuum of degree of recognition and that a state may gradually increase the number of states recognizing it. This chapter has argued that, whilst the key factor in influencing whether a unrecognized state survives beyond the initial circumstances of birth in civil war are the considerations and strategic interest of great powers, the conduct of its foreign policy may assist in its consolidation, both by demonstrating that it has the capacity to engage in foreign relations and through the practical benefits which would potentially flow from any aid, trade, or investment. It has highlighted that the foreign policy aims of unrecognized states are much the same as established states but are distinctive in that a key aim is pursuit of recognition of either de facto or a more formal kind, and the level of capability to implement will usually be far less than recognized state, except for micro-states. A final point is that unrecognized states would be well advised to continue to pursue vigorously their foreign policy capabilities as, even if they are eventually reintegrated with their parent state on a confederal, federal, or regional basis, they will have the need to pursue their aims in the form of paradiplomacy, such as that pursued by established federal regions, particularly in terms of seeking economic investment in an era of global politics.

Notes

1 See also Closson's chapter in this volume.
2 Cambridge Dictionary. Available at http://dictionary.cambridge.org/.
3 Note that a wider definition of an unrecognized state is adopted in the introduction to this volume and in several other chapters.
4 See also Anderson's chapter in this volume.
5 See also Caspersen's chapter in this volume.
6 Republic of China, Ministry of Foreign Affairs. Available at www.mofa.gov.tw/webapp/ct.asp?xItem=32514&CtNode=1861&mp=6.
7 Turkish Republic of Northern Cyprus Public Information Office. Available at www.trncpio.org/trncpio/en/index.asp.
8 EurActiv 2009. Available at www.euractiv.com/en/enlargement/turkey-accession-cyprus/article-135940.
9 Republic of South Ossetia, 'Foreign Relations'. Available at www.republicofsouthossetia.org/pages/our-government/foreign-relations.shtml.
10 Republic of South Ossetia, 'Investment Opportunities'. Available at www.republicofsouthossetia.org/pages/our-economy/investment-opportunities.shtml.

Part III

Conflict management and unrecognized states

9 The limits of international conflict management in the case of Abkhazia and South Ossetia[1]

Stefan Wolff

In August 2008, Georgia and Russia clashed in a five-day war after Georgian troops attempted to assert full control over the breakaway region of South Ossetia, in contravention of a 1992 ceasefire agreement brokered by Russia and policed by Russian troops in the guise of CIS peacekeepers. French President Nicolas Sarkozy, representing the EU Presidency, offered an impressive example of leadership and diplomacy and helped broker a ceasefire between the two countries after five days of fighting. Despite the quick end of military hostilities, the political situation escalated further, culminating in the Russian recognition of South Ossetia's and Abkhazia's independence on 26 August 2008. Sarkozy's diplomacy not only was that of a political leader who saw an opportunity to leave his mark on the European and global stage but also reflects the significance of unresolved conflicts over statehood issues that date back to the break-up of the Soviet Union. Alongside the conflicts over Transnistria (in Moldova) and Nagorno Karabakh (in Azerbaijan), the two conflicts in Georgia – Abkhazia and South Ossetia – are of critical importance, especially to the EU and its member states, as the Union engages with the region through its European Neighbourhood Policy and the Eastern Partnership. The implications of these conflicts over unrecognized states for European and EU security have also been recognized by the EU Security Strategy of 2003 (EUSS), noting that "frozen conflicts, which also persist on our borders, threaten regional stability" (Council of the European Union 2003: 5). The EUSS makes clear that "violent conflict, weak states where organized crime flourishes, dysfunctional societies or exploding population growth on its borders all pose problems for Europe" (ibid.: 7) and goes on to demand very specifically that the Union "should now take a stronger and more active interest in the problems of the Southern Caucasus" (ibid.: 8). The 2008 report on the implementation of the EUSS referred specifically to the conflicts in Georgia, claiming on the one hand that "[s]ince 2003, the EU has increasingly made a difference in addressing crisis and conflict, in places such as … Georgia" and pointing out on the other that:

> [t]he situation in Georgia, concerning Abkhazia and South Ossetia, has escalated, leading to an armed conflict between Russia and Georgia in August 2008. The EU led the international response, through mediation

> between the parties, humanitarian assistance, a civilian monitoring mission, and substantial financial support. Our engagement will continue, with the EU leading the Geneva Process.
>
> (Council of the European Union 2003: 1, 7)

One year on, the Geneva process had succeeded in keeping all sides of the conflict engaged, but had otherwise made little substantive progress, when, on 16 October 2009, Sergei Bagapsh (2009) expressed confidence "that the independence of Abkhazia not only is assured, but that we will thrive politically and economically … [and that] it is only a matter of time before we are recognized by most countries of the world". There were many remarkable things about this statement. The first was the optimism that Bagapsh displayed about Abkhazia's independence and future development. As the president of this entity, this may be expected of him, but his country remains unrecognized by all but Russia and Nauru, Nicaragua, and Venezuela, as well as by the even less recognized Transnistria. Nor has Bagapsh's election as president received any wider recognition. And even the use of the term "independence" is arguably misleading – Abkhazia and its leadership may perceive the post-August 2008 status as such, but their dependence on Russia has, if anything, increased and reduced the little room for manoeuvre that Abkhazia might have had before. Seen from this perspective, even more remarkable than the statement itself is where it was expressed: in the editorial pages of the Washington Times that also acknowledged Bagapsh's title as president. A defacto recognition, if not of Abkhazia so at least of the new status quo, giving Bagapsh such highly prestigious column space is an indication of two closely linked dimensions of the politics of unrecognized states: on the one hand, there is the frequent failure to resolve their status and to do so by peaceful means; while on the other the need persists to engage with them. This fine line between recognition and engagement – often presented as a choice between recognition and non-engagement – is what this chapter will explore in more detail in relation to the case of EU conflict management in the two separatist conflicts that have plagued Georgia and Georgian–Russian relations for most of the post-Soviet period. The focus on Abkhazia and South Ossetia is justified in that it offers an excellent case study of the dangers associated with unrecognized statehood left poorly managed in a region of significant geostrategic importance. While the EU is not solely responsible for the lack of effective conflict management, examining its role is instructive in that it can shed light on a number of core problems associated with international conflict management more generally. The chapter proceeds in three steps: it begins with an overview of EU–Georgia relations from the early 1990s to the aftermath of the Georgia–Russia war of August 2008. It then offers two complementary explanations for the ultimate failure of conflict management – the EU's lack of appropriate capabilities and the multi-layered context of the two separatist conflicts. Against this background, the chapter concludes with a broader evaluation of the utility of international conflict management strategies in relation to unrecognized states.

The EU's engagement with post-independence Georgia

EU efforts to engage with Georgia over the country's two separatist conflicts date back to the early 1990s and were initially focussed on humanitarian assistance: more than half of all ECHO funding to Georgia prior to the 2008 war and its aftermath were spent between 1992 and 1995, two-thirds of all food aid (from DG Agriculture funds), and all exceptional humanitarian assistance. From 1997 onwards, the EU also begins to commit funds to rehabilitation programmes in the two conflict zones.[2]

A major boost in the amount of EU funding received by Georgia and a significant diversification of programmatic areas in which projects are financed occurs after 1999 when relations between Georgia and the EU were put on a contractual footing with the Partnership and Cooperation Agreement (PCA) entering into force. As part of the envisioned political dialogue to be developed on issues pertaining to security, stability, economic development, institutional reform, and human and minority rights, a hope was expressed that "[s]uch dialogue may take place on a regional basis, with a view to contributing towards the resolution of regional conflicts and tensions" (European Commission 1999: 6). The Presidency Conclusions of the Cologne European Council were even more optimistic, expressing the conviction "that this will also facilitate ... the quest for lasting solutions to persisting conflicts in the region" (Council of the European Union 1999: §93.)

In 2001, the European Commission issued a Country Strategy Paper[3] for Georgia, which, apart from a gloomy overall assessment of the political and economic situation in Georgia (European Commission 2001: 4, 7–10), identified the two conflicts in and over Abkhazia and South Ossetia as a major "impediment to development in Georgia" and a contributing factor to regional instability. Noting the readiness of the EU "to look for further ways in which it could contribute to conflict resolution, as well as post-conflict rehabilitation", the paper also explicitly committed the EU to the support of "the principle of Georgian territorial integrity" (ibid.: 5). Less than two years later, the Commission published a revised country strategy, taking account of the deteriorating political and economic situation in Georgia (European Commission 2003) and restating the commitment "to support efforts to prevent and resolve conflicts as well as post conflict rehabilitation" (European Commission 2003: 4). The latest Country Strategy dates back to 2007 and is generally more upbeat about developments in Georgia after 2003, which included the appointment of an EU Special Representative for the South Caucasus and the deployment of the EU's first-ever Rule of Law mission (EUJUST Themis). While the EU's priorities vis-à-vis Georgia – poverty reduction and institutional reform – remain essentially unchanged, the language on Georgia's two conflicts is toned down, merely noting that:

> the EU attaches great importance to the resolution of conflicts in Georgia's two breakaway regions of Abkhazia and South Ossetia and is actively involved in ongoing efforts to achieve a peaceful settlement, partly through

> the offices of the EUSR for the Southern Caucasus and through providing financial assistance for reconstruction and rehabilitation projects in Georgia's conflict zones.
>
> (European Commission 2007: 7)

This is quite remarkable in light of the fact that less than a year earlier, External Relations Commissioner Ferrero-Waldner had clearly, and correctly, noted, with respect to the South Caucasus as a whole, that "[t]hree negative strands are coming together, the combination of which is, frankly, alarming", namely the failure of all parties to deliver on conflict settlement, increased defence expenditure, and ever more inflammatory rhetoric. Thus, she warned that "[a]ny further escalation of tension could re-ignite the conflicts with devastating consequences for the entire region" (European Commission 2006: 1f).

The 2007 Country Strategy must be seen in the context of the EU's European Neighbourhood Policy of which Georgia had become a participant in 2004. As a result, while the 1999 PCA remains the legal foundation of EU–Georgia relations, it is now the ENP Action Plan that provides the framework for EU assistance and it is the ENP instruments (principally, ENPI and NIF) that are primary implementation tools.[4] In the PCA, the issue of the conflicts in, and over, Abkhazia and South Ossetia only got relatively brief mentions, especially in Article 5 of Title 2 (Political Dialogue), whereas the ENP Action Plan elevated the conflicts and their settlement to a Priority Area (no. 6 among 8 priority areas in total). As a consequence, the inclusion of Georgia in the ENP in 2004 saw a general increase in the EU's engagement with the country's two secessionist conflicts. Moreover, the change in government in Tbilisi in 2004 gave the EU greater confidence that its engagement would yield positive results and more quickly so.[5] It is also important to note that this major gear shift in EU engagement in the South Caucasus also reflected a break with previous thinking on the South Caucasus more generally, which now, for the first time, became more differentiated as a region of its own, rather than being treated as a part of the post-Soviet region (Lynch 2004b).

Reflected in the policy instruments brought to bear and the funding committed to conflict resolution by the EU is a consistent EU preference for creating enabling conditions for the resolution of the conflicts in, and over, Abkhazia and South Ossetia. The bulk of EU initiatives and funding has gone to rehabilitation projects with the aim to contribute to economic and infrastructural development and thereby also build confidence between the different parties.[6] Being the largest foreign donor, the EU allocated €25 million to Abkhazia and €8 million to South Ossetia between 1997 and 2006 (European Commission 2007: 20). In addition, just over €100 million was spent on humanitarian assistance under ECHO between 1993 and 2006, primarily "targeting population groups affected by the conflict" and increasingly concentrating on food security and income generating activities for internally displaced people and other vulnerable groups (ibid.). This trend continued in 2007 and the first half of 2008 with a further €10 million committed to economic rehabilitation projects in the conflict zones of Abkhazia and South Ossetia and to a range of projects catering to the needs of Georgia's still significant number of IDPs from the two conflicts (European Union Delegation to Georgia 2010: 2). Spending on IDPs increased further in the aftermath of the 2008 war, which created an additional almost 200,000 IDPs: a total of €61 million was additionally allocated under the ENPI and a further €6 million, initially committed to the OSCE-administered economic rehabilitation programme for South Ossetia, was reassigned to IDP projects following the closing of the OSCE mission to Georgia (European Commission 2009: 5, 7).

In addition to these economic and humanitarian programmes, the EU has also been politically engaged in Georgia and in relation to its two secessionist conflicts. Apart from significant funding made available to reforms in the political and judicial institutions of the country, Joint Actions under CFSP have begun to play an increasingly important part in the EU's efforts to contribute to the peaceful resolution of the conflicts in, and over, Abkhazia and South Ossetia. When the first EU special representative (EUSR) was appointed in 2003, his mandate in relation to the conflicts in the South Caucasus was merely one of "assisting" in their resolution. The appointment of the current EUSR, Peter Semneby, in 2006 saw the mandate amended to a more proactive "contributing" to conflict resolution. This change has been reflected more generally in EU CFSP actions vis-à-vis the conflicts in, and over, Abkhazia and South Ossetia.[7] Indicative of this gear change is the first ENP Action Plan, endorsed by the EU-Georgia Cooperation Council in November 2006 and entering into force in 2007 (European Commission 2006). Under Priority Area 6 (Promote peaceful resolution of internal conflicts), Georgia and the EU commit to a range of specific actions with regard to conflict settlement in Abkhazia and South Ossetia, "based on respect of the sovereignty and territorial integrity of Georgia within its internationally recognised borders", including confidence building, economic assistance, and demilitarization (European Commission 2006: 10). "Disguised" as action items, the Commission also offers a broader assessment of the state of play at the time, pointing out that there is a "need to increase the effectiveness of the negotiating mechanisms", that "[t]he work of the Joint Control Commission [for South Ossetia] should be measured by the rapid implementation of all outstanding agreements previously reached and in particular by the start of demilitarisation", that "constructive cooperation between interested international actors in the region, including the EU and OSCE Member States" is essential for further progress towards conflict settlement (ibid.). This latter point needs to be seen also in conjunction with a reference to the peace plan for South Ossetia, endorsed at the OSCE Ministerial Council in Ljubljana in December 2005. Together with an EU commitment to support the enhancement of the mandates of the UN and OSCE in Georgia, this all clearly underlines the EU's multilateral inclination. Moreover, the EU's explicitly stated intention to "[i]nclude the issue of territorial integrity of Georgia and settlement of Georgia's internal conflicts in EU-Russia political dialogue meetings" (ibid.) reflects the clear realization that Russia is a veto-player whose support needs to be secured for any conflict settlement to have a realistic prospect of sustainability.[8]

The importance of the EU's capabilities for effective crisis management was underlined in the context and aftermath of the war in August 2008. The French presidency of the EU, together with the OSCE Chairmanship (at the time held by Finland), was instrumental in brokering the six-point ceasefire plan agreed by Russia and Georgia on 12 August. The follow-up visit by German Chancellor Angela Merkel to both Russia and Georgia between 15 and 17 August further demonstrated that two of the "Big Three" clearly saw eye-to-eye on the issue. By the time an implementation agreement was signed by Russia and Georgia on 8 September, after further shuttle diplomacy by Presidents Barroso and Sarkozy, an Extraordinary European Council meeting in Brussels on 1 September had given full backing to the ceasefire agreement and committed the Union "including through a presence on the ground, to support every effort to secure a peaceful and lasting solution to the conflict in Georgia" (Council of the European Union 2008a). The deployment of a civilian monitoring mission (EUMM) tasked with overseeing the implementation of the ceasefire agreement had its immediate significance in demonstrating the EU's capability to act quickly in terms of decision-making, financing and deployment. Longer term, the EUMM's significance was further enhanced because it soon became the only internationally mandated presence in Georgia after Russia forced the closure of both the UN and OSCE missions in Abkhazia and South Ossetia, respectively. Moreover, the political weight of the EU in the Geneva settlement negotiations (technically, talks to consolidate the August ceasefire) was considerably higher than the previous roles it had played (observer status in the JCC for South Ossetia and involvement in the UNSG Group of Friends for the Abkhazia talks through some of its member states). The EU became, alongside the UN and OSCE, an official co-chair of the Geneva process, in which the European Commission is a co-moderator (with UNHCR) of the Working Group on humanitarian and IDP issues.

The EU response to the August 2008 war between Georgia and Russia also served as a test for the Community Civil Protection Mechanism, which was mobilized to facilitate civil protection assistance provided by member states directly to Georgia and the two conflict regions. In addition, the Commission provided €9 million worth of immediate humanitarian aid for IDPs and co-hosted with the World Bank the Georgia donors' conference on 22 October where it pledged some €500 million for various rehabilitation measures, including further humanitarian assistance (€8 million), support of IDPs (€61.5 million through ENPI and €15 million through IfS), and for the EUMM (€37 million for the first 12 months to 30 September 2009).

Following this initial flurry of activity in August and September 2008, there was wide-spread enthusiasm that the EU had finally made a real breakthrough in its credibility as an international security actor. During the 12 months since, however, this perception, which was by-and-large correct at the time, has required some adjustment. While the humanitarian assistance programmes run by the EU, especially support projects for IDPs, have continued relatively successfully, the political process has stalled and a resolution of the two conflicts in, and over, Abkhazia and South Ossetia is as, if not more, remote than it was at the time of the war in August 2008. Not only has Russia gradually reneged on a number of pledges in the ceasefire agreement and implementation plan, but with its recognition of the independence of Abkhazia and South Ossetia (even though only Nicaragua, Venezuela, and Naura have so far followed suit) and the consolidation of its political and military presence in both territories, Georgia's territorial integrity and sovereignty are no more than a fiction. Georgia itself has been through a period of heightened domestic tensions, seeing a significant, yet ultimately unsuccessful, challenge to the political authority of President Saakashvili and experiencing the consequences of the global financial crisis. In addition to tense relations with Russia, Georgia's ambitions for a more concrete perspective to NATO membership, let alone an accelerated path to it, have not been fulfilled by the alliance to date. Nonetheless, Georgia continues to look to the US rather than the EU for political backing. While relations between the West and Russia have prospects of improving in the wake of a foreign policy reorientation of the US under the Obama administration, little of substance has happened, limiting both EU leverage in the Geneva talks and any incentives for Russia to make compromises. As a result, the EU, for example, had to retract proposals for an inclusion of US monitors into its mission in Georgia, strongly pushed for by Tbilisi, but equally vehemently rejected by Moscow. At the same time, within the EU, the appointment of Jacques Morel as EUSR for the Crisis in Georgia was a concession to the outgoing French EU presidency, but undermined the role of the existing EUSR for the South Caucasus, Peter Semneby, even though the latter remains tasked with providing political guidance to the EUMM. The EU thus now finds itself between several rocks and hard places in relation to the two conflicts in Abkhazia and South Ossetia: it has not been able to capitalize on its achievements in August and September 2008 by providing clear international leadership for conflict resolution but rather is involved (again) in what has become an almost meaningless settlement process in the shape of the Geneva talks. Where the EU has, however, proven its worth is the broader set of assistance measures from humanitarian aid to support for political, legal, and economic reform in Georgia. In other words, the EU has been able to maintain its engagement with both Georgia and the two unrecognized states of Abkhazia and South Ossetia while avoiding the issue of the latter's recognition, arguably by insisting on their non-recognition through the continuing emphasis on Georgia's territorial integrity. While this may have contributed to containing the conflicts, it has done little to resolve them.

Explaining the limitations of conflict management

How can we explain the lack of any tangible progress towards a negotiated settlement of the conflicts over the unrecognized states of Abkhazia and South Ossetia after close to two decades of international involvement, including by the

EU? In the case of the Union, the question could also be phrased slightly differently: how can we explain that the EU's impact was close to negligible before the summer of 2008, then for a short period of time very significant, before declining again quite steeply? As I will illustrate in the next two sections, there are two complementary sets of factors at work here – the EU's insufficient capabilities and the context in which the two conflicts are played out at local, state, regional, and global levels, and their interfaces.

Insufficient EU capabilities

Any third party involved in conflict management must possess three sets of capabilities to have any chance of succeeding in its endeavours: it must have the appropriate policy tools and be able to deploy them in a timely fashion, it must be capable of funding its efforts possibly over extended periods of time, and it must be willing and able to coordinate and cooperate within its own organizational structures and with external actors.[9] While we will assess in the next section whether the actual conflict context was conducive to an externally facilitated settlement, what follows now is an assessment of EU capabilities meant to identify also shortcomings in the Union's overall approach to conflict management and offer some recommendations of what might be done to overcome them. Our focus on EU capabilities and the external conflict context that, together, shape the likelihood of successful EU conflict management also offers a tool of gauging in which situations the Union might be able to succeed given its capabilities and the conflict context and thus to caution against over-ambitious and unrealistic expectations of what can be expected of the EU as a conflict manager in the case of Georgia, and throughout the Eastern Neighbourhood and beyond.

As noted above, the EU has markedly improved its capabilities to act and to fund. Two EU special representatives (for the South Caucasus and the crisis in Georgia) have been deployed, ENP and the Eastern Partnership have made conflict management one of their priorities, and high-level intervention, such as in the case of the (French) presidency's shuttle diplomacy during the Georgian–Russian war in August 2008, has left a positive mark. To be sure, Georgia is far from a success story for EU conflict management, but comparing the relative success of the French presidency's handling of the crisis in summer and autumn 2008 to the considerable difficulties the EU experienced in the Western Balkans throughout the 1990s indicates that the EU has come a long way in achieving some credibility as a conflict manager. Likewise, the various funding instruments available now, such as the IfS and ENPI, are working far more effectively in the short- and long-term than even the so-called Rapid Reaction Mechanism and other instruments did. Yet, even with improved capabilities, political will to engage *politically* remains a scarce commodity. The main instrument (in terms of duration and funding provided) for EU engagement to date has been the ENP. Yet, as External Relations Commissioner Ferrero-Waldner already pointed out in 2006, the ENP "is not in itself a conflict prevention or settlement mechanism", but "tackles the underlying issues which enable conflicts to fester" (European Commission 2006). Insisting, as she did at the time, that the example of Western Europe after the end of World War II has demonstrated that "promoting prosperity, stability and security is the ultimate conflict prevention policy" is empirically correct, but not a suitable analogy. Conflicts, such as those in and over Abkhazia and South Ossetia, that are based on incompatible self-determination claims of distinct ethnic groups follow a different logic that is not comprehensively captured and addressed by an approach that sees "to contribute to a more positive climate for conflict settlement" (ibid.). In other words, "impressive economic growth is not the key mechanism for turning a conflict that springs from issue of identity into a cooperative arrangement" (Coppieters 2007: 26). This is not to say that the EU approach as a whole is flawed, but rather that it lacks a comprehensive vision and strategic follow-through: unlike the UN and OSCE, the EU has significant economic and political instruments that it could deploy in support of a more active diplomatic role in seeking a negotiated settlement.[10] Rather than merely supporting existing efforts (which failed to make any progress over more than a decade), the EU should have mustered the political will to take a lead in the settlement process.

That this has not happened either before or after the 2008 Russia–Georgia war is also a reflection of the fact that the most problematic area for the EU is its internal and external capabilities to cooperate and coordinate. As already noted, being a latecomer in the arena of international conflict management, the EU has had significant difficulties finding a role for itself within the broader international conflict management efforts. This has been as much a problem in relation to the EU's internal political dynamics. Especially in the Eastern Neighbourhood, and thus in relation to the conflicts in Georgia, the Union has been unable to overcome different member state preferences on how to deal with Russia and remains fundamentally divided between a more Russia-friendly camp (comprised of those, like France and Germany, who prioritize bilateral relations with Russia over a common EU approach) and a more Russia-sceptic camp (including primarily Poland, Sweden, and the Baltic states, as well as at times the UK who prefer a much tougher line).[11] This divide within the EU has meant a repetition of a well-known EU pattern of no or insufficient action until a crisis has fully escalated, rather than the pursuit of a well-conceived, strategic, and properly resourced proactive foreign policy.

Relegated to observer status in South Ossetia and to providing support for confidence-building measures and economic reconstruction in Abkhazia, the EU's role in Abkhazia and South Ossetia was relatively marginal until summer 2008, despite a somewhat higher level of activity from spring 2008 onwards (European Commission 2009: 7), including a visit by High Representative Solana to Georgia and Abkhazia in June 2008.[12] The Georgian–Russian war in August that year, however, coincided with the French presidency of the EU and thus with an internationally heavy-weight incumbent with an experienced and well-resourced foreign office staff and a president accepted as equal in his national role by Russia. Yet, the EU needs to maintain a careful balance here, as noted by High Representative Solana, between "unity inside the EU and commitment to our principles" and realizing that "there is no alternative to a strong relationship with Russia" (Council of the European Union 2008b).[13] This was also emphasized in a Commission review of EU–Russia relations in November 2008, acknowledging that "Russia is a key geopolitical actor, whose constructive involvement in international affairs is a necessary precondition for an effective international community" and observing that the key requirement for successfully engaging Russia in conflict resolution in the common neighbourhood is "the will and the capacity of the EU to act as one, combining both Community instruments as well as those of CFSP/ESDP" (European Commission 2008: 4f.).

At the same time, the OSCE chairmanship was held by Finland, another EU member state and one not traditionally perceived as anti-Russian. Seizing the initiative, the French presidency, in cooperation with the OSCE, brokered a ceasefire and oversaw the swift agreement on, and deployment of, EU monitors to Georgia. While member states remained divided over whom to blame, Russia or Georgia or both, the French presidency of the EU managed these disagreements well enough to preserve the EU's ability to act. While this may be seen as a major breakthrough in the EU's conflict management capabilities, it also indicated some potential weaknesses, as one might wonder whether the same results would have been obtained if the war had happened during the presidency of a smaller member state anchored in the Russia-sceptic camp within the EU. Moreover, there remain question marks over whether the EU's intervention actually achieved much at all: the EU-proposed ceasefire was agreed by Georgia and Russia, but only after Russia had essentially achieved its aims; Russian recognition of the independence of South Ossetia and Abkhazia happened despite EU opposition at the end of August 2008; and thus far little, if any, progress has been made in the Geneva talks, mandated by the ceasefire agreement. Moreover, while the French presidency managed to keep EU member states in line and on course during the crisis and to get, and implement, an EU-internal agreement on the deployment of monitors to Georgia, the appointment of its own EUSR for the crisis in Georgia (the existing EUSR for Central Asia, Jacques Morel) did little to dispel perceptions of a specific French national agenda within and beyond the EU.

The conflict context

How did the conflict environment impact on failures and successes of EU conflict management in Georgia?[14] Globally, the EU is a latecomer in the area of conflict management. Throughout the 1990s, the EU was, if anything, focused on the Balkans, with little success. ESDP, the Union's major reservoir of conflict management instruments, only became fully operational in 2003 (a decade after its inception), and continues to lack military teeth. Thus, by the time the EU began to look to the Eastern Neighbourhood (ENP, too, was inaugurated only in 2003), the field of conflict management had already been carved up among other actors, such as the UN and the OSCE, who showed little enthusiasm to let the EU become a major player as well. The Union, thus, remained mostly excluded from political efforts and was relegated to providing economic support and limited confidence-building measures in Abkhazia and South Ossetia where the UN and the OSCE, respectively, were the main "drivers" of peace processes that stalled soon after ceasefire agreements were concluded in the first half of the 1990s (see below). The Union did obtain observer status in the OSCE and Russia-led Joint Control Commission in South Ossetia and appointed a Special Representative for the South Caucasus (as well as after 2008 for the crisis in Georgia). Through the presidency, held at the time by France, the EU also filled a vacuum created in the wake of the 2008 Russia–Georgia war, and provided, together with the OSCE Chairman-in-Office (Finland at the time), crucial shuttle diplomacy leading to a ceasefire agreement. However, in general, the geopolitical environment offered few concrete opportunities for the EU to play an active, let alone leading, role in managing the conflicts in Georgia. Given their prominence, it is, therefore, worth briefly exploring here the role of two international organizations – the OSCE and the UN – as part of the broader global conflict context.

As already noted, for most of the period after the outbreak of violence in Abkhazia and South Ossetia, the OSCE and the UN were the most significant external mediators involved in any of the conflict's settlement processes. Their engagement was guided by three principal objectives: to bring active hostilities to an end and to prevent their resumption; to deal with the humanitarian consequences of the two conflicts; and to achieve durable settlements. Yet, with the underlying objective of at least some of the Western members of the two organizations having been to consolidate the independence of Georgia and to effect its integration into European and transatlantic structures, tug-of-war games, in which Abkhazia and South Ossetia, as well as eventually Georgia, would become nothing more than pawns, were inevitable: locally between pro-Western and pro-Russian forces, within regional organizations (such as the OSCE and the CIS), and geopolitically between Russia and the West.

This geopolitical dimension of Georgia's contested statehood requires some further analysis of another third-party actor: the United States. US engagement was driven primarily by its own national security and energy agendas. The Baku–Tbilisi–Ceyhan (BTC) pipeline serves major US interests, including diversification of supplies and limiting Russia's (and potentially Iran's) control over Caspian hydrocarbon resources by providing alternative supply lines to world markets. The security of the pipeline, however, remained crucially dependent on stability in Georgia, which established an initial US interest in what was considered Russia's backyard throughout the first half of the 1990s. With the beginning of the "Global War on Terrorism", the region rose to higher prominence on the US security agenda because of its strategic location in relation to Afghanistan, Iraq, and the Middle East, necessitating the use of Georgian airspace and leading to the establishment of two (joint US–Turkish) airbases in Georgia. In 2002, as part of an effort to widen the coalition of countries supporting the

US-led war on terrorism, the Georgia Train and Equip programme was initiated, funded with $64 million and designed to increase the capabilities of Georgia's armed forces by training and equipping four 600-strong battalions of the Georgian army and some additional troops under the command of the ministry of the interior, including border guards. A follow-up to the Train and Equip programme was the Georgia Sustainment and Stability Operations programme, tied more specifically to Georgian troop deployments in Iraq and providing an additional $60 million in military US assistance in 2005/2006.[15] In addition, around $400 million worth of military surplus goods were delivered to Georgia.[16]

While the sustained commitment by the US to Georgia had a significant impact on the country's economic performance, especially since 2004, and arguably contributed to a number of social and political reforms, it also exacerbated Georgian–Russian tensions, especially because of US support for, if not encouragement of, Georgia's aspirations to join NATO. While US policy in the early 1990s acknowledged Russia's claims that Georgia (and other ex-Soviet republics) should be respected as part of its zone of influence, US military and energy security interests over the last decade have turned the South Caucasus into somewhat of a battleground for regional influence. In the context of generally worsening relations between Russia and the West, a perceived US agenda to press ahead with Georgia's NATO membership bid at the Bucharest Summit in April 2008 was at least a contributing factor to the outbreak of violence in South Ossetia over the summer.

These complex strategic configurations of power and the opportunities and constraints they establish for the realization of the interests of each involved player at least partly explain the failure of international conflict management efforts in facilitating a durable political settlement of the conflicts over Abkhazia and South Ossetia. Much like the EU, the UN, OSCE and US were part of the same conflict context and insufficiently able to shape it to their advantage and thus be in a better position to affect progress towards conflict settlement. Consequently, it would be unfair to lay all the blame for the lack of sustainable settlements in the two conflicts in Georgia on third parties alone. Yet, seeing them just as victims of the intransigence of local conflict parties and of the self-interested agendas of other external actors, chiefly Russia, does not tell the entire story of failure either. While the US pursued a predominantly national security agenda in Georgia which limited the degree to which it could play a more constructive role in conflict settlement, the UN and OSCE were proactively engaged as key players in international conflict management efforts, but proved themselves at the same time extremely protective of "their" settlement processes and prevented (for a long time successfully), a more multi-track and multi-actor approach. In the same way that the OSCE maintained its lead role in South Ossetia, the UN had been keen to keep other actors at bay from its efforts in Abkhazia. This exclusion of other third parties from the core conflict settlement processes limited their effectiveness in two ways. On the one hand, it deprived them from capacities that they did not, or not sufficiently, have themselves. For example, the EU's proven track record to facilitate economic reconstruction and reintegration and assist with civilian police and border management has, if anything, been activated only very late. On the other hand, despite the "protectionism" of the UN and OSCE, the number of external actors on the ground who are keen to contribute to the settlement of these conflicts has steadily increased, but the multiple efforts made by them and the respective key players have not always been sufficiently coordinated, and objectives have at times been contradictory.

Moreover, there were two further factors that added to this unfavourable global context. Kosovo's unilateral declaration of independence in February 2008, and its recognition by now all but five of the EU's 27 member states, created a welcome "precedent" for Russia as frequently emphasized by Putin, already in the run-up to February 2008.[17] While Russia's position here is ambivalent, of course, as it also backed Serbia before the ICJ challenging the legality of Kosovo's UDI, this "successful secession" further strengthened the resolve of the Abkhaz and South Ossetian elites to pursue their course of breaking away from Georgia. The second complicating factor in this respect is Georgia's aspiration to join NATO and NATO's principal openness to this idea, as expressed at the Bucharest summit in April 2008. Unsurprisingly, this was not welcomed by Russia and may well have confirmed to the Kremlin an essentially hostile agenda on the part of Georgia and NATO (in connection also with the then still ongoing US-inspired missile defence shield). The overall worsening relationship between Russia and the West clearly did not facilitate any progress on diffusing ever-increasing tensions in Georgia, thus limiting further whatever conflict prevention and resolution capabilities the EU, alone or in cooperation with other international actors, may have possessed before August 2008.[18] Moreover, as the International Crisis Group argues, defeating Georgia in the August 2008 war served several of the Kremlin's strategic goals in this respect: "to punish one nation for its NATO ambitions; to warn others, especially Ukraine, not to go down the same route; and to humiliate NATO by showing it to be indecisive and ineffective" (International Crisis Group 2008: 10).

At the regional level, constraints on EU effectiveness, by-and-large, also outweighed opportunities. The main factor here is Russia. Russia, at the same time a global player, not least through its status as permanent member of the UN Security Council, has clear security and economic interests in the area considered by the EU as its Eastern Neighbourhood, interests that are often at odds with those of the EU. The Russian military presence in South Ossetia and Abkhazia (in the form of CIS peacekeepers for much of the period after the break-up of the Soviet Union), as well as Russian political influence and economic leverage makes Russia a veto power when it comes to conflict settlement. Deteriorating relations between Russia and the West, over Kosovo and NATO expansion among others, combined with the limited leverage that the EU has over Russia, have further complicated the task for the EU. EU dependency on oil and gas from Russia and on Russia as a major transit country for energy from the Caspian region has so far outweighed Russian dependency on the EU as a major market. EU efforts to diversify supply and supply routes by investing in pipelines through the South Caucasus have significantly driven increased EU conflict management efforts in this region, and Georgia in particular, but not decreased Russian leverage, predominantly because of the continuing influence that Russia exercises in Abkhazia and South Ossetia.

The regional situation, however, is also characterized by the influence of non-state actors. The fact that, over some fifteen years, quasi-state structures have grown in Abkhazia and South Ossetia (to the extent that both regions exhibit key criteria of stateness, such as a permanent government associated with a population and a territory, yet remain largely un-integrated into international political and economic networks) has also created opportunities for transnational organized crime that has become entrenched and is closely interwoven with the local political, social, and economic structures, and in fact sustains them in many ways, financially and militarily. These criminal networks are predominantly involved with drugs smuggling and weapons trafficking and, as such, also integrated into global East–West transit routes. Moreover, throughout the 1990s, the conflict zones in Abkhazia and South Ossetia, and surrounding areas of Georgia proper, provided training and transit opportunities for jihadist fighters joining the Chechen independence struggle, thus increasing also Russian security concerns. While the EU is clearly and negatively affected by this kind of organized criminal activity, it lacks effective instruments to tackle them at their source. Moreover, from a conflict management perspective, such efforts might prove counter-productive by alienating the very local elites that will be essential for achieving a sustainable settlement.

At the state and the local levels, the factors that condition the success or failure of EU conflict management in Georgia are equally unfavourable. Local elites in Abkhazia and especially South Ossetia are deeply dependent on, and controlled by, Russia and are involved in organized criminal activity. While they may lack even a minimum of democratic legitimacy in the eyes of the EU, it is difficult to see how any continuing stabilization, let alone settlement, can be achieved without engaging them. While the EU is keenly aware of this, it remains committed to the territorial integrity of Georgia, which in turn resists any negotiations with the Abkhaz and South Ossetian elites. These elites, heavily dependent as they are on Moscow for political and military backing and for economic lifelines that help them maintain a modicum of local legitimacy for their regimes, thus have very little room for manoeuvre in potential status negotiations. In other words, even though local elites may be able to claim legitimately that they represent the interests of Abkhazia and South Ossetia, they have very limited, if any opportunity, in the existing negotiations format to do so effectively because of a regional balance of power that favours Russia from the start. The Russian position, moreover, is clearly at odds with that of Georgia and those among its supporters that insist on the country's territorial integrity. Thus, even though one of the results of the Georgia–Russia war in August 2008 was the creation of a new negotiation format involving both Russia and the EU, these so-called Geneva talks have yet to produce any concrete results. The EU has earned its place in the Geneva talks qua its efforts to broker a ceasefire, but its actual position within them is weak: limited, if any, leverage over Russia is matched by a Georgian preference for the US and NATO as backer. Moreover, the EU's role is constrained structurally.

The current agendas of the immediate conflict parties at the local and state levels in both conflicts have not only created a situation in which the EU is of relatively marginal significance but their perceptions of what their own interests in relation to security, power, and material gain are have also meant that their willingness to move beyond the status quo and towards sustainable settlement is at best limited. Security concerns in South Ossetia and Abkhazia remain high for both separatist and Georgian officials. Internal power struggles at the state level continue in Georgia. Repeated election promises by the incumbent president to restore full sovereignty over the entire territory of the Georgian state in its internationally recognized borders from the outset limited the chances of a peaceful settlement of the two conflicts there in light of entrenched positions, and Russian backing, on the other side. Moreover, the material benefits that different sections of the elites on both sides in the conflicts derive from the status quo, and thus the threats they perceive from a negotiated solution, have created significant constituencies who benefit from the lack of a solution and are thus hardly inclined to negotiate in good faith. Abkhaz and South Ossetian leaders cannot even privately contemplate any form of reintegration into Georgia, but differ with regard to their own long-term goals. Abkhaz favour independence and fear increasing Russian dominance, while South Ossetians aim at reunification with the North Ossetian republic in the Russian Federation. Yet, Russia struggles with a restive North Caucasus and is aware of the risk of further destabilization through continued Ossetian "reunification" efforts.

The international management of unrecognized states

The gradual escalation of the conflicts over Georgia's two separatist entities – the unrecognized states of Abkhazia and South Ossetia – demonstrates the dangers inherent in international efforts to manage such conflicts. As the foregoing analysis has demonstrated in its focus on the EU, there are several objective limitations to the effectiveness of international conflict management in a situation as multifaceted and complex as the context in which the conflicts over Abkhazia and South Ossetia have evolved over the past two decades. The focus on the EU, however, has also highlighted a number of capability gaps that have prevented more effective conflict management, some of which are clearly not unique to the EU but constitute a broader set of problems for third-party actors involved in conflicts related to unrecognized states. Yet, the relative failure of international conflict management in the case of these two unrecognized states in the South Caucasus also offers some important lessons.

What was crucially lacking in the case of Abkhazia and South Ossetia, on the part of the EU and third-party actors more generally, was a proper conflict management strategy. The formulation and subsequent implementation of such a strategy would need to be based on a clear definition of third-party interests vis-à-vis a specific conflict and the context in which it occurs; a context-sensitive assessment of third-party strengths and weaknesses in conflict management; and a feasible approach as to how these strengths can be best leveraged and weaknesses overcome.

In addition, there are five substantive principles that have so far not been comprehensively appreciated in their significance for the effectiveness of international conflict management in cases involving unrecognized states.

Primacy of negotiated solutions over imposed settlements

The eventual outcomes of settlement negotiations must not be prejudged, but reflect what is practical and feasible given the interests of the immediate conflict parties and other relevant players. In order to attain such outcomes, the relevant third-party actors need to stand ready to provide adequate resources for potentially protracted negotiations, as well as leadership and technical expertise as necessary to assist in crafting a sustainable settlement.

Inclusiveness of negotiations

Comparative experience of conflict management indicates more generally the need for negotiations to include all relevant parties if whatever settlement obtained is to have a chance of being fully implemented and sustainably operated. Such inclusion need not be unconditional, but conditions need to be determined and enforced with care. While a commitment by all parties to non-violence is essential, the non-prejudicial approach to negotiation outcomes outlined above, suggests that demanding prior acceptance of certain parameters of a settlement, such as continued territorial integrity or the permanence of demographic changes, might be counter-productive by undercutting the support that negotiators need from their constituencies. This point also emphasizes the need for engaging the leaderships of unrecognized states without at the same time linking such engagement to recognition.

Comprehensiveness of agreements

The two conflicts in Georgia are primarily secessionist in nature. Yet, a mere compromise about who is to control which stretch of territory will be insufficient for any settlement to be sustainable. Experience indicates that, apart from accommodating territorial claims, security, economic, and cultural concerns also need to be addressed. This will require the parties to make concessions and settle for compromises. An often painful and risky process for the negotiators personally and the parties they represent, third-party mediators need to be acutely aware of "red lines" and carefully tease out the space for compromise between them, tabling proposals at key moments. Such proposals can be specific to address a particular impasse during negotiations, but they may also be broader, considering the interests of external parties whose support will be needed for settlement implementation and operation.

Building broad coalitions of support for negotiated settlements

Difficult as it may be to reach a settlement at the negotiation table, the process of securing its implementation is often even more fraught with dangers of failure. Third-party actors will need to put significant effort into securing the support of a particular settlement from key constituencies of those represented in negotiations, external stakeholders and interested parties, as well as manage potential spoilers and limit their ability to undermine a settlement agreement once it has been negotiated. Such a broad coalition of support would need to include civil society and media, diaspora networks, regional and international organizations, neighbouring states, and relevant great powers to offer the political elites who negotiated a settlement the necessary backing and give them the room for manoeuvre to accept compromises and make concessions.

Need for long-term external assistance

Achieving a negotiated settlement in any conflict is a difficult enough task on its own, and is often additionally complicated by painful compromises over status issues involved in conflicts with unrecognized states. The subsequent implementation and operation of settlements, moreover, will be long-term projects of state and nation-building: (re-) building a single common state or consolidating two separate ones. Without external assistance, implementation and operation of settlements will almost certainly lack the necessary human and material resources to be completed successfully. Third-party actors normally have significant experience – of success and failure – in this (the EU, for example, from its engagement in the Western Balkans over the past almost two decades), and it will increase the likelihood of its success in conflict management if it commits to long-term, post-settlement engagement with the former conflict zones by providing security guarantees, development aid, and institutional capacity-building and training.

Overall, the case of international, and in particular EU involvement in the management of conflicts over the unrecognized states of Abkhazia and South Ossetia demonstrates that third-party actors rarely face the stark choice between non-engagement and recognition. Rather, to the extent that engagement can happen without recognition, the international track record of conflict management may not be that poor after all: before and after the 2008 war, economic and social reconstruction efforts and humanitarian relief for IDPs did result in some concrete benefits, even though these were clearly not enough to prevent the outbreak of war. This also illustrates that avoiding the recognition issue is no long-term strategy for conflict management either, postponing, as it does meaningful, outcome-oriented status discussions. *In extremis*, and the examples of Abkhazia and South Ossetia are cases in point here, the status issue is "resolved" by force and recognition extended partially and without broad international consensus. Sergei Bagapsh's optimism to one side, this does not do away with unrecognized states.

Notes

1 The author acknowledges the support of the Economic and Social Research Council (ESRC) through award number RES-451–26–0419 (The European Union as a Global Conflict Manager). This chapter draws, in its empirical part, on two previously published works: Whitman and Wolff (2010) and Akçakoca *et al.* (2009).
2 For detailed annual expenditures, see European Commission (2007: 33).
3 According to the Commission's 2001 Communication on Conflict Prevention, such Country Strategy Papers are "the instrument for ensuring [. . .] an integrated approach of conflict Prevention" (European Commission 2001: 11).
4 The ENP Action Plan also takes significant inspiration from the PCA and makes frequent reference to it (European Commission 2007: 5, 6, 11, 19, 21, 25, 34, 40) and clearly states that PCA implementation is the number-one priority for future assistance to Georgia (ibid.: 19).
5 Compare, for example, the EU's assessment of the situation in Georgia in the 2003 Country Strategy with that of the 2007 Country Strategy.
6 Interview with Peter Semneby and Mark Fawcett, Brussels, 16 December 2008, and John Kjaer and Stefano di Cara, Brussels, 16 December 2008.
7 Interview with Peter Semneby and Mark Fawcett, Brussels, 16 December 2008.
8 This manifests itself also in EU–Russia discussions in the framework of the Common Space External Security.
9 This argument is developed in greater detail in Wolff (2008b) and Peen Rodt and Wolff (2010).
10 Cf. International Crisis Group (2006b: 3). This report is overall highly critical of the EU's reluctance "to take on direct conflict resolution responsibilities" (ibid.: 27).
11 Cf. International Crisis Group (2008: 23f.) and Leonard and Popescu (2008: 31ff.).
12 Another high-level visit to Georgia, Abkhazia, and Russia was undertaken in July by Frank-Walter Steinmeier in his dual capacity as German foreign minister and coordinator for the five-member Friends of the UN Secretary-General (including also the United States, Britain, France, and Russia). While a peace plan presented by Steinmeier was rejected, further escalation of the conflict over Abkhazia, seen as much more likely and dangerous than the situation in South Ossetia, was averted at the time.
13 Cooperation with Russia, regardless of how reasonable it may seem from the EU's perspective, has been difficult to sustain at constructive levels. The military escalation in the summer of 2008 and the subsequent recognition by Russia of the independence of Abkhazia and South Ossetia is a clear indication that the Road Map for the Common Space of External Security is barely worth the paper on which it was written, committing the two sides, as it did, to, inter alia, cooperation in crisis management, promoting conflict prevention and settlement, regular consultation, early warning, etc. See European Commission (2005).
14 For a more detailed exploration of the dimensions of "context" and their impact, see Wolff (2008b) and Cordell and Wolff (2009).
15 Information from http://georgia.usembassy.gov.
16 Information from www.state.gov./p/eur/ci/gg/c7008.htm.
17 The International Crisis Group (2008: 8) notes in this context that soon after Kosovo's declaration of independence, Russia significantly increased the strength of pre-existing links with Abkhazia and South Ossetia.
18 The connection between the escalation of tensions between Georgia and Russia over Abkhazia and South Ossetia, on the one hand, and Kosovo's declaration of independence and the outcome of the Bucharest NATO Summit, on the other, is also emphasized by the Independent International Fact-Finding Mission on the Conflict in Georgia (European Union 2009: 31).

10 The politics of unrecognized states and the business of international peace mediation

Enablers or hindrance for conflict resolution?[1]

Antje Herrberg

States "which do not formally exist but desire to do so" pose a fundamental challenge to the international diplomatic community because they challenge the way in which international relations are being managed. The mediation of conflicts, in its various forms, has been practiced in many societies around the globe. Indeed, one could argue that conflict prevention and resolution is the greatest challenge to the international community. In 2009, more than thirty-one highly violent conflicts were being waged around the world, detrimental to human life and livelihoods (Heidelberg Institute 2009). Many of these were intrastate conflicts.

This chapter seeks to critically assess the challenges to peacemaking and the practice of international peace mediation within the contextual setting of the politics of recognition and/or non-recognition. What is mediation and how is it practiced? What are its facets and who are its actors? What role does peace mediation play in intrastate conflicts that deal with unrecognized entities? To what extent and how does conflict resolution influence recognition or non-recognition? An understanding of the practice of mediation and its strengths, opportunity and threats provides a basis for tangible venues for policy development, as well as for further areas for research.

Mediation is not a practice that is exclusive to the mediation domain of intrastate conflict. Just as conflict is part of everyday life, mediation can be practiced everyday and everywhere. It is a way to reach decisions in a cooperative way, allowing for open communication processes with little or no hierarchy. The way in which people resolve conflicts has an impact upon how a society and its institutions are governed. The practice of mediation to solve disputes is an increasingly accepted method in the Western world and is, in its variety of forms, a widespread tool-for-change in conflict situations in many parts of the world. The application of mediation is transformative for people and societies engaged in conflict and is as much about the process of deliberation or the understanding of respective perspectives, empowerment, and recognition as it is about conflict resolution (Zilleßen 1999). Often, religious and spiritual underpinnings have converged with the liberal notions of peacemaking.[2]

Mediation is one form, or a cluster of forms, of third-party intervention in conflicts. It can be differentiated from other forms of third-party intervention in that it is not based upon force and the conflict parties maintain a certain degree of ownership over the outcome in the process (Herrberg *et al.* 2009). Mediation can be defined as: *A voluntary and confidential method within a structured process where one or more impartial parties assist conflict parties to reach a mutually acceptable solution. The mediator provides the framework but makes no substantial suggestions or decisions in the case.*

The term "international peace mediation" can be used to describe the role played by an outside actor such as, for example, the United Nations or the European Union. Whilst the term "international" could be seen as redundant, it is consciously applied because international conflicts refer to third-party involvement in both interstate and intrastate conflicts. Because the abuse of human rights and the likely changes to an intra- or interstate context challenge the global order, conflicts become a concern of the international community and, in this way, a rationale for mediation and outside third-party intervention becomes relevant. The term "peace" here refers specifically to a sustainable, enduring resolution to conflict. It therefore attaches a value to international mediation as an integral and not isolated part in conflict resolution and the peacebuilding cycle.

With this in mind, there are different ways of how peace mediation is currently practiced in the field of conflict resolution. For the purpose of a framework herein, we can distinguish between the following three approaches:

- *Power-based, deal-brokering mediation* or one to which mediators bring "carrots and sticks" in order to broker an outcome. Power-based mediators usually direct the process resolutely and use manipulative tactics to get parties to reach an agreement.
- *Interest-based, problem-solving* mediation or one which uses a facilitative style and furthers the ownership by parties and the development of creative approaches which respond to the interests and needs of the parties.
- *Transformative, long-term mediation* or one in which mediators intervene at different levels to seek a change in relationships between the parties and their perception of each other. Here conflict resolution is seen as a long-term process, which happens through the empowerment and recognition of a broad variety of actors in conflicting societies (See also Herrberg *et al.* 2009: 12).

Ways of practicing mediation often depend upon whether or not the process is managed by a state or non-state actor. A distinction needs to be made between state or official actors or non-state (primarily NGOs but also private individuals endorsed by official or unofficial third actors). Whereas official talks often follow a strict hierarchy with a head of a delegation in which delegates can rarely speak without the clearance of their superiors (see also Agha *et al.* 2003: 170), informal talks have little or no hierarchy and therefore allow for a wider exploration of key issues as well as a solution at hand.

Mediation involving secession or between a parent state and an unrecognized entity have as the most basic feature three key characteristics. First, it is usually asymmetric in nature as the parent is perceived as the more powerful party. Second, the unrecognized entity has less negotiation capacity because its legitimacy is not clear, and other regional actors might intervene in the mediation process. Third, as it has been exemplified in other chapters of this book, conflicts involving unrecognized statehood have an unusual degree of "protractedness."

Presently, state-based mediation with unrecognized entities is often practiced by power-based mediators and parties and therefore usually follows the logic of a "status" frame and a "black" and "white" (independence versus territorial integrity) perspective. This often stands in the way of finding solutions that could capture the interests of all parties and stakeholders.

Each of the three mediation approaches mentioned above have their validity depending upon the conflict situation and the style and personalities of the mediators. It can be argued, however, that some conflict resolution techniques – and this does not only apply to secessionist conflicts – might produce longer-lasting agreements than others.

Mediation of intrastate conflicts which involve the question of secession and independence with mediation basing itself upon positional bargaining or interest-based approaches will, arguably, have a decisive influence over a number of issues. These include the attitude of the parties (antagonistic or issue-based), the focus of the substance of the discussion (conflict focus/contextual long-term focus), the flexibility of the parties in terms of solutions (sticking to one's own position/being open to various possible solutions), the genuineness of the parties (manipulation, pressuring, maneuvering/honesty, and open communication), the degree of openness (sticking to positions/being open about interests and needs), the relationship and contact with the other parties and the outcome (win/lose or accommodation of mutual benefit), and the degree of the relationship between the parties even after a peace agreement (damaged or destroyed versus sustained and/or enhanced) (Hoffman 2010). The issues that will be covered in a mediation process can result in positional bargaining and/or interest-bargaining. Positional bargaining is generally a win/lose or a compromise-oriented process. Interest-based mediation or negotiation, on the other hand, is pursued when solutions can be found in which all parties have their needs met (see Moore 2003: 72).

An example of positional bargaining can be seen in the case of Cyprus where the UN-led mediation process, especially between 1963 and 1974, has been considered an "exercise in frustration and futility" (Fisher 2001: 321). The antagonism of the parties results in adversarial discussions on the surface of the conflict rather than becoming a springboard for reframing or for creativity. In Cyprus – but also in many other conflict situations – the result, as Ronald Fisher has argued, is often that "parties are caught in a self-defeating process of antagonism including the blaming of the other side, attributing negative qualities to them and polarizing one's own side against them" (2001: 322). This did not concern the overall personal qualities of the mediators as much as the fact that the arguments and the formulations in the process could not offer an opportunity to address the apprehension and the deep fears of the parties. Official negotiations were based upon positions rather than interests.

The same could be argued for Georgia where the EU's approach to mediation, for example, has hitherto been dominated by a power-based – rather than an interest-based – logic. On the other hand, the EU has been financially supporting grass-roots mediation efforts conducive to both interest-based mediation approaches as well as transformative and long-term mediation. However, these still need to become a part of an overall EU approach towards interest-based mediation efforts (See also Frichova Grono 2010).

In Chapter VI (Art. 33 (1)) of the UN Charter, the UN sets forth a comprehensive list of peaceful means for the resolution of conflict. These resolutions are to help the evolution of a normative framework for the peaceful settlement of disputes between parties. On the other hand, the UN Charter prohibits its involvement in the internal affairs of member nations. This holds technically for the resolution of disputes that are status related. Mediators coming from state-based organizations, including the UN, therefore, have little opportunity to engage in an all-partial mediation process. The main challenge for international, state-based actors mediating with non-recognized entities – such as representatives of territories with state-aspirations – is conferring legitimacy and international recognition to these entities, which is not a desired normative approach. Control over one state's government or territory is the basic incompatibility of internal armed conflicts with which mediators need to struggle (Wallensteen 2007).

Mediation as a rationale for peaceful intervention

Of the total amount of the 365 political conflicts being waged today, 273 are at the intrastate level, including thirty-one highly violent conflicts. Eight of these thirty-one highly violent conflicts are secessionist conflicts (See Heidelberg Institute 2009). Literature in sociology accepts that conflicts are neither good nor bad but exist as a part of life in the continuum of the individual and the state. Indeed, some argue that the very essence of democracy is the existence of disagreements about different approaches to maintaining society. Most conflict theorists accept that conflicts are a form of societal interplay which can be a burden but also an opportunity for change. Whilst these are comforting theories, the international community is faced with the challenge of the "right to intervene" in a situation when the conflict presents a fundamental threat to human security. This "right to intervene" has been embraced through the creation of the concept of *Responsibility to Protect (R2P)* since 2005. This concept, unanimously accepted by 150 governments, asserts that sovereign states have a very explicit responsibility to protect their own people from genocide, war crimes, ethnic cleansing, and crimes against humanity, but also calls for the international community to act and take up this responsibility in case the state in question is incapable or unwilling to do so (See also Evans 2008: 283).

Whilst it is outside the scope of this chapter to test the validity of the R2P concept, it certainly warrants the questions about what type of intervention is required in which situation as well as which "cues" are available for state-based actors to offer good offices for conflicts involving secession and when states declare themselves as independent. When intervening within a human security angle, at what stage can a mediator discuss "status-related" questions with the conflict parties at the table? Is there a human security threshold that indeed calls territorial integrity into question and allows a state-based mediator, who is a subject of international law, to engage in status discussions? The inherent dilemma is exemplified by the Charter of the African Union, which provides for the right of the Union to intervene in a member state and for the right of a member state to request an intervention (Article 4 of the Act) and, at the same time, deliberating that these involve both the integrity of the African continent and the sovereignty and territorial integrity of one member state. The African Union has moved from non-intervention to the doctrine of "non-indifference" (Kioko 2003).[3]

Engaging in mediation

Parties enter into mediation for a number of reasons: the time is *ripe* for conflict resolution (also due to prolonged human suffering), the mediator is trusted and thought of as being able to deliver results, as well as because of a self-perceived inability to otherwise resolve the conflict (even by force) with the parties needing the international community to recognize their particular conflict and perceived injustice. Parties also choose to engage in a mediation process because it legitimizes status, prolongs the process and allows a party to pursue other means of gaining advantage and strength with motives, therefore, that are *not* designed to achieve a long-term political settlement (see Richmond 1998). In societies under distress and in severe conflict, Greig and Regan argue that "most offers to mediate are accepted by warring factions, any offer of mediation is better than no offer" (2008: 778). In the context of a mediation process which involves the recognition of independence on the one hand, and territorial integrity on the other – which appear to be irreconcilable positions – incentives for mediation appear to be first and foremost a cessation of hostilities and, consequently, even temporary human security.

The role of the mediator is to shape the expectations of parties in a civil war about both the consequence of rejecting mediation and the expected benefits of participation (Greig and Regan 2008: 778) but also to display in a transparent fashion the frame in which he or she is operating. In the case of Martti Ahtisaari as regards to Kosovo, for example, the frame was clear right from the beginning: due to unconstitutional actions of Serbia as regards to Kosovo, the only option available for the international contact group was that Kosovo would become an independent state.[4] Conversely, in the peace mediation with the government of Indonesia and the Free Aceh Movement in 2005, the frame was equally clear to the mediator Ahtisaari: independence was not an option to negotiate but, rather, a special autonomy status which could serve the interests of both parties. This was made clear at the very beginning of the negotiation.[5] Some mediators provide discretionary advise, as illustrated by a statement by Count Folke Bernadotte, then the UN special representative to Palestine, who was asked by the parties to provide an indication of his ideas for a possible basis for settlement:

> Notwithstanding, therefore, the complete divergence of aims and the very short time left at my disposal, I decided to submit to the two parties a set of tentative suggestions with the primary intention to discover whether there might be found at this stage a common ground on which further discussion and mediation could proceed.
>
> (Puchala 1993: 88)

In any case, whether or not the agreement will be a partial peace agreement, an agreement on "talks about talks" or one which simply covers one of the issues (such as power-sharing or consolidating state structures), this needs to be clear to the parties in order to mitigate the danger of turning the mediation process into a "battle ground" for politicians and spoilers (Wallensteen and Eriksson 2009). This context excludes the tantamount task of the mediator to convince parties to engage in comprehensive peace mediation that allows a long-term settlement. If mediation is both a science and a craft, keeping parties to a protracted conflict involved and committed is indeed an art which only a few can master.

The impartiality of the mediator in international peace mediation

How is it possible to mediate impartially between state-based and unrecognized states with which they are in conflict? Impartiality is clearly imperative, but the question merits special attention because it indicates the essential dilemma for state-based actors who are both guided by specific mandates and seek a comprehensive peace settlement with unrecognized entities. As alluded to in my introductory definition of mediation, impartiality and neutrality are critical, especially in Western-influenced practice. Impartiality refers to an absence "of bias or preference in favour of one or more negotiators, their interests or the specific solutions which they are advocating" (Moore 2003: 53).

Present approaches on impartiality in international mediation seem to confirm Gulliver's assertion that impartiality is not correct in practice and does not have a cross-cultural validity (1979: 217). Theory tells us that the mediator is to be ideally impartial even to the extent that he or she is disinterested (ibid.: 214), i.e. that he or she has no interest in or benefits from the outcome of the mediation. Whilst the range of the mediators' role may vary (Breidenbach 1995), the choice of the impartial mediator is instrumental regardless of the extent of the conflict. Some scholars in international mediation argue that the principle of impartiality does not apply to this field (Bercovitch 1996) because state actors are motivated by their relationship with one of the parties and/or have a special interest in the outcome. Some of these scholars have subsequently adjusted this view and recognize that mediation by states is evolutionary and ever changing (Bercovitch 2002). To the conflict parties, however, any perceived lack of clarity with regard to impartiality towards them might entail that "the mediators' endeavours heighten the suspicion, fear and anger and [...] are consequently ineffectual if not counter productive" (Nathan 1998). At the same time, Zartman argues that "mediators need not to be impartial but they must deliver the side to which they are perceived close" (1995b: 21). Even though the need for neutrality, impartiality, and all-partiality are core elements of Western-based mediation doctrine, however, all is not lost. Both biased and neutral as well as all partial mediators can contribute to an agreement. This plays out in the partial mediator having more leverage over the parties in conflict due to the special relationship that the mediator entertains with one of the parties (Svensson 2009).

This point is particularly pertinent in considering the role of mediation enacted by state-based actors and, more particularly, power-based mediators. As Crocker *et al.* (2004) manifest: "Just as conflict parties are not interested in achieving peace at any price, so, too, powerful mediators have a clear preference about the kind of settlement that they will support" (2004: 24).

International and regional organizations, such as the UN, the EU, and the OSCE as well as the AU, have played a number of roles in the conflicts between unrecognized states and parent states. The persistent policy of non-recognition of state-based actors at least since the end of the Cold War, however, creates a situation in which those actors are more likely to operate and engage under the framework of territorial integrity. Two issues deserving highlight are these: First, as already mentioned, when the mediators from state-based institutions *do* engage, they are likely to follow an agenda or framework (non-recognition) with regard to the outcome, in which case they become a party in the negotiation. Second, and interrelated, is the fact that eminent personalities, such as (former) statesmen (or much more rarely, women), are appointed mediators due to their standing and therefore attract the trust of all parties, but often do not consciously "apply" principles of mediation practice and proceed in the mediation process with positional bargaining. The result is that an ideally interest-based mediation, treating the genuine interest and needs of the parties, gives way to positional approaches, which follow a competitive bargaining for status. This is why Pal Kolstø has concluded that "whilst the international community is clearly in favour of peaceful, negotiated settlements to [...] conflicts, [...] its involvement, in most instances, has a quite different effect and inadvertently contributed to the prolonged existence of quasi states" (2006: 734).

The partiality of mediators, therefore, appears to show an interesting and, to mediators, counter-intuitive twist for conflict resolution. Empirical research shows that mediators who have a specific interest over one particular outcome, and can thus be labeled as "biased" mediators (also those with a stake in a conflict), are more likely to mediate a successful outcome (see Kryd 2003). According to Svensson (2009), there are three key reasons why partial mediators are more likely to come with peace agreements of higher quality as compared with neutral mediators: First, partial mediators will look for stipulations which protect their side and thus engage in deeper substantive discussions, thereby creating a greater likelihood of producing a rich agreement which fully spells out provisions for power-sharing and territorial sharing, whereas neutral mediators will hasten agreements which will put an end to fighting. Second, neutral mediators have less capacity in terms of leverage and credibility for bringing about concessions with either party as opposed to partial mediators who have this capacity. Third, parties in conflict prefer biased rather than neutral mediators in situations where substantial concessions have to be made such as power-sharing or giving up territorial integrity (see Svensson 2009).

With this in mind, it appears that formal mediation processes which revolve around status questions appear to be imbalanced in terms of the outcome and thus give rise to a genuine challenge in terms of creating balance and symmetry. The challenge for the state-based mediator, then, is how such a balance can be created. This is a question that can be answered through a policy of engagement and supporting the perceived weaker, secessionist party regardless of non-recognition. Within the continuum of extremes of recognition and non-recognition, there are alternative ways in which to engage with conflict parties, to ensure that parties in conflict and, in particular, the needs of unrecognized entities can be met.

In search of a balanced approach – and apart from a solely humanitarian dimension – it appears necessary for state-based actors to provide sufficient incentives to allow for an engagement with unrecognized states. Whilst such a strategy will not take a position on the status, it nevertheless can allow a wider dialogue with the unrecognized states in order to mend and strengthen lost confidence and reduce antagonistic behavior, which will allow for eventual balancing of third-party intervention.

The European Union's recent policy on engagement with non-recognized states is an attempt to do so. Whilst the EU has taken clear positions as to Georgia, for example, its policy of non-recognition nevertheless pursues the intent for engagement with the separatist entities in Abkhazia and South Ossetia. This includes diplomatic contacts as well as the promotion of contacts with civil society. In addition, the promotion of so-called confidence-building measures in breakaway regions is seen to promote understanding and confidence.

Not only is such a policy noteworthy – especially as it could lay a precedent as to the way in which the European Union engages with other unrecognized entities – but it also allows the approaching of the conflict vis-à-vis a human security angle to advance human security needs rather than following a policy of isolation. Whilst various commentators argue that the EU does not have the policy tools at its disposal and begs the question of whether or not this precludes its role as an effective mediator to resolve conflict,[6] it is nevertheless important to recognize such policy as a strategy to reducing overall asymmetry.

The missing link: private diplomacy

Peace "work" provides the seeds of popular involvement in non-violence and put forth the basis for the setting up of the League of Nations. We can trace back the peacebuilding work to Adam Curle's publication of his book *True Justice: Quaker Peacemakers and Peace Making* (1981), which challenged the nature of our values in peacemaking and created the beginning of the peacebuilding movement.

Since the end of the Cold War and the change of the nature of conflicts from interstate to intrastate, there has been a growth in the number of NGOs working for peace and conflict resolution. These private diplomacy actors mediate conflicts, support peace processes, and engage in dialogue with a variety of actors with the purpose of conflict resolution. The common denominator for private diplomacy actors who are NGOs specializing in mediation is that they represent private organizations and people, including former heads of state or governmental figures who practice diplomacy by using a variety of methods. These organizations and people complement the world of traditional diplomacy typically within the domain of nation-states and governments as well as regional and international organizations (Herrberg and Kumpulainen 2008).

Modern day peacebuilding and engagement with unrecognized states without civil society and its organizations is difficult to imagine, although the role of civil engagement has been quite marginalized in peace processes until recently. In the report of the UN Secretary-General on *Enhancing Mediation and Supporting Activities* (2009), the UN has recognized the multiplicity of different kinds of NGOs to support a peace process in many ways. Their "light" structures in terms of decision-making allow for early action, they appear to be less threatening, and they can influence formal processes through their facilitation of informal processes. NGOs are recognized for their long-term efforts and their specific thematic and regional or process expertise and can contribute to building constituencies for peace. At the same time, the UN points out that NGOs have fewer resources than the UN or regional or sub-regional organizations, which "makes their staying power more tenuous" (United Nations 2009: 20).

Informal peacebuilding and the peacemaking sector can be divided into two principal camps: the pragmatic one, providing a technical albeit not-for-profit service function, and the idealistic, with a focus upon values and transformative approaches. The camps can be complementary but also contrasting. They have, however, an impact upon the goals, strategy, values, and analysis of the peacebuilding organizations (see Fisher and Zimina 2008). Any analysis and appreciation of the politics of unrecognized entities needs to take account of the various roles played by international NGOs.

Provision of human security

Organizations where idealistic values dominate are more inclined to program and gear their activities towards dealing with human security, often in partnership with local, grass-roots organizations. In unrecognized entities, such organizations are likely to support a "weaker party" to the conflict, which have been deprived of the services of a state due to the politics of isolation. Their roles can range from civil disobedience to supporting a resistance movement, but their actions are difficult to assess empirically as they are rarely documented due to security concerns. The fact that they are sometimes sponsored by governments with a vested interest in the unrecognized entity only serves to confuse matters further.

Service delivery

The more pragmatic and technical services or "professional" international NGOs are often grant or service contract driven organizations, providing specific projects to conflict parties. Increasingly so, they are providing mediation and dialogue services and sometimes also offer services to one particular party. An interesting example of an organization which supports unrecognized entities is the Independent Diplomat, a NGO which works with a number of separatist entities, such as the unrecognized government of the Saharawi Arab Democratic Republic (SADR), Northern Cyprus, Somaliland, and South Sudan and provides diplomatic advice to these parties.[7] Others take the approach of providing mediation services which could serve the interests of the conflict parties, such as the Crisis Management Initiative, the Carter Center, or the Geneva-based HD Center.

Just as with states engaging in mediation, private diplomacy actors and related peacebuilding NGOs can be instrumentalized by both parent states and secessionist states. For unrecognized states, engaged international NGOs provide a forum and a form of recognition in secessionist states, whereas offering parent states an opportunity to work on an enhancement of its government policy. Here the lack of power and leverage actually becomes an advantage as it increases their potential to mediate and engage in dialogue for conflict resolution. Because there is less risk involved for the parties to participate and engage in dialogue through low-profile meetings organized by these NGOs, they provide a useful forum for contact and for understanding each other's perspective. At the same time, there is little leverage, and oftentimes not sufficient linkage with official actors for intended (need for a "safe space" and secrecy) or non-intended reasons (lack of access to official processes and/or lack of political will of the parties for conflict resolution).

There are, however, some key differences between the formal and informal practice of mediation. First and foremost, where state actors focus upon solutions (and thus status-oriented solutions), private diplomacy actors generally focus upon process. This is an important distinction as processes matter a great deal in conflict resolution efforts. This is because of "the significance that the disputants attach to their substantive demands, but also because individuals and groups want to be involved in decisions that affect their lives" (Nathan 1999).

Private diplomacy actors[8] have the advantage of engaging quickly and early in conflicts to prepare parties for negotiations; they have a different risk profile and become involved where states and international organizations are sometimes reluctant. Especially in asymmetric settings that involve the engagement with belligerents and armed groups, which sometimes creates a difficulty for engagement even if such engagement is essential, private diplomacy actors can play important intermediary roles. Oftentimes NGOs possess the local knowledge expertise and support that can be useful complements to official mediation processes. At the same time, they can build the capacities of individual conflict parties. In many situations, it can effectively be shown that NGOs have been able to create "safe spaces" for conflict parties in which parties can test ideas and relationships (Nathan 1999). A further important advantage is that private diplomacy can enhance constituencies for peace by engaging influential people and grassroots actors. These have the potential to be linked to official processes and thus create a stronger peacemaking momentum. Likewise, where official peace processes sometimes lack the ability to bring *all* stakeholders to the negotiation table, NGO mediators can convene different groups of civil stakeholders and, at the same time, also promote gender sensitivity, which is often lacking in official settings. International peacebuilding NGOs play an important complementing role in peace processes, especially in the politics of unrecognized states. Because of the asymmetric official processes, their involvement and support with weaker parties can help to balance processes. Additionally, many international NGOs have an excellent knowledge and network within and across many of the conflict areas and often do not shy away from precarious security situations.

Governments may see their main function in a conflict as contributing to an overall agreement between warring parties, such as, for example, bringing peace to a region even if it involves compromises or granting amnesties to those responsible for human rights abuses. As Jan Egeland (1999), the former UN Under Secretary for Humanitarian Affairs, argues:

> NGOs [...] tend to look at the weak spots and the consequences of peace agreements – how equitable they are, how they impact on minorities, whether human rights are protected – and, importantly and controversially, they campaign to have those responsible for human rights abuses tried and punished for their crimes.

One of the greatest challenges for effective conflict resolution, therefore, is that of creating multi-track approaches that can support and balance each other. In Cyprus, Georgia, and Somalia, for example, as in many other places in this world, sustained dialogue, conflict analysis that allows for reframing, problem-solving and involving policymaking, as well as negotiations, have the potential to put a halt to the negative conflict spiral which reigns within the politics of unrecognized states. Each failure of any peace mediation, in particular formal ones, creates further rifts between conflict parties risking to slip deeper and deeper into intractability and, possibly, even increases the likelihood of violence as the only way for self-assertion and maintenance of a status quo.

That said, the effectiveness of approaches depends upon the level of professionalism and also requires both parties (unrecognized entities and the parent state) to accept such actors as playing an intermediary role. In summary, in conflict resolution with unrecognized entities, private diplomacy actors have more opportunities for facilitating and providing venues for conflict parties, exploring issues of contention and building capacities within the parties to understand their conflict dynamics as well as acting as information brokers between parties when communications are broken.

One of the challenges that NGOs face pertains to funding mechanisms, which is often linked to governmental agencies funding diverse programs. These are sometimes politicized and complicate engagement and work with unrecognized entities. An NGO, for example, might encounter problems in arranging meetings that allow participants from parent or unrecognized states to travel to a "neutral location" due to restrictive visa issues. The funding situation often creates problems for long-term engagement, which is needed to allow for the application of transformative mediation.

As the report of the UN Secretary-General on *Enhancing Mediation and Supporting Activities* points out, although there is a small number of non-governmental organizations that provide mediation services, they nonetheless have a lack of capacity to carry out a full implementation of the agreements, including providing security arrangements and full follow-up.

Choosing the mediator: muscle and/or exploration of issues and forum shopping

Mediation is a crowded field where many actors are in stark competition with one another for access to conflict parties. This competition results, in peacemaking jargon in "forum competition," which provides the conflict parties with ample potential for manipulation. In many conflict situations and particularly those that involve protracted conflicts, it is not rare to find literally hundreds of formal and informal mediators. The question here is not if formal or informal mediation processes are the right ones. Instead it is a question of timing and cooperation between the two sectors and, self-evidently, cooperation and accord between state actors. In particular, the cooperation of NGOs and state mediators in creating genuine multi-track engagement is crucial in dealing with unrecognized states as their complementarity is readily evident and because formal processes will become "stuck" due to the danger of "losing face" on the positions of status. A mediation process is hampered by insufficient links between formal and informal processes. Even if, as in the case of Martti Ahtisaari, a non-state actor *can* be able to conclude a peace agreement with warring factions, the follow-up of a peace agreement will necessarily involve the role of the international community with state-based actors.

Ingredients for conflict resolution with unrecognized states

Is there a recipe for finding peaceful and sustainable solutions for comprehensive settlement for and with unrecognized entities? Can mediation processes proceed without the recognition of each other's claims? Will settlements, as Nina Caspersen (2008) argues, have to be "fudged?"

In order that the issues of likely concern to conflict parties involving a non-recognized state or entity are addressed, it is worth recalling my initial reference to positions and needs. It can be argued that conflict resolution can be achieved by mediators – state (formal) and non-state (informal) alike – by considering thematic issues. It follows the logic of Laurie Nathan that "the key to effective mediation lies in understanding, managing and transforming the 'psycho political dynamics' of the conflict which make adversaries so resistant to negotiations" (1999: 1). It would go beyond the scope of this chapter to appreciate the entire array of mediation intervention techniques, but it will focus instead upon those that are most likely to arise in a secessionist conflict.

With the frame that every conflict is unique and issues will always be variable, it is safe to say that most conflicts involving secession or recognition are likely to feature the issue areas of security (physical and human security). The question of governance, economic issues, and wealth sharing are areas that can provide some venues for reconciliation. If these issues can be adequately addressed and their solutions be found, a conflict *also* involving non-or-recognition could be facilitated. It is, therefore, a question of framing and approach. This impacts upon the way in which mediators might want to design their strategies; that is, some mediators work under the principle that "nothing is agreed until everything is agreed," which is applicable to highly pressurized conflict resolution such as the Aceh Peace Negotiations under Martti Ahtisaari, where the circumstances of the tsunami and the corresponding international attention to Aceh was a way to discipline and focus parties to come to an acceptable solution for all. Another strategy that could be followed is to apply a step-by-step or partial approach where different thematic areas can be agreed upon and which would gradually build upon each other and possibly spill over into

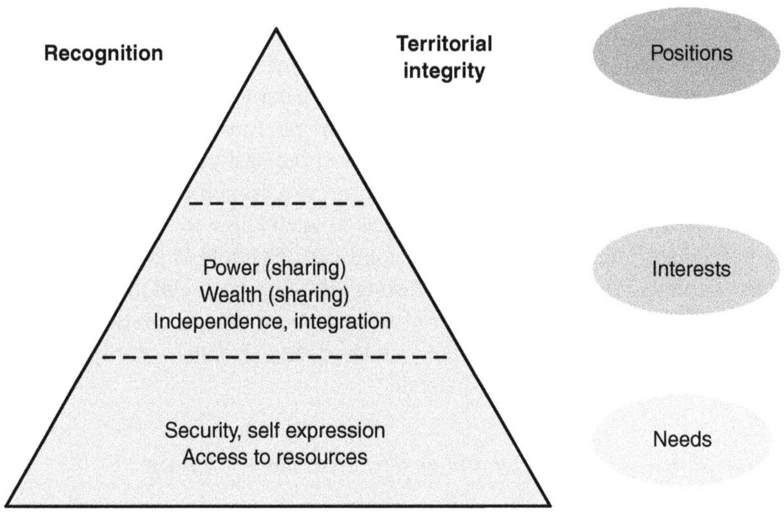

Figure 10.1 Position, interests and needs in conflict resolution.

added layers of cooperation. Such an approach allows for gradually building confidence and progressing towards a full settlement. The danger in such an approach is that, whilst certain issue areas might be agreed upon and actually facilitate rapprochement between the parties, the status of the conflict will ultimately remain as the "elephant in the living room." This confirms the argument that the role of the mediator will be to shape the expectations from the beginning of the discussions.

A basic need: security

The fact that many non-recognized states as well as their parent states have often been undergoing bloody civil wars that have shuttered human lives and livelihoods has a fundamental and strong effect upon individual and state security (of the parent and the unrecognized state). Societal threats take a variety of forms: these concern physical threats, economic threats, threats to life, and threats to position and status (see Buzan 1998). Owing to the fact that secessionist conflicts are due to, or a result of, civil wars, the perspective of providing physical security must be the first focus. Peace processes, particularly those that are the subject in this book, have as their single most important challenge to produce an enabling environment that allows for a freedom from fear for both populations.

Most mediation processes address these within the framework of *security institutions*. Effective security mechanisms are best realized through the close attention to the necessary sequencing of security transitions (Brickhill 2010: 27). The purpose is to allow for a de-escalation of violence, for the restoration of public security, and for confidence-building measures between parties. At the same time, as shown with the Somalia case, a starting point has to include an appreciation of the needs and conflict culture between parties themselves (ibid.). Disarmament, demobilization, and the reintegration of combatants are additional parts for stabilizing a post-peace agreement situation that require international support (Mason 2007). Caspersen (2011) argues that conflict resolution strategies within unrecognized states require security guarantees by the international community as a basis. Technical guarantees in the form of monitoring and peacekeeping could be and have been provided in the past in a number of cases but are not likely to come prior to the signing of a cessation of hostility agreement. It is more likely that security guarantees as such allow for a monitoring of a peace agreement once it is in place. A good case example is Georgia, where the EU has deployed over 200 monitors through the European Union Monitoring Mission (EUMM), which, even though it has only been able to monitor borders along the ceasefire lines, has been able to enhance the perceived security of local populations, albeit only on one conflict side.[9]

Control for (autonomous) action and governance: power-sharing

In 2000, Viacheslav Chirikba, now advisor to the de facto president of Abkhazia and envoy to the Geneva talks, wrote about the creation of a framework of pan-Caucasian structures with transparent borders and diminished sovereignty of central governments. Such an arrangement, he argued, would provide freedom of cultural and linguistic expression, and cross-border cultural, political and economic institutions or association, and "would lessen the importance of being separate and independent whilst enhancing the sense of greater security and opportunities within a politically, economically and financially integrated democratic and pluralistic Caucasian family of nations" (Chirikba 2000).

Effective power-sharing mechanisms in conflicts that involve secession have the potential to overcome rifts within deeply divided societies. Power-sharing describes a system of governance in which all major segments of society are provided with a permanent share of power. This can be contrasted with the government versus opposition system.[10] In secessionist conflicts, a full exploration of a future state organization by the mediator can unravel the root causes of conflicts and possibly support parties to design models and proposals to respond to these root causes (Mediation Support Project 2009). Power-sharing, however, does not equal power division. A federal or semi-federal system could allow for the division of power, whether vertical or territorial (Wallensteen and Eriksson 2009: 33). Different models of decentralization do exist and range from self and/or shared rule, symmetric or asymmetric federalism, territorial and/or ethnic federalism, and aggregation or devolution and can also include special autonomy arrangements. This said, power-sharing or division might be the only way out for sustainable peacebuilding, which could also reduce incentives for working together (ibid.: 34).[11]

Economic issues: freedom to create and share wealth

Any peace process has economic characteristics that need to be accommodated within a process. They include the agendas and conditions that shape the conflict but also conflict-induced economic transformation and costs (See also Collier and Hoeffler 1998). Economic issues are often the lowest common denominators that can provide parties with incentives for cooperation. Economic instruments can change behaviors of parties by appealing to their cost–benefit calculations (Wennmann 2009). It also moves confidence-building mechanisms from a political perspective to a (perceived) non-political, economic one in which both parties can gain benefits. Business-to-business cooperation is an opportunity to bring benefits to the population by providing access to more and possibly cheaper goods. A possible positive side-effect can also be the improved infrastructure of roads and communications to facilitate trade. These issues might not require a mediation process but might involve a facilitated back channel discussion between authorities to allow for an enabling environment for such activity.

Like power-sharing, wealth sharing and natural resource sharing arrangements are quintessential in secessionist conflicts that are often both root causes and drivers of the conflict. In the Aceh peace negotiations, for example, a challenge was the identification of the percentages of oil and gas that could be accrued to each party. Economic issues were indeed instrumental for keeping the negotiations going after a deadlock on international monitoring. This included measures to provide Aceh with the power to raise loans, to determine and impose taxes, and for local governmental authority to allocate them. In the Sudanese north–south conflict, oil has also been both a conflict driver but also a way of incentivizing parties to engage in mediation processes.

Confidentiality and agreed media outreach

Because the politics of recognition and territorial integrity is such a sensitive endeavor in which both parties require safety to protect their status and to "save face" vis-à-vis their constituents, one essential principle in conventional, albeit not always manifested in international, peace mediation pertains to the need of confidentiality. Breach of confidentiality and "leaking" content of discussions to constituencies have the potential to weaken the position of the negotiation parties on the one hand, but also weaken the mediation process on the other, because it cannot be a "safe space" for discussants, thereby deepening rifts and increasing protractedness. It is, for this reason, tantamount for the mediator to encourage parties to apply confidentiality as part of the ground rules, as well as to design a media strategy in which both parties agree upon statements to be made. This is a challenge for state-based mediators in particular, who have reporting requirements, as well as for non-state-based mediators who will have to report to their funders.

Understanding of local cultures, or let them take over

Mediators can very well also be hurdles to a process of reconciliation. Without an appreciation of local cultures, a mediator runs the danger of also overseeing the conflict culture of the parties with which he or she is dealing and runs the danger of "over-intervening" when, in fact, parties are well on their track by themselves to drive their process. Especially once the human security aspect of a conflict is achieved, parties should be encouraged and supported to solve the situation at hand. The mediating community can facilitate and provide financial support for allowing communities to grow together again, rather than insisting upon status-related talks. Such requires courage, as the interest of mediators is also to capitalize upon a sunken investment of a mediation process requiring results for their legitimacy.

Conclusion

As I have shown, the meaningful application of mediation practices in secessionist conflicts has a potential in assisting their conflict resolution by advancing the human security dimension of protracted conflicts. Because most of these conflicts are mediated by state-based actors, power approaches to mediation often result, which quickly become status-based positional bargaining and most often do not lead to comprehensive results. Whilst impartiality is a core value of mediation approaches, state-based mediators, who most often support the principle of territorial integrity, should not be "shunned" as irrelevant or incompetent as they can produce comprehensive agreements. What counts is transparency as to the approach of the mediator in question. Second, I have shown the value added by non-state actors or private diplomacy actors as qualified and complementary actors in conflict resolution, in particular those involving unrecognized entities. Better approaches, however, need to be found in order to link efforts between the formal (state) and informal (non-state) actors and to create intersecting and non-parallel tracks in conflict resolutions that run the danger of losing important confidence-building efforts or, worse yet, nullifying each other. The international community would do well to fully investigate and adopt a best practice approach in this field, which is hitherto not so evident.

The obvious weakness of my arguments presented in this chapter, although sourced from my hands-on and real-life experiences, is that although I argue that interest-based mediation is the more adequate one involving unrecognized states, it lacks solid and firm empirical testing. Such testing, however, will not be possible unless genuine interest-based mediation becomes an accepted professional practice within the field of international peace mediation. As the professionalization of this field is still in its infancy, this opportunity still lies in the future.

It is also clear that time dimensions for interest-based mediation approaches require longer time perspectives, especially if and when the human security dimension is satisfied. Exploring interests such as governance and economic issues beyond ceasefire arrangements, without pressure but with incentives, will require an enormous effort of the international community to take different perspectives in terms of continued engagement, funding, and support.

It is, perhaps, that the recognition issue will have to be "fudged" in the short term. Following the provision of security, however, and further followed by trust and confidence-building with the efforts of the engagement of the international community to support symmetry in terms of democratic governance and economic well-being of parties, alongside a recognition of cultural and ethnic values and needs, the status issue, in fact, might not matter that much anymore.

Notes

1 The author would like to express gratitude to Philippe Taflinski for able research assistance. The research was in part supported by the Initiative for Peacebuilding, funded by the European Commission, but does not commit it to any of the assertions in this paper.
2 The Quakers and Mennonites, as well as the Association of Christian Churches such as the Catholic Association of St. Egidio, have been associated with faith-based conflict resolution and mediation. In recent European history, the role of church figures has been influential, as, for example, in the Northern Irish, Kosovo or Western Papua conflicts.
3 As for the Organisation of African Unity, Williams points out that "it was somewhat contradictory for the OAU to declare secession 'a matter within a member's domestic jurisdiction which precludes external interference' and at the same time pass 'resolutions condemning secession'" (Williams 2007: 267).

4 Private discussions with Martti Ahtisaari, former president of Finland, Nobel Peace Prize laureate and chairman of the Crisis Management Initiative.
5 For a detailed account of the Aceh Peace Negotiation, see also Merikallio (2006).
6 See, for example, Wolff's chapter in this volume.
7 See www.independentdiplomat.org/our-work/.
8 This paragraph is from a workshop conducted by Swisspeace, held on 29 January 2009 in Brussels to produce findings for the Report of the UN Secretary-General on Mediation. See also Swisspeace/Centre for Security Studies (2009).
9 These are observations of the author and derive from discussions with both Monitors of the EUMM and its Head of Mission, Hans Jörg Haber.
10 See also Sisk, T.D. (2003) 'Power Sharing. Beyond Intractability': www.beyondintractability.org/essay/power_sharing/.
11 See also Anderson's chapter in this volume.

11 Reintegrating unrecognized states

Internationalizing frozen conflicts

Liam Anderson

The number of terms used to describe territorial entities that display the attributes of statehood but lack formal recognition is long and growing. Variously termed, "unrecognized states," "de facto states," "pseudo-states," "state-like entities," "states-within-states," "contested states," and even "wannabe" states, there may, by now, be more ways to refer to these entities than there are entities themselves. Nonetheless, what all of these terms reflect is a growing awareness that the simplistic vision of a world comprised solely of recognized, territorially defined, nation-states does considerable violence to a complex reality. Though sometimes assumed to be primarily a product, and, therefore, a problem of the post-Cold War world, unrecognized states have existed since the creation of the modern state system. What distinguishes the unrecognized states of today from their historical forebears, however, is that the recognized states of the contemporary state system appear more reluctant than ever to admit new members. As Samuel Huntington (1972) commented, "the bias against political divorce, that is, secession, is just about as strong as the nineteenth-century bias against marital divorce" – a contention that is strongly supported by the historical record. Aside from the new states that emerged from decolonization, and the recognized successors to the three collapsed communist federations (the Soviet Union, Yugoslavia, and Czechoslovakia), only four states have successfully seceded from parent states since the end of the World War II and been fully recognized by the international community (Bangladesh, East Timor, Eritrea, and Montenegro). There is, as one observer puts it, "an ingrained presumption against secession that pervades international law and world politics" (Geldenhuys 2009: 44). This puts today's unrecognized states in a difficult position. Most (though not all) are the product of contested secessions from recognized states. This means their prospects for admission into an increasingly exclusive community of recognized states cannot be good; but if not independence, then what? Many of today's unrecognized states were birthed in blood after a sustained period of repression (real or perceived) at the hands of the parent state. Reconciliation on any terms with the parent is, therefore, likely to be difficult. With no obvious path forward to recognized independence, and an obvious aversion to reunion with an abusive parent, unrecognized states are essentially frozen in place.

The purpose of this chapter is to examine systematically the range of "alternative destinations" for unrecognized states (Geldenhuys 2009: 45) with a particular focus on options for reintegration with the parent state. Though it is problematic to assume a priori that the other two major alternatives – recognized independence, and forced reintegration into the parent – are necessarily less normatively desirable than a peaceful reunion, there is a reasonable case to be made that some form of extensive autonomy, perhaps coupled with power-sharing arrangements, creates fewer problems than the alternatives. To this end, the analysis proceeds as follows. In section one, I use the definitional criteria outlined in the introduction to this volume to identify the universe of post-World War II unrecognized states. These include unrecognized states that are no longer with us, such as Katanga and Biafra, and those that have endured to the present day, such as South Ossetia and Somaliland. In the second section, I consider a broad range of potential destinations for unrecognized states and briefly analyze the pros and cons of each. Section three draws on the historical record to chart the fate of expired unrecognized states. The intention here is to discern *patterns* of outcomes, which can then yield plausible insights into the future of today's unrecognized states. A first cut indicates that the support of a powerful protector state is key to the survival of unrecognized states, which in turn implies that any deal to reintegrate unrecognized states into parents peacefully will depend critically on the involvement of the protector. I conclude with some constructive suggestions for what the contours of such a deal might look like.

Establishing the universe

A diverse range of territorial entities share space on planet earth with the international community of established, recognized states. These include largely unpopulated expanses of territory that belong to no state (Antarctica, for example), territories that are recognized as the property of one state but occupied by another (the Golan Heights), occupied "stateless' territory (the West Bank), freely associated "states" (the Cook Islands with New Zealand), condominiums (Andorra with Spain and France), and protected states (Liechtenstein by Switzerland), to name but a few. Unrecognized states may be the most ubiquitous and significant of these various non-state entities, but defining what constitutes an unrecognized state and, more significantly, what distinguishes them from other non-state entities is challenging. Fortunately, the introduction to this book provides a useful working definition comprised of three elements. To qualify as an unrecognized state, an entity must have achieved de facto independence and sustained it for a period of at least two years; it must not have gained broad international recognition; and it must have demonstrated a desire for full, *de jure* independence. Inevitably, none of these criteria is surgically precise. However, they are clearly sufficient to piece together an inventory of unrecognized states that either exist or have existed over the post-World War II period. Table 11.1 provides a list of all post-war unrecognized states that, I will argue, meet the definitional criteria, along with their parent states (where applicable), the dates of their existence, and the extent of their recognition.

Table 11.1 Unrecognized states since World War II

Unrecognized state	*Parent state*	*Dates*	*Breadth of recognition*
Katanga	Congo	1960–1963	None
Biafra	Nigeria	1967–1970	Five states (Gabon, Haiti, Cote d'Ivoire, Tanzania, and Zambia)
Serbian Krajina	Croatia	1991–1995	None
Chechnya	Russia	1991–1994, 1996–1999	One state (Georgia)
Tamil Eelam	Sri Lanka	1975–2009	None
Anjouan	Comoros	1997–2008	None
Gagauzia	Moldova	1991–1994	None
Republika Srpska	Bosnia and Herzogovina	1992–1995	None
KRG-Iraq	Iraq	1991–2003	None
Bougainville	Papua New Guinea	1975–1997	None
Eritrea	Ethiopia	1991–1993	Universal
East Timor	Indonesia	1999–2002	Universal
Montenegro	Federal Republic of Yugoslavia	2000–2006	Universal
Kosovo	Serbia	1990–2008?	63 states
Transnistria	Moldova	1990–	None
Nagorno Karabakh	Azerbaijan	1991–	None
Abkhazia	Georgia	1990–	Four states (Russia, Nicaragua, Venezuela, and Nauru)
South Ossetia	Georgia	1990–	Four states (Russia, Nicaragua, Venezuela, and Nauru)
Turk Cyprus	Cyprus	1983–	One state (Turkey)
Palestine	N/A	1988–	93 states
Somaliland	Somalia	1991–	None
Taiwan	China	1949–	22 states
Sahrawi Arab Democratic Republic (SADR) (Western Sahara)	Morocco?	1976–	43 states (includes the African Union)

Two cases included in the above list do not feature in the table provided in the introductory chapter; Western Sahara (SADR) and Palestine. This requires some justification and/or elaboration. To the extent that "de facto independence" requires territorial control, the inclusion of the SADR may seem somewhat questionable. The SADR possesses most of the political institutions characteristic of statehood, including a written constitution, and a president, prime minister, cabinet and parliament, but these institutions govern in exile from Algeria. Moreover, the SADR's preeminent politico-military force, the Polisario Front, controls only about 20 percent of the land area claimed by the SADR (the rest being controlled by Morocco as its "Southern Provinces"). What distinguishes the SADR from other unrecognized states, however, is that the status of Morocco as the parent state is also broadly unrecognized. To put this another way, while only twenty-three states recognize Morocco's claim to the territory of Western Sahara, more than forty states have recognized the independence of the SADR. Hence, the SADR is among the most recognized of all unrecognized states, ranking behind only Kosovo and Palestine in terms of breadth of recognition. The case of Palestine raises similar issues. Though the idea of a Palestinian state is widely recognized within the international community, control over the political institutions of the virtual Palestinian "state" is divided between Hamas (Gaza) and Fatah (the West Bank). Moreover, much of the territory of the West Bank (up to 40 percent, by some estimates) is also controlled by an occupying force (Israel), whose sovereignty over the territory is almost universally unrecognized by the international community. It would, therefore, be incongruous to include Palestine and exclude the SADR.

I make no claim that this is *the* definitive, indisputable inventory of post-war unrecognized states and there are certainly points of debate surrounding both omissions and inclusions. Clear-cut omissions include the Mahabad Republic – the stillborn Kurdish state established in northern Iran in 1947, and the Republic of Crimea, neither of which satisfy the criterion for two-year duration. Less clear-cut are omissions such as Puntland (Somalia) and Adjara (Georgia). Although both entities clearly satisfy the requirements of de facto statehood in that both are (were) self-governing and in control of defined territory for periods longer than two years, neither expressed a desire to secede from their respective parent. Also omitted are a significant number of insurgencies and uprisings that may have been inspired by a desire for independence, but in which the aspiring state never exerted sufficient political control over territory to qualify as de facto independence.

A further series of caveats apply to the dates identified for the beginnings and (in some cases) ends of unrecognized states. In some cases, Somaliland, for example, a formal declaration of independence accompanied by unambiguous political control of territory makes identifying the birth date relatively straightforward. In other cases, such as Montenegro, the absence of such a formal declaration complicates the dating of the birth. In still other cases, Chechnya and Kosovo, for example, the on–off nature of the conflict in both territories over time makes it difficult to determine with precision over which periods of time the "de facto independence" criterion applied. During the time of the First Chechen war (1994–1996), for example, it would be difficult to argue that anyone really *controlled* the territory of Chechnya in any meaningful sense (though the same case could also be made about the 1996–1999 period). Hence, the dates provided in Table 11.1 should best be viewed as approximations.

With these caveats in mind, a trawl through the post-World War II history of unrecognized states yields an inventory of twenty-three entities that fit the definitional criteria. Thirteen of these are no longer with us, while ten continue to the present day, and it is the range of options for dealing with the extant ten to which the analysis now shifts.

Possible destinations for unrecognized states

There are three broad categories of destination for unrecognized states. First, their independence may be broadly recognized by the international community, transforming their status from unrecognized to recognized states; second, they may be forcibly reintegrated into their parent state; and, third, they may be peacefully reintegrated with their parent through a negotiated settlement that involves some form of autonomy and/or power-sharing. Not all options are available for all unrecognized states. Self-evidently, unrecognized states that lack a parent state (Palestine and, arguably, the SADR) cannot be reintegrated into a parent either forcibly or voluntarily. Likewise, this list does not exhaust the possibilities. For example, some scholars have suggested incorporation into a protector state as a possible alternative destination for unrecognized states (Kolstø 2006). This option is not considered more fully here for several reasons. First, it obviously cannot provide a plausible option for unrecognized states that lack a protector (Somaliland, Palestine). Second, even for those unrecognized states that are protected, this is not a plausible option for most, either because the protector has expressed no interest in incorporating the entity (Abkhazia), or due to the lack of territorial contiguity between entity and protector (Transnistria and Taiwan). Third, as Kolstø (2006) notes, "so far, there are no examples of successful inclusion into the external patron state." Hence, the empirical evidence suggests that the option of incorporation into a parent is an even less plausible destination for an unrecognized state than recognition of its full independence. Table 11.2 replicates the list of post-World War II unrecognized states along with the outcomes in each case.

Full independence

Based on the post-war historical record, the path that ends with universal international recognition of independence for unrecognized states is the least plausible of the three possibilities. Aside from the decolonization process and the disintegration of the three communist federations, only four states have successfully navigated the path from secession to full independence. In one case, Bangladesh, recognition of independence resulted from Pakistan's military defeat at

Table 11.2 Fate of unrecognized states since World War II

Unrecognized state	*Parent state*	*Outcome*
Katanga	Congo	Forced reintegration into parent
Biafra	Nigeria	Forced reintegration into parent
Serbian Krajina	Croatia	Forced reintegration into parent
Chechnya	Russia	Forced reintegration into parent
Tamil Eelam	Sri Lanka	Forced reintegration into parent
Anjouan	Comoros	Forced reintegration into parent
Gagauzia	Moldova	Voluntary reintegration into parent
Republika Srpska	BiH	"Voluntary" reintegration into parent
KRG-Iraq	Iraq	Voluntary reintegration into parent
Bougainville	PNG	Voluntary reintegration into parent
Eritrea	Ethiopia	Independence
East Timor	Indonesia	Independence
Montenegro	FRY	Independence
Kosovo	Serbia	Contested independence
Transnistria	Moldova	Undetermined
Nagorno Karabakh	Azerbaijan	Undetermined
Abkhazia	Georgia	Undetermined
South Ossetia	Georgia	Undetermined
Turk Cyprus	Cyprus	Undetermined
Palestine	N/A	Undetermined
Somaliland	Somalia	Undetermined
Taiwan	China	Undetermined
SADR	Morocco?	Undetermined

the hands of Bangladeshi and Indian forces. In the other three cases, East Timor, Eritrea, and Montenegro, secession was essentially uncontested by the parent state, though in the case of East Timor, only after a sustained period of brutal civil war. The absence of successful examples of contested secessions (those to which the parent state does not consent) is striking and reflects a powerful normative bias in international relations in defense of territorial integrity. More precisely, the unwritten rules of international relations effectively preclude the recognition of new states that claim independence *against* the wishes of a parent. Hence, according to Kolstø (2006), "the community of recognized states has … been closed at both ends. While no members are thrown out, the entrance gate has been strictly guarded and new applicants are routinely turned away." Unless unrecognized states have the military capacity to defeat a parent on the battlefield, or can successfully convince a parent to consent to a voluntary separation, the independence prospects for unrecognized states look bleak. It is as yet unclear whether the recognition of Kosovo's independence in the teeth of vociferous opposition from its Serbian parent will change this dynamic. Kosovo is now recognized as fully independent by over sixty states, including the United States and most of the members of the European Union. This blatant violation of the long-standing international norm against the recognition of contested secessions triggered reprisal recognitions by Russia (of South Ossetia and Abkhazia) and a desperate struggle in Western capitals to justify why Kosovo is a "unique" case that does not set a precedent for the future.[1] It remains unclear, however, what it is about Kosovo's experiences with an abusive parent that distinguishes it in any meaningful way from other unrecognized states, such as South Ossetia and Abkhazia. The Kosovo example does serve to highlight an important point regarding recognition in contemporary international relations. The recognition of Kosovo by over sixty states, including most of the world's major powers, provides strong evidence in favor of Glendenhuys' (2009) contention that "recognition is an act of political discretion, not a legal or moral duty." Arguably, Kosovo has no more legal or moral right to be recognized as independent than most other unrecognized states and it is significantly less capable of independence than many (Taiwan, for example); hence, the calculation underlying the decision to recognize Kosovo's independence and not that of, say, Abkhazia, is inherently political. The politicized nature of recognition inevitably leads to "egregious double standards," whereby in certain cases, "recognition is granted readily or, more typically, persistently maintained in spite of conditions on the ground which are tantamount to legal fiction" (Bachcheli *et al.* 2004). Meanwhile, in other cases, "recognition is stubbornly withheld even though the realities on the ground themselves expose the legal fictions which the international community supports in the defence of the principle of territorial integrity" (Bachcheli *et al.* 2004). This has important implications for the independence prospects of unrecognized states because it suggests that, regardless of the strengths (or weaknesses) of the legal or moral case for recognition, the outcome will be driven by political expediency.

There are, in fact, some quite powerful legal and moral arguments in favor of recognized independence for unrecognized states and a right to secession more broadly (Buchanan 1991; Crawford 1979; Macedo and Buchanan 2003). This is not the appropriate place to delve deeply into the circumstances under which there is, or should be, a right to secession/self-determination that trumps an existing state's right to territorial integrity. The legal/moral issues associated with state recognition are essentially irrelevant for current purposes. In purely practical terms, the vast majority of the world's recognized states are "multinational" and, therefore, have a shared vested interest in refusing to recognize a right to secession and preserving the territorial status quo. The body of international law that relates to issues such as state recognition, rights to secession/self-determination, and territorial integrity has been composed, interpreted, and implemented by *states* and their legal representatives. By definition, unrecognized states are, therefore, excluded from participating in the creation of the rules that govern their status and prospects for recognition. Thus, the major drawback with full independence as a future destination for unrecognized states has almost nothing to do with its normative desirability (or otherwise), and everything to do with its practical implausibility. In essence, fully recognized independence is implausible because it depends on acquiring recognition from recognized states that have a powerful collective interest in denying this. As former UN Secretary-General U Thant bluntly stated in 1970:

> As far as the question of secession of a particular section of a Member State is concerned, the United Nations' attitude is unequivocal. As an international organization, the United Nations has never accepted and does not accept and I do not believe it will ever accept the principle of secession of a part of its Member State.[2]

Forced reintegration

Statistically speaking, the most likely fate for an unrecognized state is defeat on the battlefield and reintegration into the parent. As well as the cases of forcible reintegration listed in Table 11.2 – Katanga, Biafra, Serbian Krajina, Chechnya, Tamil Eelam, and Anjouan – it should be noted that the Republika Srpska's reintegration into BiH (Bosnia and Herzegovina) was, if not forced, then at least, "strongly encouraged" by a NATO campaign of strategic bombing against the Republika Srpska's armed forces during 1995. In several other past cases, such as Kurdistan-Iraq, Bougainville, and East Timor, parent states made strong efforts to defeat their unruly children militarily, but were unable to deliver the decisive blow.

Though forced reintegration may be a plausible destination for unrecognized states, an obvious question mark hangs over its normative desirability as an option. Views on this will vary depending on how grave a threat to international stability one perceives successful secession to be. No less a figure than UN Secretary-General Boutros Boutros-Ghali (1992) observed that, "if every ethnic, religious or linguistic group claimed statehood, there would be no limit to fragmentation, and peace, security and economic well-being for all would become ever more difficult to achieve."[3] Presumably, a similar sort of "slippery slope" argument could be used to provide normative justification for the violent eradication of unrecognized states on the part of the parent. At a minimum, the violent eradication of an unrecognized state can serve as a powerful deterrent to other groups contemplating secession. Certainly after 11 September 2001, it helps if the parent state can present the struggle as one between the "legitimate" forces of a sovereign state and the "illegitimate" forces of terrorism. Once the armed forces of an unrecognized state are classified as terrorists, as was most obviously the case with the Tamil Tigers in Sri Lanka, the international community seems quite willing to tolerate their brutal suppression.

In practice, the international community of recognized states has several options for dealing with military conflict between unrecognized state and its parent. These range from collective military support for the parent, to collective support of varying kinds (including military) for the unrecognized state. Katanga represents the sole example of the former (Lemarchand 1962).[4] In this case, the UN's response to Katanga's declaration of independence in July 1960 was to pass UNSCR 161, which urged the withdrawal of all Belgian forces from Congo and authorized "all appropriate measures to prevent the occurrence of civil war in the Congo, including … the use of force, if necessary, in the last resort."[5] Although the resolution did not explicitly endorse offensive UN military operations, UN forces played a vital role in the final military defeat of Katanga's bid for independent status. The international community (or important elements of it) has also taken military action on occasion in defense of an unrecognized state. Notable here is NATO's military intervention against Serbia (FRY) in defense of Kosovo. In other cases, such as East Timor and Bougainville, the international community has played a role in mediating an end to violence between child and parent, but normally long after the worst of the violence has occurred. Indeed, the most common response of the international community has been to do nothing. Excepting Katanga, in all other cases listed as "forced reintegration into parent" in Table 11.2, the international community did more or less nothing to either support or impede the parent state. For the recognized states of the international community, there is an inherent tension raised by secession conflicts that pits a powerful vested interest in defending the territorial integrity of member states against the violent excesses that often accompany the military suppression of unrecognized states. For example, the Biafran secession that triggered the Nigerian civil war led to the deaths of an estimated one to three million people. Based on Milton Leitenberg's (2006) figures, a rough estimate of the total deaths associated with parental suppressions (or attempted suppressions) of the unrecognized states listed in Table 11.2 would be somewhere between four and five million. Combined with the atrocities (on both sides) that frequently accompany wars of secession/suppression – such as the use of chemical weapons against the Kurds of Iraq, or the ethnic cleansing of Serbs from Kraijina by Croatian forces – it seems reasonable to conclude that the human cost of preserving the territorial integrity of recognized states has been high, perhaps unreasonably so. As a solution to the problem of unrecognized states then, the option of forced reintegration may be plausible in many cases, but it is normatively problematic.

Voluntary reintegration

As options for unrecognized states, full independence may (or may not) be normatively desirable, but is practically implausible, while forced reintegration is plausible, but normatively problematic. The option of voluntary reintegration, via some form of deal that provides power-sharing and/or autonomy to the unrecognized state would seem to offer an important point of compromise. It is more normatively desirable than forced reintegration, in that it resolves the status of the unrecognized state without violence and bloodshed, but it is also more plausible than full independence because it does not disturb the territorial integrity of the international community of recognized states. It is, therefore, the only option that is likely to be unambiguously supported by most, if not all, members of the international community. Of course, the desirability of this option for the unrecognized state itself is an open question.

There is obviously a close affinity between power-sharing arrangements and group autonomy (federalism) as options for the alleviation of tension within deeply divided societies. The former is a means of sharing power *within* the institutions of the central government, and the latter a mechanism for sharing power *across* levels of government. The two approaches are most obviously united in the well-established concept of consociational democracy (for example, Lijphart 1968, 1969; O'Leary 2005). Yet the two are separable. Majoritarian federations, such as Canada, involve sharing power across levels of government, but may provide few, if any, formal arrangements for sharing power at the federal level. Conversely, in political systems such as Lebanon's, power-sharing norms and mechanisms are deeply entrenched at the central level, but the system is unitary rather than federal in nature.

Power-sharing

In ethnically divided societies, power-sharing arrangements are generally designed to provide one or more of the following: a sense of inclusion for previously excluded minorities; a share in the material benefits that flow from access to positions of political power; and, the capacity to exert influence over the political process, normally in the negative sense of being able to prevent deleterious changes to the status quo. This has clear relevance for today's unrecognized states, most of which are populated by an ethnic minority that has, in some way, suffered at the hands of the majority ethnicity. A broad range of possible arrangements are subsumed under the term power-sharing; power-sharing can be applied broadly or narrowly across the range of political and administrative positions; the degree to which power is shared can vary widely; and power can be shared either formally, or informally.

In terms of breadth of application, the principle of power-sharing can be applied to one specific part of the political infrastructure, or across the whole range of governing institutions (including the bureaucracy and security forces). Iraq's election law for the 2009 provincial council elections – which set aside six out of a total 440 seats on councils for various ethnic and religious minorities – offers an example of the former. The sole concession on the part of the Moldovan government to sharing power with its Gagauzian minority is the provision that the governor of Gagauzia has guaranteed (ex-offico) membership of the Moldovan cabinet. The Northern Ireland peace agreement (the so-called "Good Friday Agreement") and the political system of BiH are both examples of power being shared among communities across an extensive range of governing institutions.

In terms of the degree to which power is shared, there are two basic options – either power is shared proportionally, or it is shared equally. Under the former, institutional mechanisms are put in place to ensure that a minority that comprises, say, ten percent of the population, obtains ten percent of the seats in the legislative branch, ten percent of executive posts, and so on. Equal power-sharing, meanwhile, assigns political power equally among communal groups regardless of their respective numerical presence in the population. In practice, there are no existing cases of political systems in which pure equality of power-sharing is applied across all institutions. The closest to this ideal are probably the

Lebanese system – in which seats in parliament are assigned equally between Christians and Muslims, and the three key power positions (president, prime minister, and speaker) are shared among the three main communities – and the Bosnian system. In the Bosnian example, a three-person collegial presidency guarantees that each of the three communities achieves executive representation, and ethnic quotas determine the membership of the two chambers of the federal parliament. Of the 15 delegates to the House of Peoples, five are reserved for each group and a quorum requirement of nine delegates, providing there are at least three delegates in attendance from each group, means that three delegates of any ethnicity can effectively paralyze the chamber. A similar, though more limited veto provision applies in the House of Representatives. Ultimately, any proposed law can be rejected by a two-thirds majority in either of the parliaments of the two entities and there is no provision for overriding this veto.

Finally, power-sharing can be formal, in the sense of being legally or constitutionally mandated, or it can be informally based on norms of behavior that may (or may not) be deeply entrenched. Bosnia is a clear example of the former, as is the Belgian constitution's requirement that the council of ministers (cabinet) must contain equal numbers of French and Dutch speakers. The composition of Iraq's presidency council provides an example of informal power-sharing. Though nowhere mandated in the constitution, the three-member council has, since its inception, comprised a Kurd, a Sunni Arab, and a Shi'a Arab.

In the context of unrecognized states, the potential for power-sharing arrangements to smooth the way toward a peaceful reintegration into a parent may seem obvious. In many cases, the original grievance of an unrecognized state involves the exclusion of its population from participating meaningfully in the exercise of power at the level of the parent state. Moreover, many of the most trenchant criticisms of power-sharing on the basis of group identity are significantly less compelling in the context of unrecognized states than they may be in other cases. The argument, for example, that group-based power-sharing arrangements like consociational democracy serve to "lock in" group identity as the defining principle of politics may be valid, but it is also trivial in the context of unrecognized states. In most cases, the relationship between an unrecognized state and its parent has deteriorated significantly beyond the point at which other non-group based approaches, such as integrationism, are even remotely feasible. The "60–40" incentives problem identified by Horowitz (2002) as a major weakness of the consociational approach is also of only limited relevance. A parent state (representing the majority of the state's overall population) has a powerful incentive to concede generous power-sharing arrangements to an unrecognized state (the minority) because, presumably, it wishes to restore or retain its territorial integrity and is unable to achieve this by other means.[6]

There are, however, several issues that will likely complicate the forging and sustenance of any power-sharing agreement between an unrecognized state and its parent. Most obviously, the two parties are likely to diverge significantly on the details. Broadly speaking, the most preferred arrangement for an unrecognized state that is willing to rejoin a parent will be a formalized agreement that provides for *equal* power-sharing across the broadest possible range of governing institutions. All else being equal, the most preferred outcome for the parent state is likely to be the inverse of this – that is, an informal agreement for proportional power-sharing across a limited range of institutions. It seems reasonable to assume that some sort of compromise position is possible between these two extremes, the exact nature of which to be determined by the leverage each side can bring to the table. For example, one possible option is to allow the unrecognized state to be numerically over-represented in certain of the governing institutions. To take Abkhazia as an example; based on the 2003 census, Abkhazia's population constitutes approximately five percent of Georgia's total population. A seemingly generous power-sharing deal might set aside ten percent of the seats in the Georgian parliament for Abkhaz representatives, and even, perhaps, an equivalent percentage of guaranteed cabinet posts. While this may allow Abkhazia to enjoy a disproportionate share of the benefits accruing from access to positions of power, it clearly does not, of itself, allow Abkhazian representatives to block deleterious changes to the status quo. Most decisions in democratic political systems are made on the basis of simple majority vote, and a ten percent share of legislative and/or executive posts is obviously insufficient to block the will of the majority. This becomes particularly problematic in the context of the power-sharing agreement itself. The strongest protection for a power-sharing agreement between an unrecognized state and its parent is to embed it into the constitution of the parent. Assuming, as is almost always the case, that supermajorities are required to amend the constitution, this gives the agreement a degree of protection above and beyond that of a normal law. In Georgia's case, however, the constitution can be amended by a two-thirds majority vote in parliament, which cannot be blocked by Abkhazia's hypothetical ten percent of the vote. In the absence of subsidiary provisions, therefore, Abkhazia's share of power is insufficient to prevent the passage of harmful legislation, and, in any case, is perpetually susceptible to revocation by a two-thirds majority of the Georgian parliament.

The standard remedy for this is to endow minority groups with veto power. Limited vetoes – those that can be overturned by a supermajority – provide no protection for a small minority group confronted by a large coherent majority, unless the supermajority requirement is raised to absurdly high levels. In the hypothetical case above, the requirement for overturning an Abkhazian veto would have to be something in the order of 91 percent of parliament in order to offer real protection to the Abkhaz minority. Alternatively, a veto may be absolute, in which case it would seemingly provide clear protection to a minority, but would likely generate resentment on the part of the majority, and risks condemning the political system to permanent gridlock (as has been the case for much of the time in post-war BiH). Moreover, it is not clear that furnishing a minority group with absolute veto power does, in practice, provide the group with enhanced protection. Presumably any constitutionally specified power-sharing agreement that endows a minority group with absolute veto power can be changed by constitutional amendment. The only way to guarantee that a majority cannot use its numerical strength to revoke this veto power is to furnish the minority group with absolute veto power over constitutional amendments. In the case of Abkhazia, this would mean that approximately five percent of the population would have the capacity to block a constitutional amendment supported by 95 percent of Georgia's population. There is no political system in the world that requires anything close to this for constitutional amendments. The current system in Iraq, which *temporarily* allows the three Kurdish-dominated provinces to block a package of amendments to the 2006 constitution is probably the closest. Predictably, the Kurds have used this power as a weapon to push a range of other demands, such as control over Kirkuk, and the process has been totally gridlocked since mid-2008 (Anderson and Stansfield 2009).

In many ways, then, the core problem with power-sharing as part of a deal that peacefully reintegrates unrecognized states into their parents is one of numbers. The populations of unrecognized states are generally small relative to the overall population of their parent states. Using approximate population figures, Somaliland's population constitutes about 39 percent of Somalia's total, while Northern Cyprus contains roughly 25 percent of Cyprus' total. Other than these two, all of the populations of other recognized states constitute less than five percent of their parents' total. This has two implications for any power-sharing deal with a parent. First, assigning absolute veto power to groups representing, in some cases (Nagorno-Karabakh and South Ossetia, for example), less that two percent of the total population seems barely plausible. Second, absent absolute veto power, there is no way to *guarantee* that a parent state will not use the power of numbers to renege on a power-sharing deal at some point in the future. Mutual trust is an essential commodity in political deal-making, but it is a commodity in desperately short supply in the context of relations between an unrecognized state and a parent.

Group autonomy (federalism)

The terms "group autonomy" and federalism are not identical, but for current purposes they can be treated as synonymous. Federalism is among the most frequently advocated approaches to dealing with states that suffer deep divisions along ethnic lines, and a significant body of literature has emerged to champion its merits. Federalism, as Elazar (1993) notes, "is a genus that includes several species," and federations are, by some distance, the most common species of the genus. Most definitions of the term "federation" share common features – at least two levels of government (federal and regional), with separate powers or competencies allocated to each level via a written constitution (though powers may also be shared between levels). In meaningful federations, the constitutional division of powers between levels cannot be altered unilaterally by either level of government and the consent of both levels is required, usually via constitutional amendment. Beyond this, there is little consensus regarding specifics, indeed almost every aspect of federalism is a topic of controversy.[7] It is almost inevitable that any deal to reintegrate unrecognized states peacefully into parents will require some form of federal arrangement.

The two most important issues to address in the design of any federal system are; how are the subunits to be defined?; and, how should powers be shared across levels of government – in short, who gets to govern themselves, and to what extent? The first of these questions leads into a debate that is not entirely relevant for current purposes. In the context of ethnically divided states, there is a fundamental difference of opinion between scholars who advocate a "territorial" form of federalism and those who champion "ethnic" (or plurinational) federalism. In the former, the boundary lines of subunits are drawn to maximize the ethnic heterogeneity of the subunit populations, whereas in the latter, subunit boundary lines are designed to maximize ethnic homogeneity. In the context of the voluntary reintegration of an unrecognized state into its parent, the subunit is already territorially defined, and it is unthinkable that the leaders of the unrecognized state would consent to having its borders redefined to any significant degree. The starting point for analysis, then, is that the identity of at least one of the subunits in any prospective federation is set in stone. With respect to the definition of subunits, therefore, the only remaining issue to address is whether the unrecognized state is the *only* entity (or one among few) to enjoy a federal relationship with the parent, or whether it is one among many. In the former case, the unrecognized state federates with an otherwise unitary parent to form an asymmetrical federation; in the latter, it becomes one among several autonomous subunits in a fully-fledged federal system, either asymmetrical or symmetrical. Looking at the list of parents of today's unrecognized states, it is clear that none is currently organized as a system-wide federation, but that several already have autonomy arrangements in place with other individual subunits – Moldova with Gagauzia, Georgia with Adjara, and China with Hong Kong and Macao. In practice, therefore, reintegrating unrecognized states into parents via the federal option seems certain to result in asymmetrical federations. As defined by John McGarry (2005), asymmetrical federalism exists when "one part of a country enjoys a formally distinct degree of autonomy from the rest." Further, according to McGarry, asymmetrical federalism

> can occur in federations, when one or more of the federal units have a distinct status, or in (partly decentralized) unitary states, when only one part of the state enjoys autonomy or when it enjoys a distinct type of autonomy.

This latter version of asymmetrical federalism (where one, or a small number of subunits are federated with an otherwise unitary state) is sometimes termed a *federacy*, and appears to be the option of choice for most of those formerly unrecognized states that have reintegrated with parents. Of the four examples of reintegrated unrecognized states, only Republika Srpska is unambiguously part of a symmetrical, system-wide federation. Gagauzia and Bougainville are both distinct autonomous units within an otherwise unitary parent, while Iraq's status is ambiguous. Though constitutionally defined as a "federation," Iraq functions in practice as a de facto federacy. The basic building blocks of the Iraqi "federal" system are the 18 governorates; according to Article 119 of the Iraqi constitution, these may vote to become regions either individually or collectively and thereby acquire enhanced autonomy. Technically, governorates are also supposed to exercise autonomy (though at a lesser level than regions) as part of a system-wide federation, but in practice, the scope for autonomy is severely limited. The Baghdad government controls the revenue stream to governorates, governorates are not allowed to write their own constitutions, the federal government determines the timing of elections and the electoral system used, and the Iraqi parliament can vote to remove the governors of governorates from office. The idea that governorates are meaningfully self-governing under the Iraqi system is, therefore, technically true, but empirically false.

In terms of the division of competences between federal and subunit governments, there is obviously huge variation possible in both theory and practice. Of the reintegrated unrecognized states, Gagauzia is, by some distance, the least autonomous. Gagauzia's autonomous status is detailed in three separate documents – the Moldovan constitution, the Moldovan government's "Law on the Special Status of Gagauzia" (1994), and the "Code of Gagauzia." In terms of legal significance, the Law is defined as an "organic law" which, theoretically grants it the same legal status as the Moldovan constitution. It seems clear from the terms of all three documents, however, that the provisions of Moldovan constitution take precedence over those of the other two in cases of conflict (Venice Commission 1998). The real problem with all three documents is that they do not clearly articulate the power divisions between the Moldovan government and that of Gagauzia. The Law allows the Gagauzian People's Assembly to adopt laws in a range of areas, including education, "taxation activities," and "economy," but does not define these as exclusive competences of the Gagauzian government. By contrast, the Moldovan constitution bestows powers on the central government that are vague and potentially extensive. Along with a range of specific powers, Article 66 of the constitution empowers the Moldovan parliament "to approve the main directions of the state's internal and external policy" (Article 66, d), "to provide legislative interpretations and insure the legislative unity of regulations throughout the country," and "to exercise other powers, as provided for by the Constitution and the Law." It is not clear what any of these provisions really mean in practice, but they seem to provide ample scope for the Moldovan government to restrict the autonomy of Gagauzia. With respect to Gagauzia's autonomy, the Moldovan constitution contains only one reference, and even here the reference is indirect.[8] In reality, therefore, Gagauzia's autonomy seems limited to having the right to elect its own three-branch government, the power to adopt the paraphernalia of nationhood (flag, coat of arms, and so on), and perhaps most importantly, the right of "external self-determination" in the event of a "change of the status of the Republic of Moldova as an independent state."

In contrast to the meager grant of autonomy to Gagauzia, the Autonomous Region of Bougainville enjoys extensive, perhaps unrivalled, autonomy in its relations with the government of Papua New Guinea (PNG). The broad outlines of Bougainville's autonomy are contained in the Peace Agreement, and then fleshed out in the lengthy (241 articles) Constitution of Bougainville. Unlike Gagauzia's arrangement with Moldova, the powers of the PNG government are specifically listed in Article 51 of the Peace Agreement; all other powers are reserved for the government of Bougainville. Bougainville's list of reserved powers is extensively detailed in Schedule 4 of the Bougainville constitution, and includes "trade, industry and commerce," education, language, health, mining, natural resources, and "land, sea and air transport." The Peace Agreement also grants Bougainville the power to regulate foreign investment, and, critically, control over internal security (though not national defense). Strikingly, the Peace Agreement also grants Bougainville the right to hold a referendum on independence within a period of between ten and fifteen years.

The Kurdistan Region of Iraq occupies a more ambiguous place within the Iraqi political system, partly because the Iraqi constitution is vague (even internally contradictory) and partly because the contents of the constitution itself are still being disputed. Article 110 of the Iraqi constitution lists the exclusive powers of the federal government, while Article 114 lists competences shared between federal and subunit governments. Article 115, meanwhile, states that, "all powers not stipulated in the exclusive powers of the federal government belong to the authorities of the regions and governorates that are not organized in a region." This seemingly clear statement of a reserved powers doctrine is controversial because the management of oil and gas resources is not listed as an exclusive power of the federal government in Article 110. Reasonably enough, the Kurds have interpreted this to mean that regions have the power to manage oil and gas on their territory. In addition to those powers not assigned to the federal government, regions also have a range of other powers, including the power to draft constitutions, the right to diplomatic representation abroad, and control over internal security for the region. Further, Article 121 (2) states that in cases of conflict between federal and regional law in an area outside the exclusive powers of the federal government, the regional government "shall have the right to amend the application of the national legislation within that region." Once again, this strongly suggests that regional law trumps federal law in the management of oil and gas. Depending on how the Iraqi constitution is interpreted, therefore, the Kurdistan Region can have its own government, its own army (thinly disguised as internal security forces) and can manage its own extensive reserves of oil and gas. If this interpretation were universally accepted within Iraq, the Kurdistan Region would be one of the more powerful federated entities anywhere; but this interpretation is disputed, notably with respect to the management of oil and gas, and the basic legitimacy of the constitution itself is questioned by many.

Finally, Republika Srpska (RS) forms one of two constituent entities in the fully federated system of BiH. The basic division of competences between the federal government and the two entities was detailed in BiH's constitution that formed Annex 4 of the 1995 Dayton Peace Accord (DPA). Aside from provision allowing the entities "the right to establish special parallel relationships with neighboring states," and the de facto problem that each of the three communities was allowed to maintain its army, if only temporarily, there was nothing particularly unusual or radical about the division of powers between the federal government and the entities. The powers of the federal government are "expressly assigned" in Article III (1) and include standard responsibilities such as foreign policy and the regulation of inter-entity transportation. All powers not listed in this article are reserved for the entities, including internal security. In terms of the division of powers, the federal government of BiH is not notably weaker than the central governments of many other federations. The key difference lies in the elaborate power-sharing mechanisms in place at the federal level that have allowed representatives of the RS to block the strengthening of federal (inter-entity) institutions in the face of determined efforts by Bosniaks to centralize power at the federal level. The limited progress made to date to strengthen federal institutions at the expense of the RS's autonomy has been largely due to the actions of the Office High Representative (OHR). Created as part of the DPA, the OHR has broad powers to "maintain close contact with the Parties to promote their full compliance with all civilian aspects of the peace settlement," and "to ensure the efficient implementation of the civilian aspects of the peace settlement." The DPA's stipulation that the OHR has "the final authority in theater regarding interpretation of this Agreement on the civilian implementation of the peace settlement" means that, in practice, the OHR has been able to exercise dictatorial powers over any individual or entity that is judged (by the OHR) to be impeding the implementation of the DPA. Assessing the extent of the RS's autonomy within the BiH's federal system is, therefore, complicated. Its autonomy probably depends less on constitutional allocations of power and more on its capacity to block the strengthening of federal institutions at the center. At the same time, the RS's autonomy is severely compromised by the overarching authority of the OHR.

This brief assessment of the four examples of unrecognized states that peacefully reintegrated with parents suggests that, unlike power-sharing, some form of federal arrangement appears to be an essential part of any peace deal. The case of Gagauzia excepted, the degree of autonomy demanded by an unrecognized state as the price for reintegration is also likely to be high; but the case of the Peace Agreement between PNG and Bougainville, and, to a lesser extent, the Kurds with Iraq, illustrate this need not be an insurmountable problem. Though a number of asymmetrical federations have collapsed over the years, many more appear to have withstood the test of time (McGarry 2005). Moreover, in the context of unrecognized states, the starting point is not an entity that seeks greater autonomy within a unified state, but an entity that already exercises de facto independence from its parent. Hence the argument that granting high levels of autonomy to an entity risks encouraging secessionist ambitions is not relevant because the status quo is an entity that has already effectively seceded.

A deeper problem with any federal arrangement that forms part of a deal to reintegrate an unrecognized state is similar to the problem with power-sharing arrangements. Put simply, what guarantee does an unrecognized state have that an autonomy agreement in the present will not be unilaterally revoked by the majority at some point in the future? In the case of Gagauzia, for example, the Law that details Gagauzia's autonomy can be amended by a three-fifths majority of the Moldovan parliament. Similarly, the standard procedure for amending the Iraqi constitution requires a two-thirds majority in the Iraqi parliament and the people's approval in a referendum. The Kurds have never controlled enough seats in the parliament to block a constitutional amendment and nor are they likely to in the future. In an effort to address this problem, the Kurds insisted on the inclusion in the constitution of Article 126 (4), which forbids constitutional amendments that take away powers from the regions without the consent of the regional government concerned. The obvious problem with provisions such as these is that they too are susceptible to amendment (or deletion) by a determined supermajority.[9]

This problem is especially acute for an autonomous subunit in an otherwise unitary state. In a fully federal state, there are powerful forces with a vested interest in protecting the autonomy of subunits against federal government encroachment; frequently these interests have institutional protection in the form of powerful upper legislative chambers with veto power over legislation. In a unitary state, the federated region is devoid of natural allies to help protect against erosions of autonomy on the part of the federal government. Assuming that an unrecognized state has an interest in reintegrating with its parent, the main problem with this option is that the institutional mechanisms that are likely to be required as part of the deal – autonomy and/or power-sharing – are vulnerable to revocation at a later date. As the Kurds learned to their cost in 1970, a weak central government that makes major concessions in the present may have few incentives to abide by the terms of the deal once its strength has been regained.

Evaluating the options

To summarize briefly, of the three options described above – full independence, forced reintegration, and voluntary reintegration – only the third would appear to qualify as both normatively desirable *and* plausible as a destination for unrecognized states. But if full independence is deeply implausible for most unrecognized states, why have today's unrecognized states not opted for the least bad of the remaining two options? Or to ask the question another way, what is it that prevents unrecognized states from having to choose between forced and voluntary reintegration? In some cases, the answer is obvious. Palestine has no parent, the paternity of the SADR's parent is itself unrecognized, and Somaliland has nothing viable into which to reintegrate. For the others, though, there is something that enables the status quo to endure. King (2001) suggests that "statelike entities" persist in Eurasia due to mutual self-interest on the part of individuals in both entity and parent. As King argues, "In many cases both the separatists and their erstwhile opponents in central governments benefit from the untaxed trade and production flowing through the former war zones," and further, that these conflicts have reached a "dark version of Pareto efficiency" in which a peaceful settlement cannot be reached without making key interest groups on both sides worse off (525–6). Kolstø (2006), meanwhile, explains the "sustainability" of unrecognized states as the product of five factors – nation-building, military power, the weakness of the parent, the role of the international community, and the existence of an "external patron" (733). The critical role of an external patron, or protector state, in sustaining the status of unrecognized states is also recognized by a number of other scholars and is worthy of further consideration.[10] Table 11.3 replicates the list of post-World War II unrecognized states, past and present, along with the fate of each and the identity of a protector state, if one existed.

The data in Table 11.3 reveal some striking, though not altogether surprising patterns. If "protector state" is defined as an external power that is willing to defend an unrecognized state against a military assault from a parent, the first clear pattern is that, with the marginal exception of Katanga, no unrecognized state that has been forcibly reintegrated into a parent has had a protector. This does not necessarily mean that the absence of a protector inevitably leads to

Table 11.3 Protectors of unrecognized states since World War II

Unrecognized state	*Parent state*	*Outcome*	*Protector*
Katanga	Congo	Forced reintegration into parent	None (Belgium initially)
Biafra	Nigeria	Forced reintegration into parent	None
Serbian Krajina	Croatia	Forced reintegration into parent	None (Serbia initially)
Chechnya	Russia	Forced reintegration into parent	None
Tamil Eelam	Sri Lanka	Forced reintegration into parent	None
Anjouan	Comoros	Forced reintegration into parent	None
Gagauzia	Moldova	Voluntary reintegration into parent	None
Republika Srpska	BiH	"Voluntary" reintegration into parent	None (Serbia initially)
KRG-Iraq	Iraq	Voluntary reintegration into parent	USA, UK, (France)
Bougainville	PNG	Voluntary reintegration into parent	None
Eritrea	Ethiopia	Independence	None
East Timor	Indonesia	Independence	None
Montenegro	FRY	Independence	None
Kosovo	Serbia	Contested independence	NATO
Transnistria	Moldova	Undetermined	Russia
Nagorno Karabakh	Azerbaijan	Undetermined	Armenia
Abkhazia	Georgia	Undetermined	Russia
South Ossetia	Georgia	Undetermined	Russia
Turk Cyprus	Cyprus	Undetermined	Turkey
Palestine	N/A	Undetermined	None
Somaliland	Somalia	Undetermined	None
Taiwan	China	Undetermined	USA
SADR	Morocco?	Undetermined	Algeria?

forced reintegration. Bougainville, East Timor, and Montenegro are all examples of unrecognized states that met with different fates, despite lacking a protector. A related pattern is that no parent has successfully forced the reintegration of an unrecognized state that is under external protection. This would, by definition, require a parent to defeat a protector state on the battlefield, and presumably, a protector would be unlikely to offer protection if it were militarily weaker than the parent. Again this may seem obvious, but it does have one important implication. If a powerful protector is willing to defend an unrecognized state against its parent, then forced reintegration is not an option, and the unrecognized state does not need to confront the choice between forced or voluntary reintegration. The status quo becomes a viable alternative option. It is currently a viable option for six of the world's nine remaining unrecognized states. The corollary of this is that, where powerful protectors are present, no attempt to resolve the status of the unrecognized state is likely to succeed without the support of the protector.

This does not necessarily impose an additional obstacle in the path of a peaceful settlement, however. In fact, it might best be seen as an opportunity.

Internationalizing frozen conflicts

If an unrecognized state prefers to fight to the death rather than be peacefully reintegrated into a parent, or a protector state prefers the status quo to resolving the status of the protected state permanently, then there is probably no solution to the problem. If neither condition holds, there are possibilities. A federal arrangement that grants significant autonomy to the reintegrating state is essential to any peaceful settlement. Beyond this, power-sharing arrangements may be desirable for both parties, but from the perspective of the reintegrating state, they are only *necessary* in so far as they allow the state to safeguard its autonomy against future revocation by the parent. As discussed above, it is extremely difficult in practice to guarantee political arrangements by embedding them in the documents of the parent state. Laws and constitutions can always be amended without the consent of the minority. One possible solution to this is to embed arrangements in a higher level document that transcends the parent state. Embedding political arrangements in a document that has the status of international law, for example, provides an extra layer of protection for the reintegrating state.

There are numerous real-world examples of domestic political arrangements (power-sharing and/or autonomy) being internationally "guaranteed" in this way. The relationship between Finland and the Åland Islands provides an exemplar case of a durable, and successful, federacy arrangement.[11] In 1917, over 90 percent of the Swedish-speaking Ålanders voted to secede from Finland and reunify with Sweden. The dispute was ultimately resolved by a decision of the Council of the League of Nations in 1921, in which sovereignty over the islands was awarded to Finland, but Finland was also required to codify certain guarantees to the Ålanders aimed at "the preservation of the Swedish language in the schools, at the maintenance of the landed property in the hands of the Islanders … and at ensuring the appointment of the Governor who will possess the confidence of the population."[12] These guarantees were subsequently embedded in an Act of Autonomy, the most recent version of which entered into force in 1993. Less important, for current purposes, than the degree of autonomy granted by the act is the legal status it enjoys in the eyes of the international community. During negotiations over Finland's accession to the EU, for example, the Finnish government referred to the "internationally recognized status" of Åland's autonomy and requested that the terms of the Accession Treaty not be applied to the islands without the assent of the islanders in a referendum. In turn, the EU's "common position" on the issue recognized the "special status that the Åland Islands enjoy under international law," and accepted that the terms of the treaty would not apply without the consent of the islands' population.[13] Experts are divided on the issue of whether the 1921 agreement between Sweden and Finland rises to the level of a binding international treaty, but there is a general consensus "that the international status of Åland has won general recognition within the international community," and that Åland's autonomy is "deeply rooted in international customary law" (Hannikainen 1997).

Other prominent examples include the Northern Ireland peace process and the settlement of the status of South Tyrol. The 1998 peace agreement in Northern Ireland that outlined details of political power-sharing arrangements for the two main communities (Catholic and Protestant) was folded into the provisions of an international treaty signed by governments of both Ireland and the United Kingdom. In theory, violations of the agreement, therefore, can be arbitrated by a relevant international legal institution, such as the European Court of Justice. This provides both communities in Northern Ireland an extra layer of protection above and beyond the terms of the agreement itself. In the case of South Tyrol, the status of this disputed majority German-speaking Italian province was initially hammered out in the Paris Peace Treaty of 1946, which incorporates the terms of a prior agreement between the Italian and Austrian governments (the Gruber-Degasperi Agreement [GDA]). The GDA granted, among other things, autonomous legislative and executive powers to the province, equality of rights among language groups, and special provisions to protect the ethnic character of South Tyrol's German population. The failure of the Italian government to implement the terms of the agreement led to significant and, at times, violent unrest among South Tyrol's German-speaking population during the 1950s and 1960s and prompted the Austrian government to intervene on behalf of the South Tyroleans at the United Nations in 1960. This led to the tripartite "package" agreement of 1969 (endorsed by the Italian and Austrian governments and the South Tyrolean People's Party [SVP]), and, subsequently, an enhanced Autonomy Statute of 1972. The package outlined the terms of South Tyrol's autonomy and the sequence in which these were to be implemented (the "Operational Calendar"), to culminate in a formal declaration to the United Nations on the part of the Austrian government (with the approval of the SVP) that the conflict had been resolved. This declaration was duly submitted in 1992. The Operational Calendar included a provision that required any dispute resulting from the implementation of the package to be resolved at the International Court of Justice (ICJ) in the Hague, and in 1992, the Italian government finally acknowledged that the terms of the package transcended domestic law. In effect, the autonomy of South Tyrol and the various rights granted to its inhabitants had been internationalized. According to Medda-Windischer (2008), the linkage of the package to various international organizations "was indeed a guarantee, especially for the future, that the South Tyrol issue was not merely a domestic affair." The "international anchoring" of the South Tyrol dispute was sufficient to persuade a large majority of the SVP to endorse the settlement "provided that an international guarantee was included" (Medda-Windischer 2008: 30).

These three cases are by no means unique. Table 11.4 provides a number of examples of cases where domestic arrangements (power-sharing, autonomy, the right to self-determination, and so on) are, or have been, provided with what Stefan Wolff (2008a) terms "hard" international guarantees.

There are probably many plausible ways to internationalize a deal to reintegrate an unrecognized state into a parent, but ideally any deal will involve both protector and parent state. An international treaty between the two, as in the cases of South Tyrol and Northern Ireland, would be the obvious vehicle. The reintegrating state obtains a deal that cannot be unilaterally revoked by the parent and a guarantee of enduring protection of its status from the protector; the parent reintegrates its wayward offspring, thereby restoring its sovereignty and territorial integrity; the international community gets to eliminate a latent or actual

Table 11.4 Examples of domestic arrangements with "hard" international guarantees

Territory	*International guarantee*
South Tyrol	Treaty between Italy and Austria guaranteeing status
Northern Ireland	Treaty between UK and Republic of Ireland guaranteeing terms of "Good Friday Agreement"
Hong Kong	Treaty between China and UK ("Joint Declaration") guaranteeing special status of Hong Kong
Macao	Treaty between China and Portugal ("Joint Declaration") guaranteeing special status of Macao
Bosnia and Herzegovina	DPA (containing BiH's constitution) signed by heads of state of UK, USA, France, and Russia
Andorra	"Condominium" – sovereignty shared by France and Spain; rights and liberties guaranteed by both
East Timor	1999 Treaty ("Agreement") between Portugal and Indonesia guaranteeing self-determination for East Timorese
Åland Islands	Agreement between Finland and Sweden guaranteeing autonomy of islands

"black spot" whilst avoiding the potentially negative consequences of recognizing independence; finally, the protector state gets a guaranteed influence over the future status of the protected state without incurring the international approbation that typically accompanies protection of unrecognized states. On paper, this is a win–win solution. In practice, of course, the scale of the potential pitfalls and problems should not be underestimated. Most obviously, this approach is not directly applicable to unrecognized states that lack a parent and/or a protector; but in these cases (Palestine and Somaliland, for example) it is presumably not beyond the wit of the international community to devise alternative international guarantees. Nor can this approach necessarily guarantee success. Notably, a tripartite agreement among the UK, Greece, and Turkey guaranteeing power-sharing arrangements in post-independence Cyprus had fallen apart within three years.

It also needs noting that this approach assumes that all parties are interested in finding a peaceful solution. However, the unrecognized state may be adamantly opposed to reintegration with a parent on any terms; the parent may be unwilling to tolerate an arrangement that gives an adversarial protector a guaranteed say in what it views as a matter of internal concern; and the protector may prefer the prevailing status quo because it provides greater leverage over the parent. These are serious potential problems. Nonetheless, if resolving the status of unrecognized states were easy, then presumably, there would be no unrecognized states. Of the three possible destinations for unrecognized states, general recognition remains extremely implausible in most cases, and forced reintegration by the parent is normatively problematic and, in any case, implausible in the presence of a powerful protector. This leaves voluntary reintegration as the one viable alternative to the status quo. If in the end, as King (2001) suggests, all parties prefer the status quo to a peaceful settlement, then the problem of unrecognized states is inherently insoluble.

Notes

1 For example, the UK's foreign secretary, David Miliband, described Kosovo as "unique" because "for nine years there's been a UN protectorate within the independent country of Serbia" ("Kosovo case unique, says Miliband." BBC News, available at http://news.bbc.co.uk/2/hi/uk_news/politics/7252212.stm). Why this in any way justifies recognizing Kosovo as an independent state, in apparent violation of UNSCR 1244, which reaffirmed "the commitment of all Member States to the sovereignty and territorial integrity of the Federal Republic of Yugoslavia" was left unclear.

2 UN Monthly Chronicle, 1970, No. 2, p. 2; quoted in Geldenhuys (2009).

3 Boutros-Ghali was certainly not condoning the use of violence to suppress secessionist movements; indeed his "solution" was to urge a "commitment to human rights with a special sensitivity to those of minorities, whether ethnic, religious, social or linguistic," in order to enhance the situation of minorities as well as the stability of states.

4 Repbublika Srpska, which was subjected to both military and political pressure to come to the peace table, might also qualify as an example here.

5 Full text available at http://daccess-dds-ny.un.org/doc/RESOLUTION/GEN/NR0/171/68/IMG/NR017168.pdf?OpenElement.

6 Another problem that is sometimes used to attack power-sharing arrangements in ethnically divided societies is how to identify the groups to be included in any power-sharing arrangement. This is obviously not an issue in the case of unrecognized states because the identity of the group is already clearly defined.

7 The literature on various elements of federalism is extensive. Notable examples include: Elazar (1987); Watts (1999); King (1982); Franck (1966); Earle (1968); Duchacek (1970); and Riker (1964). For a useful summary article of the state of the discipline, see Elazar (1993).

8 Article 111 states, "The places on the left bank of the Nistru river, as well as certain other places in the south of the Republic of Moldova may be granted special forms of autonomy according to special statutory provisions of organic law."

9 Whether constitutional articles that state themselves to be "unamendable" have a deeper status than other articles in a constitution is a complex issue that lies beyond the scope of this paper. Suffice it to say, it seems implausible that article 126 (4) would be perceived by many Arabs in Iraq as a serious impediment to the drive for recentralization. For a detailed treatment of the status of the US constitution's two "unamendable" provisos, see Linder (1981).

10 See Caspersen's chapter in this volume.

11 The Åland Islands were part of Sweden until after the Russo-Swedish War of 1808–1809, when Sweden was forced to relinquish control over the islands and Finland to the Russian Empire. The islands remained under Russian control, governed as part of the Grand Duchy of Finland until the collapse of the Empire in 1917.

12 "Decision of the Council of the League of Nations on the Åland Islands Including Sweden's Protest," September 1921. Available at www.kultur.aland.fi/kulturstiftelsen/traktater/eng_fr/1921a_en.htm.

13 "Finland's Request and EU Common Position on Åland at the Accession of Finland to the European Union," 21 February 1994. Available at www.kultur.aland.fi/kulturstiftelsen/traktater/eng_fr/1994a_en.htm.

Appendix: maps of unrecognized states

Map 1 Georgia, Abkhazia.

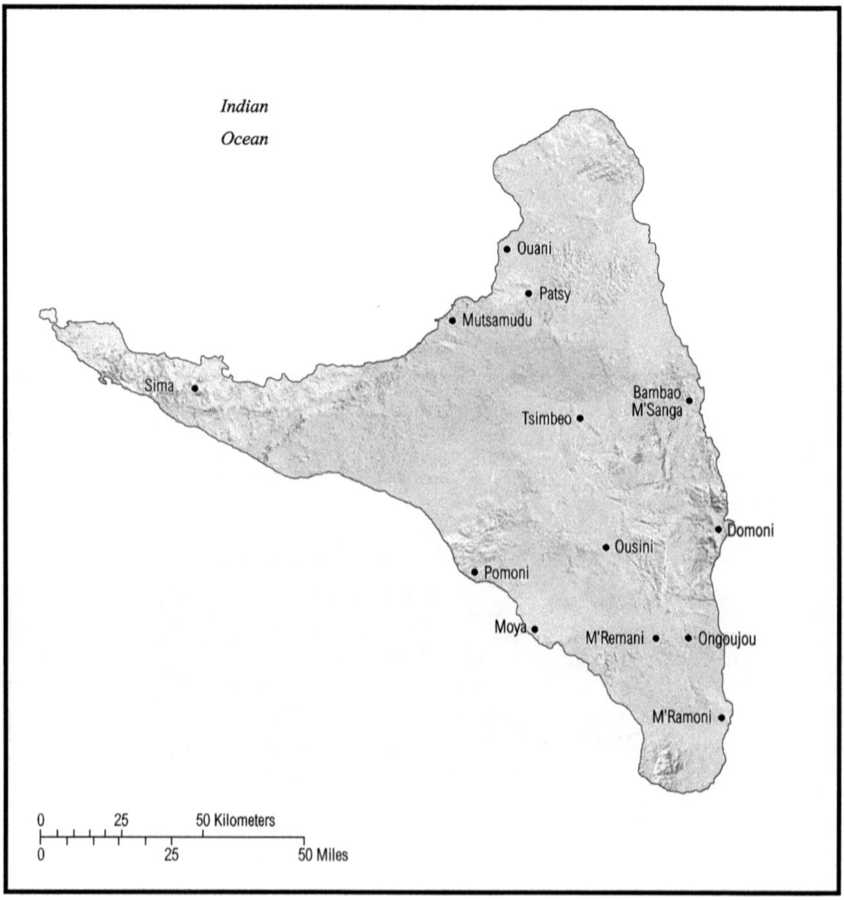

Map 2 Comoros, Anjouan.

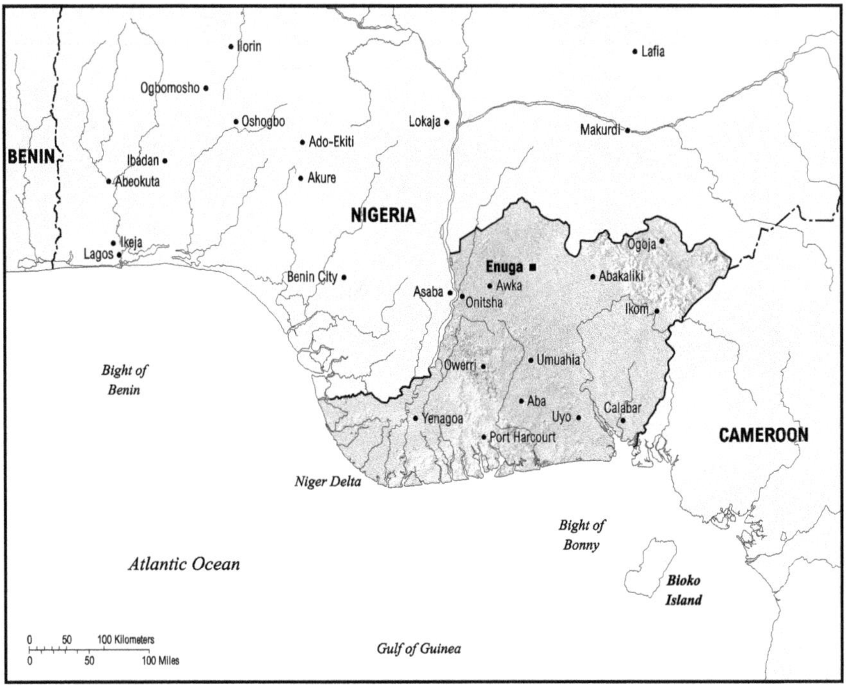

Map 3 Nigeria, Biafra.

Map 4 Papua New Guinea, Bougainville.

Map 5 Russia, Chechnya.

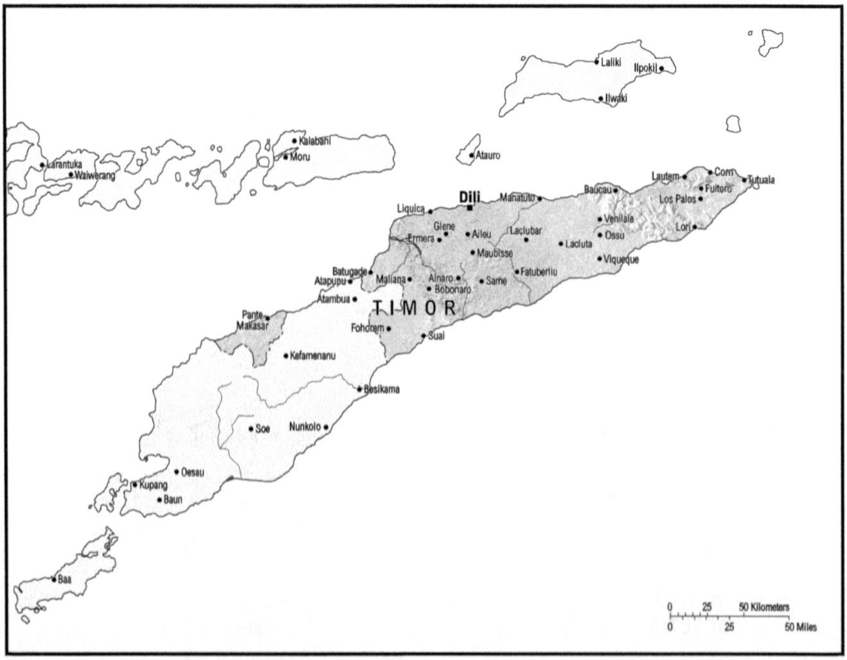

Map 6 Indonesia, East Timor.

Map 7 Ethiopia, Eritrea.

Map 8 Moldova, Gagauzia.

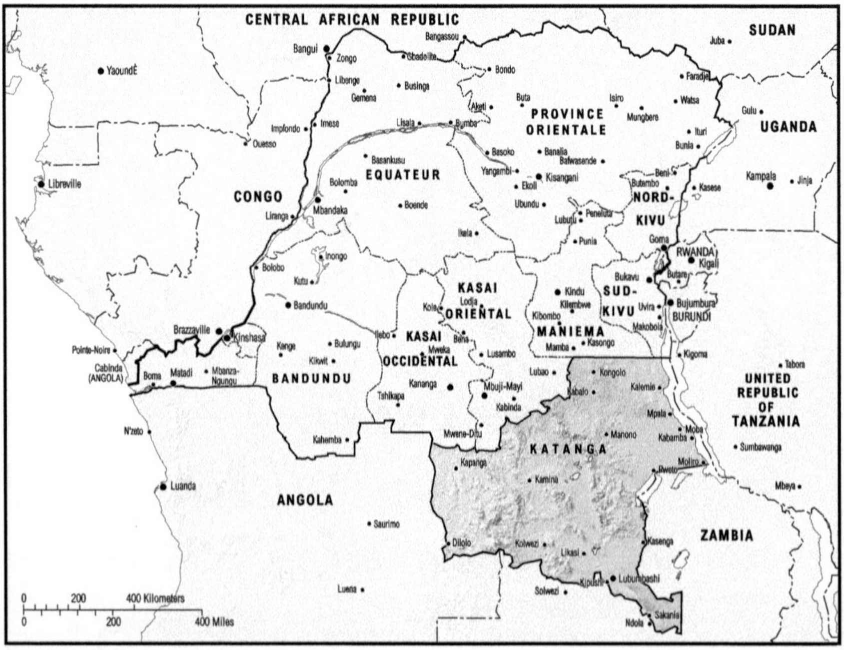

Map 9 Congo, Katanga.

Map 10 Serbia, Kosovo.

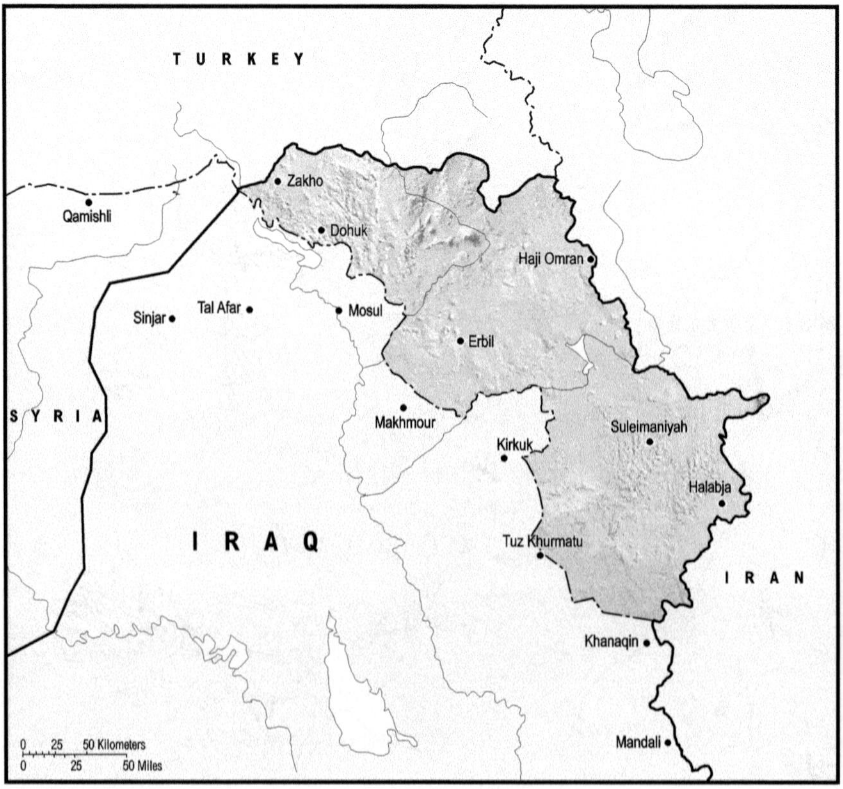

Map 11 Iraq, Kurdistan Region.

Map 12 Federal Republic of Yugoslavia, Montenegro.

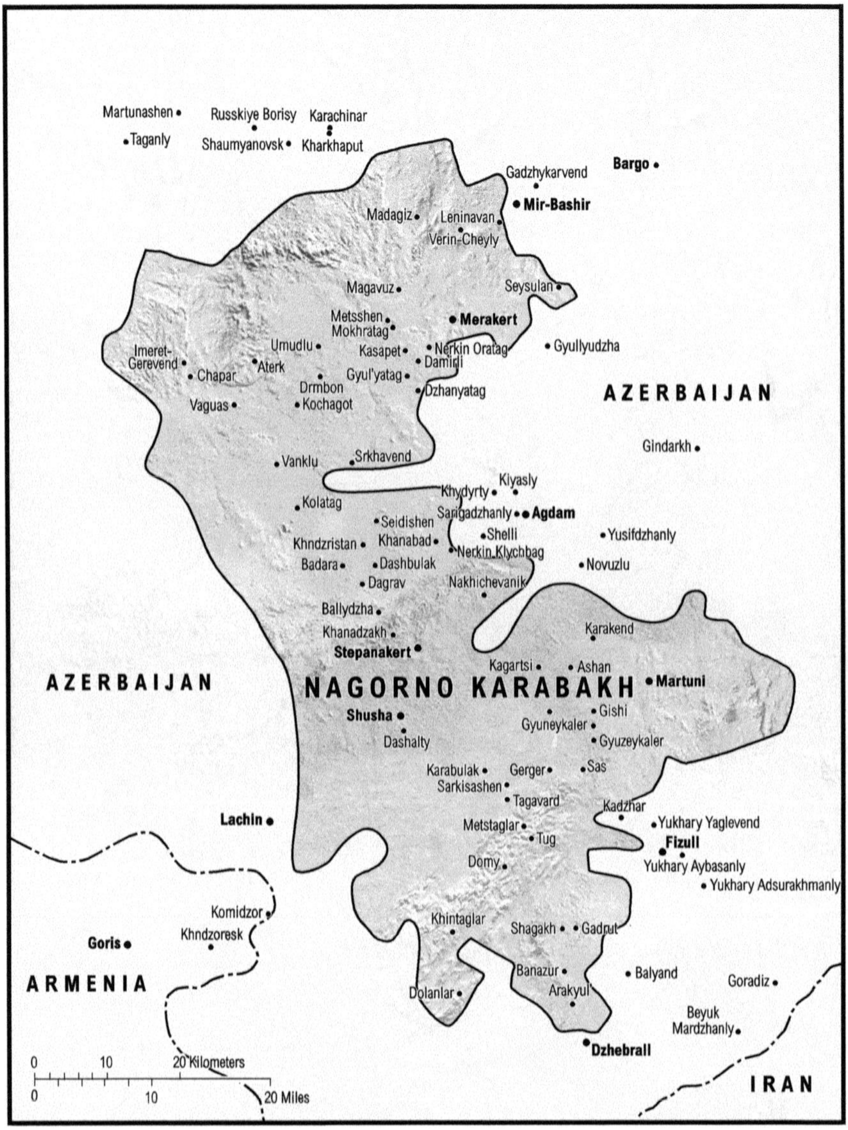

Map 13 Azerbaijan, Nagorno Karabakh.

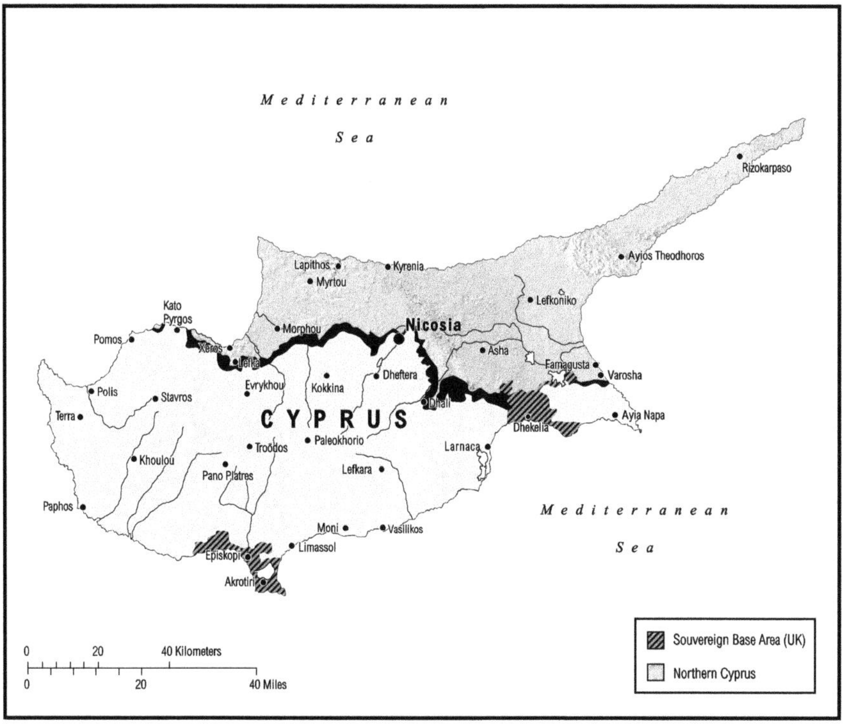

Map 14 Cyprus, Northern Cyprus.

Map 15 Bosnia, Republika Srpska.

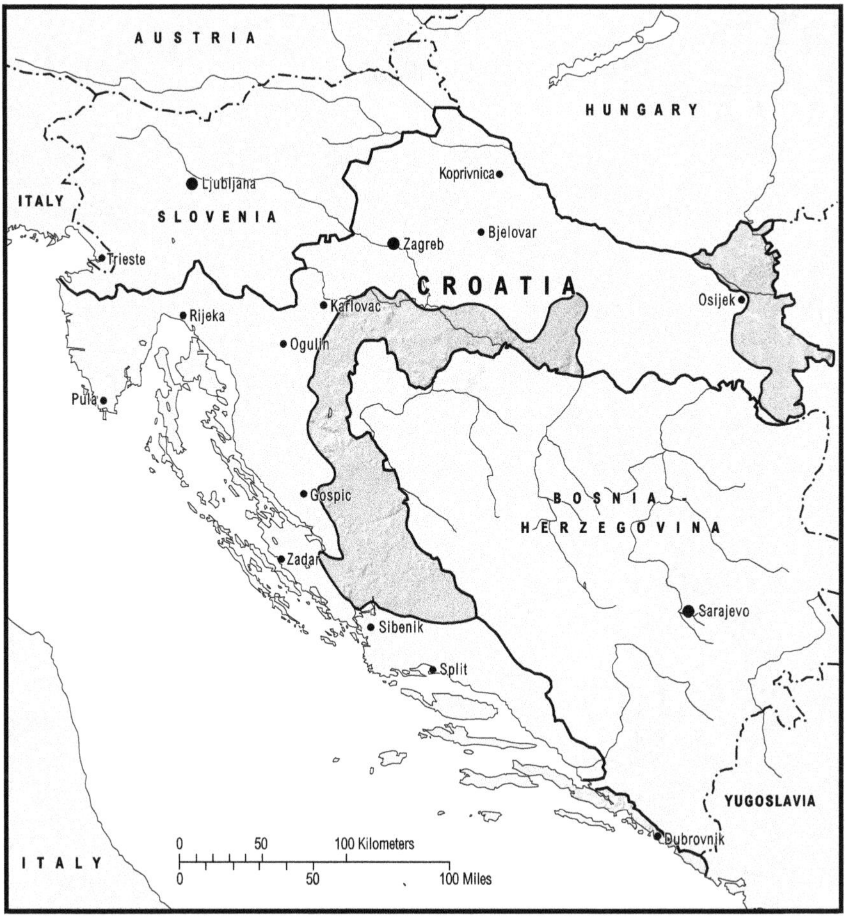

Map 16 Croatia, Republika Srpska Krajina.

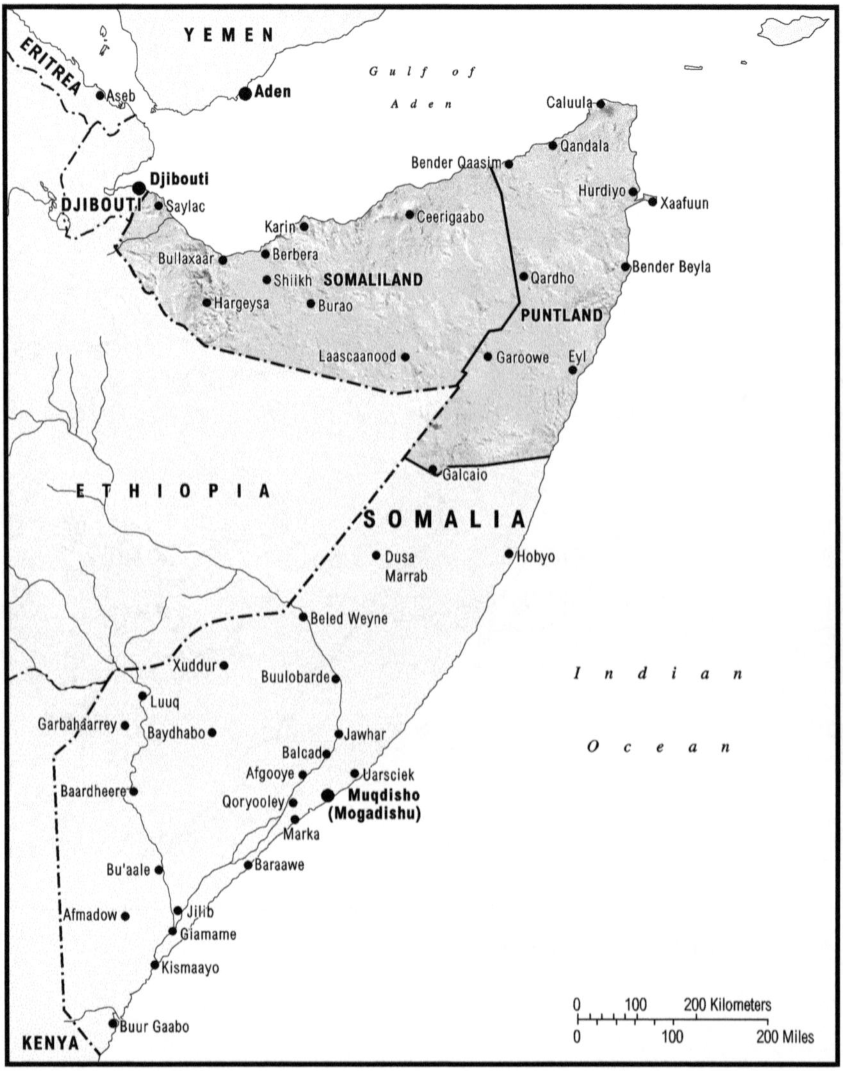

Map 17 Somalia, Puntland and Somaliland.

Map 18 Georgia, South Ossetia.

Map 19 China, Taiwan.

Map 20 Sri Lanka, Proposed Tamil Eelan.

Map 21 Moldova, Transnistria.

Bibliography

Aalberts, T.E. (2004) 'The Sovereignty Game States Play: (Quasi-) States in the International Order', *International Journal for the Semiotics of Law*, Vol. 17: 245–57.

Adler-Nissen, R. and Gammeltoft-Hansen, T. (eds) (2008) *Sovereignty Games: Instrumentalizing State Sovereignty in Europe and Beyond*, London: Palgrave Macmillan.

Agha, H., Feldman, S., Khalidi, A., and Schiff, Z. (2003) *Track – II Diplomacy: Lessons from the Middle East*, London: MIT Press.

Agnew, J. and Corbridge, S. (1995) *Mastering Space: Hegemony, Territory, and International Political Economy*, New York: Routledge.

Ahmedbeyli, S. and Beglarian, A. (2008) 'Karabakh Truce Breaks Down', *Caucasus Reporting Service*, 20 November, Institute of War and Peace Reporting.

Akçakoca, A., Vanhauwaert, T., Whitman, R.G., and Wolff, S. (2009) *After Georgia: Conflict Resolution in the EU's Eastern Neighbourhood*, Brussels: European Policy Centre.

Akhmedli, Z. (2001) 'Azerbaijan-Based Institute Works on Anti-Terror Program', *RFE/RL Azerbaijan Report*. Available at www.rferl.org/content/Article/1340900.html.

Aliyev, H. (2001) *Address at the Session of the Parliamentary Assembly of the Council of Europe (Strasbourg, 25 January 2001)*. Available at www.azerbembassy.org.cn/rus/statements5.html.

Aliyev, I. (2001a) *Address to the PACE on Item 'Europe's Fight against Economic and Transnational Organized Crime' (Strasbourg, 23–27 April 2001)*. Available at www.azerbembassy.org.cn/rus/statements4.html.

Aliyev, I. (2001b) *Speech by Mr. Ilham Aliyev, Head of the Delegation of the Parliament of the Republic of Azerbaijan to Parliamentary Assembly of Council of Europe (PACE) (Strasbourg, 25 September 2001)*. Available at www.azerbembassy.org.cn/rus/statements3.html.

Allison, G. (2000) 'The Impact of Globalization on National and International Security', in J.S. Nye Jr. and J.D. Donahue (eds) *Governance in a Globalizing World*, Washington, DC: Brookings Institution.

Allison, G. (2006) 'Globalization, Terrorism, and the U.S. Relationship with Russia,' in R.N. Rosecrance and A.A. Stein (eds) *No More States? Globalization, National Self-Determination, and Terrorism*, New York: Rowman & Littlefield Publishers.

Almond, G. and Verba, S. (1963) *The Civic Culture: Political Attitudes and Democracy in Five Nations*, Princeton, NJ: Princeton University Press.

Amnesty International (2004) 'Moldova: School Closures in Self-Proclaimed Dnestr Moldavian Republic Violate Right to Freedom of Expression', Amnesty International Available at www.amnesty.org/en/library/info/EUR59/002/2004/en.

Anderson, L. and Stansfield, G. (2009) *Crisis in Kirkuk: The Ethnopolitics of Conflict and Compromise*, Philadelphia: University of Pennsylvania Press.

Andrejevich, M. (1992) 'Bosnia and Herzegovina: A Precarious Peace', *RFE/RL Research Report 1*, No. 9, 28 February.

Anjaparidze, Z. (2004) 'Infighting Plagues Abkhaz Separatist Camp', *Eurasia Daily Monitor*, 24 June.

Appadurai, A. (1996) *Modernity at Large: Cultural Dimensions of Globalization*, Minneapolis: University of Minneapolis Press.

Arbour, L. (2009) 'Bosnia's Continuing Chaos', *Foreign Policy*, 18 November.

Armenian News Network (2004) 'The Rise and Fall of Samvel Babayan', 6 October.

Armstrong, D., Farrell, T., and Lambert, H. (2007) *International Law and International Relations*, Cambridge: Cambridge University Press.

Ashley, R. (1989) 'Living on Border Lines: Man, Poststructuralism, and War', in J.D. Derian and M. Shapiro (eds) *International/Intertextual Relations*, Lexington: Lexington Books.

Atlas, P.M. and Licklider, R. (1999) 'Conflict Among Former Allies after Civil War: Sudan, Zimbabwe, Chad, and Lebanon', *Journal of Peace Research*, 36 (1): 35–54.

Austin, J.L. (2001) *How to Do Things With Words*, Cambridge, MA: Harvard University Press.

Avioutskii, V. and Mili, H. (2003) 'The Geopolitics of Separatism: Genesis of Chechen Field Commanders', *Central Asia and the Caucasus: Journal of Social and Political Studies*, 2 (20): 7–13.

Bagapsh, S. (2009) 'Abkhazia will succeed', *Washington Times*, 16 December 2009.

Bahcheli, T. (2004) 'Under Turkey's Wings: The Turkish Republic of Northern Cyprus, The Struggle for International Acceptance', in T. Bahcheli, B. Bartmann, and H. Srebrnik (eds) *De Facto States: The Quest for Sovereignty*, London: Routledge.

Bahcheli, T., Bartmann, B. and Srebrnik, H. (eds) (2004) *De Facto States: The Quest for Sovereignty*, London: Routledge.

Bakke, K.M. (2009). *Preserving Peace? Decentralization and Intrastate Struggles*, Unpublished manuscript, Department of Political Science, University College London.

Bakke, K.M. (2010) 'The Turn to Violence in Chechnya and Punjab: Self-Determination Struggles in Decentralized States', in A. Lawrence and E. Chenoweth (eds) *Rethinking Violence*, Cambridge, MA: MIT Press.

Bakke, K.M., O'Loughlin, J., and Ward, M.D. (2009) 'Reconciliation in Conflict-Affected Societies: Multilevel Modeling of Individual and Contextual Factors in the North Caucasus of Russia', *Annals of the Association of American Geographers*, 99 (5): 1012–21.

Barbarosie, A., Nantoi, O., Botan, I., Gremalschi, A., Lupan, V., Cibotaru, V., Revenco, E., Minzarari, D., and Vrabie, R. (2008) *Synthesized Vision over the Transnistrian Issue*. Available at www.ipp.md/files/Publicatii/2008/Summary_11_1_.09.2008_eng.doc.

Bartelson, J. (2006) 'The Concept of Sovereignty Revisited', *The European Journal of International Law*, 17 (2): 463–74.

Bartelson, J. (2008) 'Sovereignty Before and After the Linguistic Turn', in R. Adler-Nissen and T. Gammeltoft-Hansen (eds) *Sovereignty Games: Instrumentalizing State Sovereignty in Europe and Beyond*, London: Palgrave Macmillan.

Bartkus, V.O. (1999) *The Dynamic of Secession*, Cambridge: Cambridge University Press.

Bartmann, B. (2004) 'Political Realities and Legal Anomalies: Revisiting the Politics of

International Recognition', in T. Bahcheli, B. Bartmann, and H. Srebrnik (eds) *De facto States: The Quest for Sovereignty*, London: Routledge.

BBC (1999) 'Chechen Parliament in Exile's Top Man Scorns President's "Useless" Peace Plan', *BBC Monitoring Service*, 11 October.

Ben-Dor, G. (1988) 'Ethnopolitics and the Middle Eastern State', in M.J. Esman and I. Rabinovich (eds) *Ethnicity, Pluralism, and the State in the Middle East*, Ithaca, NY: Cornell University Press.

Bercovitch, J. (1996) 'Understanding Mediation's Role in Preventive Diplomacy', *Negotiation Journal*, 12: 241–58.

Bercovitch, J. (2002) (ed.) *Studies in International Mediation*, New York: Palgrave.

Biersteker, T.J. and Weber, C. (1996) 'The Social Construction of State Sovereignty', in T.J. Biersteker and C. Weber (eds) *State Sovereignty as Social Construct*, Cambridge: Cambridge University Press.

Blank, S. (2008) 'Russia and the Black Sea's Frozen Conflicts in Strategic Perspective', *Mediterranean Quarterly*, 19: 23–54.

Bobbitt, P. (2002) *The Shield of Achilles: War, Peace, and the Course of History*, New York: Anchor Books.

Bohlen, C. (1999) 'Russia Severs Ties to Republic of Chechnya', *New York Times*, 2 October.

Bose, S. (2003) 'Flawed Mediation, Chaotic Implementation: The 1987 Indo-Sri Lanka Peace Agreement', in J. Stedman, D. Rothchild, and E.M. Cousens (eds) *Ending Civil Wars: The Implementation of Peace Agreements*, Boulder: Lynne Rienner.

Boutros-Ghali, B. (1992) *An Agenda for Peace*. Available at www.un.org/Docs/SG/agpeace.html.

Boyle, M. (2009) 'Explaining Strategic Violence after Wars', *Studies in Conflict and Terrorism*, 32: 209–36.

Bradbury, M. (2008) *Becoming Somaliland*, London: Progressio.

Brehm, J. and Rahn, W. (1997) 'Individual-Level Evidence for the Causes and Consequences of Social Capital', *American Journal of Political Science*, 41 (3): 999–1023.

Breidenbach, S. (1995) *Mediation. Struktur, Chancen und Risiken von Vermittlung im Konflikt*, Köln: Dr. Otto Schmidt.

Brickhill, J. (2010) 'Security and Stabilisation in Somalia. Learning from Local Approaches', in M. Bradbury and S. Healy (eds) *Whose Peace is it Anyway? Connecting Somali and International Peacemaking*, Conciliation Resources, ACCORD issue 21.

Broers, L. (2005) *The Politics of Non-recognition and Democratization*, London: Conciliation Resources. Available at www.c-r.org/our-work/accord/nagorny-karabakh/democratization-abstract.php.

Brooks, R.E. (2005) 'Failed States, or the State as Failure?', *University of Chicago Law Review*, 72 (Fall).

Brzezinski, Z., Ignatius, D., and Scowcroft, B. (2008) *America and the World: Conversations on the Future of American Foreign Policy*, New York: Basic Books.

Buchanan, A. (1991) *Secession: The Morality of Political Divorce from Fort Sumter to Lithuania and Quebec*, Boulder, CO: Westview Press.

Bull, H. (2002) *The Anarchical Society: A Study of Order in World Politics*, 3rd edition, London: Palgrave Macmillan.

Burton, J. (1993) 'Conflict Resolution as a Political System', Working paper, George Mason University. Available at www.gmu.edu/departments/ICAR/wp_1_burton.pdf.

Buzan, B. (1983) *People, States and Fear: The National Security Problem in International Relations*, Brighton: Wheatsheaf.

Buzan, B., Wæver, O., and de Wilde, J. (1998) *Security: a New Framework for Analysis*, Boulder, CO: Lynne Rienner.

Caplan, R. (2005) *Europe and the Recognition of New States in Yugoslavia*, Cambridge: Cambridge University Press.

Caspersen, N. (2008) 'Separatism and Democracy in the Caucasus', *Survival*, 50 (4): 113–36.

Caspersen, N. (2009) 'Playing the Recognition Game: External Actors and De facto States', *International Spectator*, 44(4): 21–34.

Caspersen, N. (2010) *Contested Nationalism: Serb Elite Rivalry in Croatia and Bosnia in the 1990s*, Oxford: Berghahn.

Caspersen, N. (2011) *Unrecognised States: The Struggle for Sovereignty in the Modern International System*, Cambridge: Polity Press (forthcoming).

Cassese, A. (1995) *Self-Determination of Peoples*, Cambridge: Cambridge University Press.

Castells, M. (2000) *The Information Age: Economy, Society and Culture*, Malden: Blackwell.

Castells, M. (2004) 'Informationalism, Networks, and the Network Society: a Theoretical Blueprint', in M. Castells (ed.) *The Network Society: A Cross-cultural Perspective*, Northampton: Edward Elgar Publishing.

Chiclet, C. (2004) 'The Armenian Genocide', in O. Roy (ed.) *Turkey Today: A European Country?*, London: Anthem Press.

Chirikba, V. (2000) 'Georgia and Abkhazia: Proposals for a Constitutional Model', in B. Coppieters, D. Darchiashvili, and N. Akaba (eds) *Federal Practice. Exploring Alternatives for Georgia and Abkhazia*, Brussels: VUB University Press.

Chorev, M. (2007) 'Iraqi Kurdistan: Internal Dynamics and Statecraft of a Semistate', Master's Thesis, Medford: Tufts University.

Ciobanu, C. (2004) *NATO/EU Enlargement: Moldova and the 'Frozen and Forgotten' Conflicts in Post-Soviet States*. Available at www.ipp.md/download.php?file=cHVibGljL2JpYmxpb3RlY2EvNzQvcm8vUmVwb3J0IEp1bHkgMjUsIHJldmlzZWQuZG9j.

Ciobanu, C. (2008) *Frozen and Forgotten Conflicts in the Post-Soviet States: Genesis, Political Economy and Prospects for Solution*. Available at www.ipp.md/public/files/Publicatii/2008/USIP_manuscript_MAR13_08__Moldova_.doc.

Clogg, R. (2008) 'The Politics of Identity in Post-Soviet Abkhazia: Managing Diversity and Unresolved Conflict', *Nationalities Papers*, 36 (2): 305–29.

Collier, P. (2006) 'Post-Conflict Economic Recovery', unpublished manuscript, Department of Economics, Oxford University. Available at http://users.ox.ac.uk/~econpco/research/pdfs/IPA-PostConflictEconomicRecovery.pdf.

Collier, P. and Hoeffler, A. (1998) 'On Economic Causes of Civil War', *Oxford Economic Papers*, 50: 563–73.

Collier, P., Elliott, V.L., Hegre, H., Hoeffler, A., Reynal-Querol, M., and Sambanis, N. (2003) *Breaking the Conflict Trap: Civil War and Development Policy*, Washington, DC: The World Bank and Oxford University Press.

Coppieters, B. (2007) *The EU and Georgia: Time Perspectives in Conflict Resolution*, Paris: EU Institute for Security Studies.

Cordell, K. and Wolff, S. (2009) *Ethnic Conflict: Causes – Consequences – Responses*, Cambridge: Polity.

Council of the European Union (1999) 'European Council, Cologne, 3–4 June 1999: Presidency Conclusions', Cologne, 4 June 1999. Available at www.consilium.europa.eu/ueDocs/cms_Data/docs/pressData/en/ec/kolnen.htm.

Council of the European Union (2003) *A Secure Europe in a Better World. European Security Strategy*, Brussels, 12 December 2003. Available at www.consilium.europa.eu/uedocs/cmsUpload/78367.pdf.

Council of the European Union (2008a), 'Extraordinary European Council, Brussels, 1 September 2008: Presidency Conclusions,' Brussels, 6 October 2008. Available at: www.consilium.europa.eu/uedocs/cms_Data/docs/pressdata/en/ec/102545.pdf.

Council of the European Union (2008b) 'Summary of Remarks by EUHR Solana to EU Parliament Foreign Affairs Committee and Chairs of Foreign Affairs and Defence Committees of National Parliaments', Brussels, 5 November 2008. Available at www.europa-eu-un.org/articles/en/article_8274_en.htm.

Crawford, J. (1979) *The Creation of States in International Law*, Oxford: Clarendon Press.

Crocker, C.A., Hampson, F.O., and Aall, P. (2004) *Taming Intractable Conflicts. Mediation in the Hardest Cases*, Washington, DC: United States Institute for Peace Press.

Cunningham, K.G. (2008) 'Strategic Accommodation', Working Paper, Department of Political Science, Iowa State University.

Cunningham, K.G., Bakke, K.M., and Seymour, L. (2010) 'Shirts Today, Skins Tomorrow: The Effects of Fragmentation on Conflict Processes in Self-Determination Disputes', paper presented at the Annual Meeting of the International Studies Association, New Orleans.

Curle, A. (1981) *True Justice: Quaker Peacemakers and Peace Making*, Swathmore Lecture, Quaker Books.

Day.Az (2007) 'Kyamil' Salimov: "Ugrozy PKK o sovershenii teraktov v Azerbaijane dayut nam vozmozhnost' realizovat' nashi zadachi po osvobozhdeniyu okkupirovannoi territorii"', 19 December. Available at www.dayaz.com/news/politics/101936.html (last accessed 3 May 2009).

De Mel, N. (2007) *Militarizing Sri Lanka: Popular Culture, Memory and Narrative in the Armed Conflict*, New Delhi: Sage.

Devdariani, J. (2003) 'South Ossetian Leader Tightens Control over Breakaway Georgian Province', *Eurasia Insight*, 11 July.

De Waal, T. (2003) 'Karabakh Ceasefire Under Strain', *Caucasus Reporting Service*, 3 August, Institute of War and Peace Reporting.

De Waal, T. (2004) *Black Garden: Armenia and Azerbaijan through Peace and War*, New York: New York University Press.

Doob, L.W. (1986) 'Cypriot Patriotism and Nationalism', *Journal of Conflict Resolution*, 30 (2): 383–96.

Downes, A.B. (2006) 'Desperate Times, Desperate Measures: The Causes of Civilian Victimization in War', *International Security*, 30 (4): 152–95.

Duchacek, I. (1970) *Comparative Federalism: The Territorial Dimensions of Politics*, New York: Holt, Rinehart and Winston.

Dunér, B. (1981) 'Proxy Intervention in Civil Wars', *Journal of Peace Research*, 18 (4): 353–61.

Dunlop, J.B. (1998) *Russia Confronts Chechnya: Roots of a Separatist Conflict*, New York: Cambridge University Press.

Earle, V. (1968) *Federalism: Infinite Variety in Theory and Practice*, Itasca, IL: F.E. Peacock.

Easton, D. (1981) 'The Political System Besieged by the State', *Political Theory*, 9 (3).

The Economist (2009) 'The Blame Game', 1 October.

Edmundson, M.R. (2005) 'The Political Economy of Secession Without Recognition: The Case of Somaliland', Economics Department Honours Thesis, Tufts University, June.

Egeland, J. (1999) 'Peace-making and the Prevention of Violence: the Role of Governments and Non-governmental Organizations', *International Review of the Red Cross*, 833: 73–83.

Elazar, D.J. (1987) *Exploring Federalism*, Tuscaloosa, AL: The University of Alabama Press.

Elazar, D.J. (1993) 'International and Comparative Federalism', *PS: Political Science and Politics*, 26 (2).

Embassy of the Republic of Azerbaijan in Poland (n.d.) 'Armenian terrorism'. Available at http://azembassy.pl/index.php?section=53>.

Etzioni, A. (1993) 'The Evils of Self-Determination', *Foreign Policy*, 89: 21–35.

European Commission (1993) 'Accession Criteria'. Available at http://ec.europa.eu/enlargement/enlargement_process/accession_process/criteria/index_en.htm.

European Commission (1996/9) 'Partnership and Cooperation Agreement between the European Communities and their Member States, of the one part, and Georgia, of the other part', Luxembourg, 22 April 1996. OJ L205 of 4 August 1999, pp. 3–52. Available at http://ec.europa.eu/world/agreements/downloadFile.do?fullText=yes&treatyTransId=632.

European Commission (2001) 'Communication on Conflict Prevention', Brussels, 11 April 2001. Available at http://ec.europa.eu/external_relations/cfsp/crisis_management/docs/com2001_211_en.pdf.

European Commission (2003) 'Country Strategy Paper 2003–2006' and 'Tacis National Indicative Programme 2004–2006: Georgia'. Available at http://eeas. europa.eu/georgia/csp/03_06_en.pdf.

European Commission (2005) 'Road Map for the Common Space of External Security', Annex 3 to the 2005 Moscow Summit Declaration. Available at http://ec.europa.eu/external_relations/russia/docs/roadmap_economic_en.pdf.

European Commission (2006) 'Speech by EU Commissioner Ferrero-Waldner: Political Reform and Sustainable Reform in the South Caucasus', Bled Strategic Forum, Slovenia, 28 August 2006. Available at http://europa.eu/rapid/pressReleasesAction.do?reference=SPEECH/06/477&format=HTML&aged=0&language=EN&guiLanguage=en.

European Commission (2007) 'Georgia Country Strategy Paper 2007–2013', Brussels. Available at www.delgeo.ec.europa.eu/en/trade/enpi_csp_georgia_en1.pdf.

European Commission (2008) 'Communication from the Commission to the Council: Review of EU-Russia Relations', Brussels, 5 November 2008. Available at http://ec.europa.eu/external_relations/russia/docs/com_08_740_en.pdf.

European Commission (2009) 'Commission Staff Working Document accompanying the Communication from the Commission to the European Parliament and Council: Implementation of the European Neighbourhood Policy in 2008, Progress Report Georgia', Brussels, 23 April 2009. Available at http://ec.europa.eu/world/enp/pdf/progress2009/sec09_513_en.pdf.

European Community (1991) 'D 85 Criteria for the Recognition of States, Declaration on the Guidelines on the Recognition of new States in Eastern Europe and the Soviet Union', Brussels, 16 December.

European Union Delegation to Georgia (2010) 'Overview of ECAssistance to People Affected by Conflict in Georgia'. Available athttp://ec.europa.eu/delegations/georgia/documents/projects/overview_post_conflict_ec_assistance_may10_en.pdf.

European Union (2009) 'Independent International Fact Finding Mission on the Conflict in Georgia', Volume 1, Brussels. Available at http://91.121.127.28/ceiig/pdf/IIFFMCG_Volume_I.pdf.

Evans, G. (2008) 'Responsibility to Protect: An Idea Whose Time has Come … and Gone?' *International Relations*, 22(3): 283–98.

Fabry, M. (2008) 'Secession and State Recognition in International Relations and Law', in A. Pavkovic and P. Radan (eds) *On the Way to Statehood: Secession and Globalization*, Aldershot: Ashgate.

Ferguson, Y.H. and Barry Jones, R.J. (eds) (2002) *Political Space: Frontiers of Change and Governance in a Globalizing World*, New York: State University of New York Press.

Fisher, R. (2001) 'The Failure of Mediation and the Escalation of an Identity-Based Conflict to an Adversarial Impasse', *Journal of Peace Research*, 48(3): 307–26.

Fisher, S. and Zimina, L. (2008) *Just Wasting our Time? An Open Letter to Peacebuilders*, Berlin, Berghof Foundation for International Peace Support.

Franck, T. (1966) *Why Federations Fail: An Inquiry into the Requisites for a Successful Federation*, New York: New York University Press.

Frichova Grono, M. (2010) *Georgia's Conflicts: What Role for the EU as a Mediator?*, Brussels: Initiative for Peacebuilding.

Galtung, J. (1969) 'Violence, Peace, and Pace Research', *Journal of Peace Research*, 6 (3): 167–91.

Garcelon, M., Walker, E.W., Wood, A., and Radovich, A. (eds) (1998) *The Geopolitics of Oil, Gas, and Ecology in the Caucasus and Caspian Basin*, Berkeley: University of California Press.

Geldenhuys, D. (2009) *Contested States in World Politics*, London: Palgrave Macmillan.

German, T.C. (2003) *Russia's Chechen War*, New York: RoutledgeCurzon.

Ghemawat, P. (2007) 'Why the World Isn't Flat', *Foreign Policy*, March/April.

Giragosian, R. (2000) 'Nagorno Karabakh Democracy', *CACI Analyst*, 26 April.

Gleditsch, N.P., Wallensteen, P., Eriksson, M., Sollenberg, M., and Strand, H. (2002) 'Armed Conflict 1946–2001: A New Dataset', *Journal of Peace Research*, 39 (5): 615–38.

Glenny, M. (1992) *The Fall of Yugoslavia: The Third Balkan War*, London: Penguin.

Goltz, T. (1993) 'Letter from Eurasia: The Hidden Russian Hand', *Foreign Policy*, 92 (3).

Gottlieb, G. (1994) 'Nations without States', *Foreign Affairs*, 73 (3).

Gow, J. (2003) *The Serbian Project and Its Adversaries: A Strategy of War Crimes*, London: Hurst.

Greenhill, K. and Major, S. (2006/7) 'The Perils of Profiling: Civil War Spoilers and the Collapse of Intrastate Peace Accords', *International Security*, 31 (3): 7–40.

Greig, M. and Regan, P. (2008) 'When Do They Say Yes? An Analysis of the Willingness to Offer and Accept Mediation in Civil Wars', *International Studies Quarterly*, 52: 759–81.

Gribincea, M. (2006) *Russian Troops in Transnistria – a Threat to the Security of the Republic of Moldova*. Available at http://politicom.moldova.org/news/russian-troops-in-transnistria-a-threat-to-the-security-of-the-republic-of-moldova-20998-eng.html.

Guibernau, M. (2000) *Nations Without States*, Cambridge: Polity Press.

Gulliver, P.H. (1979) *Disputes and Negotiations. A Cross-Cultural Perspective*, London: Academic Press.

Gurgulia, M (2004) 'Democratisation in Conditions of a non-Recognized State', paper presented at the conference *Abkhazia in the Context of Contemporary International Relations*, July. Available at www.circassianworld.com/Gurgulia.html.

Gurr, T.R. (2000) *Peoples versus States*, Washington, DC: United States Institute of Peace Press.

Hakki, M.M. (2008) *The Cyprus Issue: A Documentary History 1878*–2006, London: I.B. Tauris.

Halbach, U. (2007) 'Eingefrorene Konflikte im Südkaukasus: Probleme und Grenzen der Europäisierung', *Osteuropa*, 57: 83–94.

Hale, H. (2008) *The Foundations of Ethnic Politics: Separatism of States and Nations in Eurasia and the World*, New York: Cambridge University Press.

Halliday, F. (2005) *The Middle East in International Relations: Power, Politics and Ideology*, Cambridge: Cambridge University Press.

Halliday, F. (2008) *Tibet, Palestine and the Politics of Failure*, Open Democracy News Analysis. Available at www.opendemocracy.net.

Hannikainen, L. (1997) 'The International Legal Basis of the Autonomy and Swedish Character of the Åland Islands', in L. Hannikainen, and F. Horn (eds) *Autonomy and Demilitarisation in International Law: The Aland Islands in a Changing Europe*, The Hague: Kluwer Law International.

Hannum, H. (1996) *Autonomy, Sovereignty, and Self-Determination: The Accommodation of Conflicting Rights*, Philadelphia: University of Philadelphia Press.

Hansen, S. and Bradbury, M. (2007) 'Somaliland: A New Democracy in the Horn of Africa?' *Review of African Political Economy*, 34(113): 461–76.

Harbom, L., Högbladh, S., and Wallensteen, P. (2006) 'Armed Conflict and Peace Agreements', *Journal of Peace Research*, 43 (5): 617–31.

Hechter, M. (1992) 'The Dynamics of Secession', *Acta Sociologica*, 35: 267–83.

Hechter, M. (2000) *Containing Nationalism*, New York: Oxford University Press.

Hedges, C. (1998) 'Stari Tng Journal; Below It All in Kosovo, A War's Glittering Prize', *New York Times*, 8 July.

Heidelberg Institute for International Conflict Research (2009) *Conflict Barometer 2009*, Heidelberg, University of Heidelberg.

Held, D., McGrew, A., Goldblatt, D., and Perraton, J. (1999) *Global Transformations: Politics, Economics, and Culture*, Stanford: Stanford University Press.

Herbst, J. (1996) 'Responding to State Failure in Africa', *International Security*, 21 (3): 120–44.

Herrberg, A. and Kumpulainen, H. (2008) *The Private Diplomacy Survey 2008. Mapping of 14 Private Diplomacy Actors in Europe and America*, Brussels, Crisis Management Initiative.

Herrberg, A., Gündüz C., and Davis, L. (2009) *Engaging the EU in Mediation and Dialogue. Reflections and Recommendations. Synthesis Report*, Brussels, Initiative for Peacebuilding.

Hewitt, J.J., Wilkenfeld, J. and Gurr, T.R. (2010) *Peace and Conflict 2010*, Boulder: Paradigm Publishers.

Hill, C. (2003) *The Changing Politics of Foreign Policy*, Basingstoke: Palgrave.

Hinnebusch, R. (2003) *The International Politics of the Middle East*, Manchester: Manchester University Press.

Hoffman, B. (2010) *Lecture at the Peace Mediation Course*, 7–19 March 2010, Oberhofen.

Holbrooke, R. (1996) 'The Road to Sarajevo', *The New Yorker*, 21 and 28 October.

Holbrooke, R. (1998) *To End a War*, New York: Random House.

Horowitz, D. (1981) 'Patterns of Ethnic Separatism', *Comparative Studies in Society and History*, 23 (2): 165–95.

Horowitz, D.L. (2002) 'Constitutional Design: Proposals versus Processes', in A. Reynolds (ed.) *The Architecture of Democracy*, Oxford: Oxford University Press.

Hughes, J. (2001) 'Managing Secession Potential in the Russian Federation', *Regional Federal Studies*, 11 (3): 36–68.

Hughes, J. (2007) *Chechnya: From Nationalism to Jihad*, Philadelphia: University of Pennsylvania Press.

Human Rights Watch (1995) *Georgia/Abkhazia: Violations of the Laws of War and Russia's Role in the Conflict.* Available at www.hrw.org/en/reports/1995/03/01/georgiaabkhazia-violations-laws-war-and-russia-s-role-conflict.

Humphreys, M. (2005) 'Natural Resources, Conflict, and Conflict Resolution: Uncovering the Mechanisms', *Journal of Conflict Resolution*, 49: 508–37.

Huntington, S.P. (1972) 'Foreword', to E.A. Nordlinger *Conflict Regulation in Divided Societies*, Occasional Papers in International Affairs, Cambridge, MA: Centre for International Affairs, Harvard University.

Hussain, S.R. (2010) 'Liberation Tigers of Tamil Eelam: Failed Quest for a "Homeland" ', in K. Mulaj (ed.) *Violent Non-State Actors in World Politics*, London: Hurst and New York: Columbia University Press.

Ibragimov, N. (n.d.) *Armyanskii terrorizm: ser'eznaya ugroza regionu v usloviyakh globalizatsii*. Available at www.anl.az/el/q/qarabag_2/q-38.htm.

Ilgen, T.L. (ed.) (2003) *Reconfigured Sovereignty. Multi-Layered Governance in the Global Age*, Aldershot: Ashgate.

Infotag (2005) *Prezident Voronin vyskazalsya za razrabotku i vnedrenie individual'nogo plana deistvii RM–NATO.* Available at http://politicom.moldova.org/news/prezident-vladimir-voronin-viskazalsya-za-razrabotku-i-vnedrenie-individualinogo-plana-deistvii-rm-nato-3050-rus.html.

International Alert (2004) *From War Economies to Peace Economies*, London.

International Crisis Group (2004) *Georgia: Avoiding War in South Ossetia*, Europe Report, No. 159, 26 November.

International Crisis Group (2005) *Nagorno-Karabakh: Viewing the Conflict from the Ground*, Europe Report No. 166, 14 September.

International Crisis Group (2006a) *The Cyprus Stalemate: What Next?*, Europe Report No. 171, 8 March.

International Crisis Group (2006b) *Conflict Resolution in the South Caucasus: The EU's Role*, Europe Report No. 173, 20 March.

International Crisis Group (2006c) *Moldova's Uncertain Future*, Europe Report No. 175, 17 August.

International Crisis Group (2006d) *Abkhazia Today*, Europe Report No. 176, 15 September.

International Crisis Group (2006e) *Georgia: Avoiding War in South Ossetia*, Europe Report No. 159, 26 November.

International Crisis Group (2007a) *Nagorno-Karabakh: Risking War*, Europe Report No. 187, 14 November.

International Crisis Group (2007b) *Georgia's South Ossetia Conflict: Making Haste Slowly*, Europe Report No. 183, 7 June.

International Crisis Group (2008) *Russia vs Georgia: The Fallout*, Europe Report No. 195, 22 August.

International Crisis Group (2009) *Europe Briefing No. 57*, 12 November.

International Crisis Group (2010a) *Abkhazia: Deepening Dependence*, Europe Report No. 202, 26 February.

International Crisis Group (2010b) *Crisis Watch*, No. 81, 1 May.

Isachenko, D. (2009) ' "Symptoms" of Democracy in Transdniestria', *S+F – Sicherheit und Frieden*, 27 (2): 96–101.

Iyer, P. (2007) *Coming to the Table: Decisions and Decision-Making in a Non-State Armed Group, The Liberation Tigers of Tamil Eelam*, Ph.D. dissertation, George Mason University.

Jackson, R.H. (1987) 'Quasi-States, Dual Regimes, and Neoclassical Theory: International Jurisprudence and the Third World', *International Organization*, 41 (Autumn).

Jackson, R.H. (1990) *Quasi-States: Sovereignty, International Relations and the Third World*, Cambridge: Cambridge University Press.

Kaldor, M. (2003) *Global Civil Society: An Answer to War*, Cambridge: Polity Press.

Kalyvas, S.N. (2003) 'The Ontology of Political Violence', *Perspectives on Politics*, 1 (3): 475–94.

Kalyvas, S.N. (2006) *The Logic of Violence in Civil War*, New York: Cambridge University Press.

Kalyvas, S.N. (2008) 'Ethnic Defection in Civil War', *Comparative Political Studies* 41 (8): 1043–68.

Kang, S. and Meernik, J. (2009) 'Civil War Destruction and the Prospects for Economic Growth', *Journal of Politics*, 67 (1): 88–109.

Karabakh Open (2008) 'Karabakh Has Serious Grounds for International Recognition of Sovereignty', 20 February. Available at www.armeniandiaspora.com/archive/index.php/t-122518.html.

Keating, J. (2008) 'How to Start your own Country in Four Easy Steps', *Foreign Affairs*, 26 February.

Keating, M. and Aldecoa, F. (1999) *Paradiplomacy in Action: The Foreign Relations of Subnational Governments*, London: Frank Cass.

Keen, D. (2001) 'War and Peace: What's the Difference', *International Peacekeeping*, 7 (4): 1–22.

Kemp, W. (2005) 'Selfish Determination: The Questionable Ownership of Autonomy Movements', *Ethnopolitics*, 4 (1): 88–9.

Keohane, R.O. and Nye Jr., J.S. (2000) 'Introduction', in J.S. Nye, Jr. and J.D. Donahue (eds) *Governance in a Globalizing World*, Washington, DC: Brookings Institution Press.

Khalil, L. (2009) 'Stability in Iraqi Kurdistan: Reality or Mirage?' *Saban Centre Working Paper* 2, Washington, DC: Brookings Institution.

Khashig, I. (2003) 'Abkhazia: Veterans Challenge President', *Caucasus Reporting Service*, 31 July.

Khashig, I. (2004) 'Abkhazia's Political Roulette Goes On', *Caucasus Reporting Service*, 17 November.

Khashig, I. (2009) 'Abkhaz Opposition Fear Growing Russian Influence', *Caucasus Reporting Service*, 7 August.

King, C. (2001) 'The Benefits of Ethnic War: Understanding Eurasia's Unrecognized States', *World Politics*, 53 (July): 524–52.

King, P. (1982) *Federalism and Federation*, Baltimore: The Johns Hopkins University Press.

Kingston, P. and Spears, I. (eds) (2004) *States Within States: Incipient Entities in the Post-Cold War Era*, London: Palgrave Macmillan.

Kioko, B. (2003) 'The Right of Intervention under the African Union's Constitutive Act: From Non-interference to Non-intervention', *International Review of the Red Cross*, 85 (852): 807–25.

Klip, A. and Sluiter, G. (eds) (1999) *Annotated Leading Cases of International Criminal Tribunals, Volume I, The International Criminal Tribunal for the Former Yugoslavia 1993–1998*, Antwerp: Intersentia.

Klip, A. and Sluiter, G. (eds) (2001) *Annotated Leading Cases of International Criminal Tribunals, Volume III, The International Criminal Tribunal for the Former Yugoslavia 1997–1999*, Antwerp: Intersentia.

Kniga pamyati zashchitnikov Pridnestrov'ya (1995) Tiraspol: Tiraspol'skoe knizhnoe izdatel'stvo.

Kohen, M.G. (2006) *Secession, International Law Perspectives*, Cambridge: Cambridge University Press.

Kolossov, V. and O'Loughlin, J. (1999) 'Pseudo-states as Harbingers of a New Geopolitics: the Example of the Transdniestr Republic (TMR)', in D. Newman (ed.) *Boundaries, Territory and Post-modernity*, London: Frank Cass.

Kolstø, P. (2006) 'The Sustainability and Future of Unrecognized Quasi-States', *Journal of Peace Research*, 43 (6): 723–40.

Kolstø, P. and Blakkisrud, H. (2008) 'Living with Non-recognition: State- and Nation-building in South Caucasian Quasi-states', *Europe-Asia Studies*, 60(3): 483–509.

Krasner, S. (1999) *Sovereignty: Organized Hypocrisy*, Princeton, NJ: Princeton University Press.

Krasner, S. (2001) *Problematic Sovereignty: Contested Rules and Political Possibilities*, New York: Columbia University Press.

Krueger, H. (2009) 'Implications of Kosovo, Abkhazia and South Ossetia for International Law: The Conduct of the Community of States in Current Secession Conflicts', *Caucasus Review of International Affairs*, 3 (2): 121–42.

Kryd, A. (2003) 'Which Side Are You On? Bias, Credibility, and Mediation', *American Journal of Political Science*, 47(4): 597–611.

KSAM (2005) *Nezakonnaya deyatel'nost' Armenii na okkupirovannykh territoriyakh Azerbaidzhana.* Available at www.ksam.org/index.php?mtype=news1&mid=341.

Kumar, R. (1997) *Divide and Fall? Bosnia in the Annals of Partition*, London: Verso.

Lake, D.A. and Rothchild, D. (1996) 'Containing Fear: The Origins and Management of Ethnic Conflict', *International Security*, 21 (2): 41–76.

Lamb, R. (2007) 'Ungoverned Areas and Threats from Safe Havens', Final Report of the Ungoverned Areas Project, Prepared for the Office of the Under Secretary of Defense for Policy, December. Available at www.cissm.umd.edu/papers/files/ugash_report_final.pdf.

Lapidus, G. (1998) 'Contested Sovereignty: The Tragedy of Chechnya', *International Security*, 23 (1): 5–50.

Lapidus, G. (2002) 'Accommodating Differences in Post-Soviet Eurasia', in M. Beissinger and Y. Crawford (eds) *Beyond State Crisis: Post-Colonial Africa and Post-Soviet Eurasia in Comparative Perspective*, Baltimore: Johns Hopkins University Press.

Lawrence, A. (2010) 'Triggering Nationalist Violence: Competition and Conflict in Uprisings against Colonial Rule', *International Security*, 35 (2): 88–122.

Leitenberg, M. (2006) *Deaths in Wars and Conflicts in the 20th Century*, Cornell University Peace Studies Program, Occasional Paper No. 29, 3rd edition.

Lemarchand, R. (1962) 'The Limits of Self-Determination: The Case of the Katanga Secession', *American Political Science Review*, 56(2): 404–16.

Leonard, M. and Popescu, N. (2008) *A Power Audit of EU-Russia Relations*, London: European Council on Foreign Relations.

Licklider, R. (1995) 'The Consequences of Negotiated Settlements in Civil Wars, 1945–1993', *American Political Science Review*, 89 (3): 681–91.

Lieven, A. (1998) *Chechnya: Tombstone of Russian Power*, New Haven: Yale University Press.

Lijphart, A. (1968) *The Politics of Accommodation: Pluralism and Democracy in the Netherlands*, Berkeley: University of California Press.

Lijphart, A. (1969) 'Consociational Democracy', *World Politics*, 21.

Lijphart, A. (1990) 'The Power-Sharing Approach', in J.V. Montville (ed.) *Conflict and Peacemaking in Multiethnic Societies,* Lexington, MA: Lexington Books.

Linder, D. (1981) 'What in the Constitution Cannot be Amended', 23 *Arizona Law Review*, 117. Available at www.law.umkc.edu/faculty/projects/ftrials/conlaw/unamendable.html.

Lobjakas, A. (2005) 'Moldova: Western Diplomats Say Reports of Smuggling from Transdniester Likely Exaggerated', *Radio Free Europe/Radio Liberty*. Available at www.rferl.org/content/Article/1062030.html.

Loizides, N.G. and Antoniades, M.A. (2009) 'Negotiating the Right to Return', *Journal of Peace Research*, 46 (5): 611–22.

Lynch, D. (2002) 'Separatist States and Post-Soviet Conflicts', *International Affairs*, 78 (4): 831–48.

Lynch, D. (2004a) *Engaging Eurasia's Separatist States: Unresolved Conflicts and De facto States*, Washington, DC: United States Institute of Peace Press.

Lynch, D. (2004b) *The EU-Russia Partnership in the Shared Neighbourhood.* Paris: European Institute for Security Studies.

Lyons, T. (2004) 'Transforming the Institutions of War: Postconflict Elections and the Reconstruction of Failed States', in R.I. Rotberg (ed.) *When States Fail: Causes and Consequences*, Princeton: Princeton University Press.

Macedo, S. and Buchanan, A. (eds) (2003) *Secession and Self-Determination*, New York: New York University Press.

Mallinson, W. (2008) *Cyprus: A Modern History*, revised edition, London: I.B. Tauris.

Marshall, M.G. and Gurr, T.R. (2005) *Peace and Conflict 2005: A Global Survey of Armed Conflicts, Self-Determination Movements, and Democracy*, College Park: Center for International Development and Conflict Management, University of Maryland.

Mason, A.S. (2007) *Mediation and Facilitation in Peace Processes*, Mediation Support Project, ETH Zürich, Centre for Security Studies.

Mathews, J.T. (1997) 'Power Shift', *Foreign Affairs*, 76 (1).

Mayall, J. (1992) *Nationalism and International Society*, Cambridge: Cambridge University Press.

McColl, R.W. (1969) 'The Insurgent State: Territorial Bases of Revolution', *Annals of the Association of American Geographers*, 59 (4): 613–31.

McDowall, D. (1996) *A Modern History of The Kurds*, London: I.B. Tauris.

McGarry, J. (2005) 'Asymmetrical Federalism and the Plurinational State', position paper, 3rd International Conference on Federalism, Brussels.

Meadwell, H. (1999) 'Secession, States and International Society', *Review of International Studies*, 25: 371–87.

Medda-Windischer, R. (2008) 'Minorities Under International Law and in South Tyrol', in J. Woelk, F. Palermo, and J. Marko (eds) *Tolerance Through Law: Self Governance and Group Rights in South Tyrol*, Leiden: Martinus Nijhoff Publishers.

Mediation Support Project (2009) *Federalism and Peace Mediation*, Peace Mediation Essentials, Zürich: Swisspeace.

Merikallio, K. (2006) *Making Peace. Ahtisaari and Aceh*, Helsinki: WS Bookwell Oy.

Meurs, W. van (2007) 'Eingefrorene Konflikte: Wie weiter mit den Quasistaaten?', *Osteuropa*, 57: 111–20.

Michael, M.S. (2009) *Resolving the Cyprus Conflict: Negotiating History*, Houndmills: Palgrave Macmillan.

Mihalkanin, E. (2004) 'The Abkhazians: A National Minority in their own Homeland', in T. Bahcheli, B. Bartmann, and H. Srebrnik (eds) *De Facto States: The Quest for Sovereignty*, London: Routledge.

Ministerstvo Natsional'noi bezopasnosti (2005) *Armyano-azarbaidzhanskii, nagorno-karabakhskii konflikt*. Available at www.mns.gov.az/ermenistaninfealiyyeti_ru.html.

Ministry of Foreign Affairs (MOFA) (2010) Foreign Policy Guidelines, Republic of China, Ministry of Foreign Affairs. Available at www.mofa.gov.tw/webapp/ct.asp?xItem=32514&CtNode=1861&mp=6.

Mnogostoronnaya gruppa po mezhdunarodnomu sotrudnichestvu v bor'be s terrorizmom (GMT). Dostizheniya na natsional'nom urovne – Azerbaidzhan (2002) Strasbourg: Council of Europe. Available at www.mns.gov.az/download/GMT-rus.doc.

Moldova's Transnistrian Conflict: 3D Strategy (Demilitarization, Decriminalization, Democratization) (2004) Available at http://foundation.moldova.org/pages/eng/136.

Moore, C.W. (2003) *The Mediation Process. Practical Strategies for Resolving Conflicts*, San Francisco: Jossey Bass.

Mulaj, K. (2008) *Politics of Ethnic Cleansing: Nation-State Building and Provision of In/Security in Twentieth-Century Balkans*, Lanham, MD: Lexington Books/Rowman & Littlefield.

Mulaj, K. (2010) 'Violent Non-State Actors: Exploring their State Relations, Legitimation, and Operationality', in K. Mulaj (ed.) *Violent Non-State Actors in World Politics*, London: Hurst and New York: Columbia University Press.

Muller, E.N. and Seligson, M.A. (1994) 'Civic Culture and Democracy: the Question of Causal Relationships', *American Political Science Review*, 88 (3): 635–52.

Munteanu, A. and Munteanu, I. (2007) 'Transnistria: a Paradise for Vested Interests', *South East Europe Review of Labour and Social Affairs*, 10: 51–66.

Munteanu, I. (2004) *Between Failed States Syndrome and Non-conventional Threats to Regional Security in the Black Sea Area*. Available at www.viitorul.org/public/373/en/Casa%20NATO%20September%202004.doc.

Mustafayev, R. (ed.) (2002) *Prestupleniya armyanskikh terroristicheskikh i banditskikh formirovanii protiv chelovechestva (XIX–XXI vv.)*, Baku: Elm.

Mustafayeva, S. (2003) 'Azerbaidzhan lider v antiterrore: Antiterroristicheskii tsentr SNG blokiruet progressivnye initsiativy po pros'be Armenii', *Ekho*, 25 July. Available at http://karabakh-doc.azerall.info/ru/anti-terror/ater01.htm.

Nadler, A., Malloy, T.E., and Fisher, J.D. (2008) 'Intergroup Reconciliation: Dimensions and Themes', in A. Nadler, T.E. Malloy, and J.D. Fisher (eds) *The Social Psychology of Intergroup Reconciliation: From Violent Conflict to Peaceful Coexistence*, New York: Oxford University Press.

Nantoi, O. (2005) 'Pridnestrovskii konflikt – ot konsensusa deklaratsii k konsensusu deistvii', *Ekonomicheskoe obozrenie*, 15 April. Available at http://logos.press.md/Weekly/Main.asp?IssueNum=606&IssueDate=15.04.2005&YearNum=14&Theme=8&Topic=15843.

Natali, D. (2005) *The Kurds and the State: Evolving National Identity in Iraq, Turkey, and Iran*, Syracuse: Syracuse University Press.

Natali, D. (2008) 'The Kirkuk Conundrum', *Ethnopolitics*, 7 (4): 433–43.

Nathan, L. (1998) *A Case of Undue Pressure: International Mediation in African Civil Wars*, paper presented at the African Mediation Seminar, 3–5 November, Johannesburg, Independent Mediation Service of South Africa and Centre for Conflict Resolution.

Nathan, L. (1999) '"When Push Comes to Shove". The Failure of International Mediation in African Civil Wars', *Track Two* 8(2), Cape Town, Centre for Conflict Resolution.

National Security Strategy of the United States of America (2002) The White House, Washington, DC.

Necatigil, Z.M. (1993) *The Cyprus Question and the Turkish Position in International Law*, Oxford: Oxford University Press.

NEWSru.com (2006) 'Prezident Moldavii Voronin ob''yasnil v Germanii pochemu Rossiya boikotiruet moldavskoe vino', 16 May. Available at http://newsru.com/world/16may2006/vorong.html.

Nezavisimaya Moldova (2002) 'Prezident PM Vladimir Voronin vystupil na prazhskom forume NATO', 26 November. Available at www.nm.md/daily/news/2002/11/26.html (last accessed 1 December 2009).

Nezavisimaya Moldova (2003) 'Vstrecha glavy gosudarstva s prestavitelyami sudebnykh instantsii', 1 April. Available at www.nm.md/daily/article/2003/04/01/0104.html (last accessed 1 December 2009).

Nezavisimaya Moldova (2007) 'Vladimir Voronin: "V nashei sotsial'noi politike: vse prozhivayushchie v Pridnestrov'e – eto grazhdane Respubliki Moldova"', 23 May. Available at www.nm.md/daily/article/2007/05/23/0102.html.

Nilsson, D. (2008) 'Partial Peace: Rebel Groups Inside and Outside of Civil War Settlements', *Journal of Peace Research*, 45 (4): 479–95.

Nivat, A. (2001) *Chienne de Guerre: A Woman Reporter in Chechnya*, New York: Public Affairs.

Norwegian Refugee Council/Global IDP Project (2003) *Profile of Internal Displacement: Georgia*, Global IDP Database, Geneva, Switzerland.

Novruzoglu, R. (2003) 'Karabakh: "Chernyi rynok" dlya mezhdunarodnogo terrorizma'. Available at www.kitab.az/cgi-bin/catlib2/item.cgi?lang=ru&item=20051123172659214 (last accessed 24 November 2009).

Ohanian, K., Ahmedbeyli, S., and Muradyan, S. (2008) 'Mutual Recriminations After Karabakh Clash', *Caucasus Reporting Service*, 7 March.

O'Leary, B (2005) 'Debating Consociational Politics: Normative and Explanatory Arguments', in S. Noel (ed.) *From Power Sharing to Democracy: Post-conflict Institutions in Ethnically Divided Societies*, Montreal: McGill-Queen's University Press.

O'Loughlin, J. and Ó Tuathail, G. (G. Toal) (2009) 'Accounting for Separatist Sentiment in Bosnia-Herzegovina and the North Caucasus of Russia: A Comparative Analysis of Survey Responses', *Ethnic and Racial Studies*, 32 (4): 591–615.

O'Loughlin, J., Kolossov, V., and Tchepalyga, A. (1998) 'National Construction, Territorial Separatism and Post-Soviet Geopolitics: The Example of the Transdniester Moldovan Republic', *Post Soviet Geography and Economics*, 38: 332–58.

O'Loughlin, J., Toal, G., and Ward, M.D. (2008) 'The Dynamics of Unrecognized Quasi-States: Eurasian Secessionist Regions and the Independence of Kosovo', research project funded by the National Science Foundation's Initiative on 'Human and Social Dynamics', based at the University of Colorado, Boulder, CO.

Ottoway, M. (1995) 'Democratization in Collapsed States', in I.W. Zartman (ed.) *Collapsed States: The Disintegration and Restoration of Legitimate Authority*, Boulder: Lynne Rienner.

Owen, E. (2007) 'Domestic Debate Marks Karabakh Presidential Vote', *Eurasianet*, 19 July.

Panossian, R. (2001) 'The Irony of Nagorno-Karabakh: Formal Institutions versus Informal Politics', *Regional and Federal Studies*, 11 (3): 143–64.

Parish, M. (2009) 'Republika Srpska: After Independence', *Balkan Insight*, 19 November. Available at www.balkaninsight.com.

Pearlman, W. (2009) 'Spoiling Inside and Out: Internal Political Contestation and the Middle East Peace Process', *International Security*, 33 (3): 79–109.

Pearlman, W. (forthcoming) *Violence, Nonviolence, and the Palestinian National Movement, 1918–2008*, New York: Cambridge University Press.

Peebles, P. (2006) *The History of Sri Lanka*, Westport: Greenwood.

Peen Rodt, A. and Wolff, S. (2010) 'The Reactive Crisis Management of the European Union in the Western Balkans: Policy Objectives, Capabilities and Effectiveness', in U. Rabi (ed.) *International Intervention in Local Conflicts: Crisis Management and Conflict Resolution since the Cold War*, London, I.B. Taurus.

Pegg, S. (1998) *International Society and the De facto State*, Brookfield: Ashgate.

Pegg, S. (1999) 'The Nonproliferation of States: A Reply to Pascal Boniface', *The Washington Quarterly*, 22 (2): 139–47.

Pegg, S. (2004) 'From De facto States to States-Within-States: Progress, Problems and Prospects', in P. Kingston and I. Spears (eds) *States Within States: Incipient Entities in the Post-Cold War Era*, London: Palgrave Macmillan.

Pełczynska-Nałęcz, K., Strachota, K., and Falkowski, M. (2008) 'Para-States in the Post-Soviet Area from 1991 to 2007', *International Studies Review*, 10 (2): 370–87.

Politkovskaya, A. (2001) *A Dirty War: A Russian Reporter in Chechnya*, London: The Harvill Press.

Politkovskaya, A. (2003) *A Small Corner of Hell: Dispatches from Chechnya*, Chicago: University of Chicago Press.

Popescu, N. (2006a) *Democracy in Secessionism: Transnistria and Abkhazia's Domestic Policies*, Budapest: Open Society Institute.

Popescu, N. (2006b) 'Outsourcing De facto Statehood: Russia and the Secessionist Entities in Georgia and Moldova', Center for European Policy Studies (CEPS), Policy Brief, No. 109, July.

Pratap, A. (1984) 'If Jayawardene was True Buddhist, I Would Not Be Carrying a Gun: Prabhakaran Interview', *Sunday*, 11–17 March.

Puchala, D.J. (1993) 'The Secretary General and his Special Representatives', in B. Rivlin and L. Gordenker (eds) *The Challenging Role of the UN Secretary General: Making 'The Most Impossible Job in the World' Possible*, Westport: Praeger.

Radan, P. (2008) 'Secession: A Word in Search of a Meaning', in A. Paković and P. Radan (eds) *On The Way to Statehood: Secession and Globalization*, Aldershot: Ashgate.

Reno, W. (2000) 'Clandestine Economies, Violence and States in Africa', *Journal of International Affairs*, 53 (2): 433–59.

Reno, W. (2002) 'Mafiya Troubles, Warlord Crises', in M. Beissinger and Y. Crawford (eds) *Beyond State Crisis: Post-Colonial Africa and Post-Soviet Eurasia in Comparative Perspective*, Baltimore: Johns Hopkins University Press.

RFE/RL (2010) 'Abkhazia appoints new "foreign minister" ', 28 February.

Rich, P. and Stubbs, R. (eds) (1997) *The Counter-Insurgent State: Guerrilla Warfare and State Building in the Twentieth Century*, London: Macmillan.

Richmond, O. (1998) 'Devious Objectives and the Disputants' View of International Mediation: A Theoretical Framework', *Journal of Peace Research*, 35 (6): 707–22.

Riker, W.H. (1964) *Federalism: Origin, Operation, Significance*, Boston: Little, Brown.

Rimple, P. (2007) 'Gali: A Key Test Case for Georgia's Separatist Abkhazia Region', *Eurasianet*, 5 March.

Robinson, G. (2007) 'The Palestinians', in D.E. Long, B. Reich, and M. Gasiorowski (eds) *The Government and Politics of the Middle East and North Africa*, Boulder: Westview Press.

Roeder, P.G. and Rothchild, D. (eds) (2005) *Sustainable Peace: Power and Democracy after Civil Wars*, Ithaca, NY: Cornell University Press.

Rogel, C. (2003) 'Kosovo: Where it all Began', *International Journal of Politics, Culture and Society*, 17 (1): 167–82.

Roper, S.D. (2001) 'Regionalism in Moldova: The Case of Transnistria and Gagauzia', *Regional and Federal Studies*, 11 (3): 101–22.

Rosecrance, R.N. (2006) 'Who Will Be Independent?', in R.N. Rosecrance and A.A. Stein (eds) *No More States? Globalization, National Self-Determination, and Terrorism*, New York: Rowman & Littlefield Publishers.

Rosecrance, R.N., Solingen, E., and Stein, A.A. (2006) 'Globalization and Its Effects: Introduction and Overview', in R.N. Rosecrance and A.A. Stein (eds) *No More States? Globalization, National Self-Determination, and Terrorism*, New York: Rowman & Littlefield Publishers.

Rosenau, J.N. (2002) 'NGOs and Fragmented Authority in Globalizing Space', in Y.H. Ferguson and R.J. Barry Jones (eds) *Political Space: Frontiers of Change and Governance in a Globalizing World*, New York: State University of New York Press.

Rosenau, J.N. (2006) *The Study of World Politics: Globalization and Governance*, vol. 2, London: Routledge.

Rotberg, R.I. (1996) 'The Failure and Collapse of Nation-States: Breakdown, Prevention, and Repair', in R.I. Rotberg (ed.) *When States Fail: Causes & Consequences*, Boulder: Lynne Rienner.

Rotberg, R.I. (1999) *Creating Peace in Sri Lanka: Civil War and Reconciliation*, Washington, DC: Brookings Institution.

Rotberg, R.I. (ed.) (2004) *When States Fail: Causes and Consequences*, Princeton: Princeton University Press.

Ruggie, J.G. (1998) *Constructing the World Polity: Essays on International Institutionalization*, New York: Routledge.

Rutland, P. (2007) 'Frozen Conflicts, Frozen Analysis', paper presented at the ISA's 48th Annual Convention, Chicago, 1 March.

Sarkees, M.R, Wayman, F.W., and Singer, D.J. (2003) 'Inter-State, Intra-State, and Extra-State Wars: A Comprehensive Look at Their Distribution over Time, 1816–1997', *International Studies Quarterly*, 47 (1): 49–70.

Schaeffer, R. (1990) *Warpaths: The Politics of Partition*, New York: Hill and Wang.

Sevdimaliev, R. (2004) *Mezhdunarodnyi terrorizm – global'naya problema sovremennosti*, Baku: Elm.

Seymour, L. (2008) 'Pathways to Secession: Mapping the Institutional Effects of Conflicts of Self-Determination', Ph.D. dissertation, Political Science Department, Northwestern University.

Sheehy, A. (1991) 'Power Struggle in Checheno-Ingushetia', *RFE-RL Report on the USSR*, 15 November.

Sloane, R. (2002) 'The Changing Face of Recognition in International Law: A Case Study of Tibet', *Emory International Law Review*, 16: 107–86. Available at www.bu.edu/law/faculty/scholarship/workingpapers/documents/SloaneR110906.pdf.

Smith, S. Hadfield, A., and Dunne, T. (2007) *Foreign Policy: Theories, Actors and Cases*, Oxford: Oxford University Press.

Snow, D. (1996) *Uncivil Wars*, Boulder: Lynne Rienner.

Socor, V. (2006) 'Kosovo and the Post-Soviet Conflicts: No Analogy Means No Precedent', *Eurasia Daily Monitor*, 14 April.

Sørensen, G. (1999) 'Sovereignty: Change and Continuity in a Fundamental Institution', *Political Studies*, 47: 590–604.

Spears, I.S. (2002) 'Africa: The Limits of Power-Sharing', *Journal of Democracy*, 13 (3): 123–36.

Spiegel, P. (2008) 'Pakistan Tribal Area Called Likely Source of Next Attack on U.S.', *Los Angeles Times*, 11 June.

Stanislawski, B. (eds) (2008) 'The Forum: Para-States, Quasi-States and Black Spots: Not States, But Not "Ungoverned Territories" Either', *International Studies Review*, 10 (2): 366–96.

Stansfield, G. (2003) *Iraqi Kurdistan: Political Development and Emergent Democracy*, London: RoutledgeCurzon.

Stedman, J. (1997) 'Spoiler Problems in Peace Processes', *International Security*, 22 (2): 5–53.

Stephen, M. (2001) *The Cyprus Question*, London: Northgate.

Strange, S. (1996) *The Retreat of the State: The Diffusion of Power in the World Economy*, Cambridge: Cambridge University Press.

Suhrke, A. (2007) 'Reconstruction as Modernization: The "Post-Conflict" Project in Afghanistan', *Third World Quarterly*, 28 (7): 1291–308.

Suhrke, A., Strand, A., Samset, I., Knudsen, A.J., and Chaudhary, T.W. (2006). 'Violence in the Post-Conflict State', program at the Chr. Michelsen Institute, Bergen, Norway. Available at www.cmi.no/research/project/?886=violence-in-the-post-conflict-state.

Svensson, I. (2009) 'Who Brings Which Peace? Neutral versus Biased Mediation and Institutional Peace Arrangements in Civil Wars', *Journal of Conflict Resolution*, 53 (3): 446–69.

Swisspeace/Centre for Security Studies (2009) *Towards Realizing the Strengths and Mitigating the Challenges of NGO Mediators (Final Report of Consultation Process)*, Mediation Support Project.

Talmon, S. (1998) *Recognition of Governments in International Law: With Particular Reference to Governments in Exile*, Oxford: Oxford University Press.

Tamás, G. (1996) 'Ethnarchy and Ethno-Anarchism', *Social Research*, 63 (1): 147–90.

Tchilingirian, H. (1999) 'Nagorno Karabagh: Transition and The Elite', *Central Asian Survey*, 18 (4): 435–61.

Thomson, J.E. (1995) 'State Sovereignty in International Relations: Bridging the Gap between Theory and Empirical Research', *International Studies Quarterly*, 39 (2): 213–33.

Tilly, C. (1985) 'War Making and State Making as Organized Crime', in P.B. Evans, D. Rueschemeyer and T. Skocpol (eds) *Bringing the State Back In*, Cambridge: Cambridge University Press.

Tishkov, V. (2004) *Chechnya: Life in a War-Torn Society*, Berkeley: University of California Press.

Toft, M.D. (2003) *The Geography of Ethnic Violence: Identity, Interests, and the Indivisibility of Territory*, Princeton: Princeton University Press.

Tuathail, G. (G. Toal) (2008) 'Russia's Kosovo: A Critical Geopolitics of the August 2008 War over South Ossetia', *Eurasian Geography and Economics*, 49 (6): 670–705.

Turan Information Agency (2001) *Bor'ba s terrorizmom ne oznachaet, chto reshenie armyano-azerbaidzhanskogo konflikta dolzhno byt' otlozheno, schitaet Geidar Aliev*, 25 October. Available at http://karabakh-doc.azerall.info/ru/news/turan1001.htm#t1001_28.

Twining, D.C. (2004) 'Beware Russia's Pocket Empire', *The Christian Science Monitor*, 1 July.

UCDP Peace Agreement Dataset v. 1.0, 1989–2005 (2005) Available at http://infoglue.uu.se/research/ucdp/datasets.

United Nations (2009) *Report of the Secretary-General on Enhancing Mediation and Its Supporting Activities*, S/2009/189, New York, United Nations.

Unrepresented Nations People's Organization (2010a) *Somaliland: President Rayale Meets With International Agencies Representatives*. Available at www.unpo.org/content/view/10728/236.

Unrepresented Nations People's Organization (2010b) *Somaliland: A New US and EU Partner in the Horn of Africa*. Available at www.unpo.org/content/view/10928/236.

Unrepresented Nations People's Organization (2010c) *Somaliland: Israel Says Ready to Recognize Somaliland*. Available at www.unpo.org/content/view/10712/81.

United States Department of State (2000) 'Moldova: Country Report on Human Rights Practices'. Available at www.state.gov/g/drl/rls/hrrpt/1999/347.htm.

United States Mission to the OSCE (2004) 'Statement on Schools and Linguistic Cleansing in Transnistria, Moldova'. Available at http://osce.usmission.gov/media/pdfs/2004-statements/linguistic_cleansing_07_29_2004.pdf.

Uyangoda, J. (2007) *Ethnic Conflict in Sri Lanka: Changing Dynamics*, Policy Studies 32, Washington, DC: East-West Centre.

Valiyev, A. (2008) 'Foreign Terrorist Groups and the Rise of Home-grown Radicalism in Azerbaijan', *HUMSEC Journal* no. 2. Available at www.etc-graz.at/cms/fileadmin/user_upload/humsec/Journal/Valiyev.pdf.

Venice Commission (1998) 'Opinion on the Legal Code of Gagauzia'. Available at www.venice.coe.int/docs/1998/CDL(1998)041-e.asp.

Wæver, O. (1995) 'Securitization and desecuritization', in R.D. Lipschutz (ed.) *On Security*, New York, NY: Columbia University Press.

Walker, E. (1998) 'No Peace, No War in the Caucasus: Secessionist Conflicts in Chechnya, Abkhazia, and Nagorno-Karabakh', Occasional Paper, Belfer Center for Science and International Affairs, Harvard University.

Walker, R.B.J. (1992) *Inside/Outside: International Relations as Political Theory*, Cambridge: Cambridge University Press.

Walker, R.B.J. (2008) 'The Variety of Sovereignty', in R. Adler-Nissen, and T. Gammeltoft-Hansen (eds) *Sovereignty Games: Instrumentalizing State Sovereignty in Europe and Beyond*, London: Palgrave Macmillan.

Wallensteen, P. (2007) *Understanding Conflict Resolution*, London: Sage.

Wallensteen, P. and Eriksson, M. (2009) *Negotiating Peace. Lessons from Three Comprehensive Peace Agreements*, Uppsala: Uppsala University.

Walter, B. (1999) 'Designing Transitions from Civil War', in B.F. Walter and J. Snyder (eds) *Civil Wars, Insecurity, and Intervention*, New York: Columbia University Press.

Walter, B. (2002) *Committing to Peace*, Princeton: Princeton University Press.

Warrick, J. (2003) 'Dirty Bomb Warheads Disappear', *Washington Post*, 3 December.

Watts, R.L. (1999) *Comparing Federal Systems*, Montreal & Kingston: School of Policy Studies, Queen's University.

Webber, M. and Smith, M. (2002) *Foreign Policy in a Transformed World*, Upper Saddle River: Prentice Hall.

Weber, C. (1995) *Simulating Sovereignty: Intervention, the State and Symbolic Exchange*, Cambridge: Cambridge University Press.

Weinstein, J. (2007) *Inside Rebellion: The Politics of Insurgent Violence*, New York: Cambridge University Press.

Wennmann, A. (2009) *Charting the Economic Dimensions of Peace Mediation*, background paper for the workshop 'Economic Issues and Wealth Sharing in Mediation Processes', New York, 8–9 December.

Werner, S. (1999) 'The Precarious Nature of Peace: Resolving the Issues, Enforcing the Settlement, and Renegotiating the Terms', *American Journal of Political Science*, 43 (3): 912–34.

Werner, W.G. and De Wilde, J.H. (2001) 'The Endurance of Sovereignty', *European Journal of International Relations*, 7 (3): 283–313.

Whitman, R.G. and Wolff, S. (2010) 'The EU as a Conflict Manager? The Case of Georgia and its Implications', *International Affairs*, 86 (1): 87–107.

Widner, J. (2004) 'Building Effective Trust in the Aftermath of Severe Conflict', in R.I. Rotberg (ed.) *When States Fail: Causes and Consequences*, Princeton: Princeton University Press, 222–36.

William, P.R. and Pecci, F.J. (2004) 'Earned Sovereignty: Bridging the Gap between Sovereignty and Self-Determination', *Stanford Journal of International Law*, 1–40.

Williams, P.D. (2007) 'From Non-Intervention to Non-Indifference: The Origins and Development of the African Union's Security Culture', *African Affairs*, 106 (423): 253–79.

Wolff, S. (2008a) 'Complex Power Sharing as Conflict Resolution: South Tyrol in Comparative Perspective', in J. Woelk, F. Palermo and J. Marko (eds) *Tolerance Through Law: Self Governance and Group Rights in South Tyrol*, Leiden: Martinus Nijhoff Publishers.

Wolff, S. (2008b) 'Learning the Lessons of Ethnic Conflict Management? Conditional Recognition and International Administration in the Western Balkans since the 1990s', *Nationalities Papers*, 36 (3): 553–71.

Woodward, S.L. (1995) *Balkan Tragedy: Chaos and Dissolution after the Cold War*, Washington, DC: The Brookings Institution.

Yuzhnyi Kavkaz (2005) *Nezakonnaya deyatel'nost' Armenii na okkupirovannykh territoriyakh Azerbaidzhana.* Available at http://analitika.az/articles.php?item_id=20060521043143274&sec_id=17.

Zahar, M-J. (2004) 'Republika Srpska', in T. Bacheli, B. Bartmann, and H. Srebnik (eds) *De Facto States: The Quest for Sovereignty*, London: Routledge.

Zartman, I.W. (1995a) 'Putting Things Back Together', in I.W. Zartman (ed.) *The Elusive Peace: Negotiating an End to Civil War*, Washington, DC: The Brookings Institution.

Zartman, I.W. (1995b) 'Dynamics and Constraints in Negotiations in Internal Conflicts', in I.W. Zartman (ed.) *The Elusive Peace: Negotiating an End to Civil War*, Washington, DC: The Brookings Institution.

Zilleßen, H. (1999) 'Die Stellung der Mediation im politischen System der Demokratie', *Zeitschrift für Mediation*, 2 (5): 278–82.

Zinecker, H. (2006) 'Violence in Peace: Forms and Causes of Violence in Postwar Guatemala', PRIF Reports No. 76, Peace Research Institute Frankfurt.

Žunec, O. (2001) 'Operations Flash and Storm', in B. Magaš and I. Žanić (eds) *The War in Croatia and Bosnia Herzegovina*, London: Frank Cass.

Zürcher, C. (2007) *The Post-Soviet Wars: Rebellion, Ethnic Conflict, and Nationhood in the Caucasus*, New York: New York University Press.

Index

Note: Page numbers in **bold** denote figures or illustrations, those in *italics* denote tables.

eBooks

eBooks – at www.eBookstore.tandf.co.uk

A library at your fingertips!

eBooks are electronic versions of printed books. You can store them on your PC/laptop or browse them online.

They have advantages for anyone needing rapid access to a wide variety of published, copyright information.

eBooks can help your research by enabling you to bookmark chapters, annotate text and use instant searches to find specific words or phrases. Several eBook files would fit on even a small laptop or PDA.

NEW: Save money by eSubscribing: cheap, online access to any eBook for as long as you need it.

Annual subscription packages

We now offer special low-cost bulk subscriptions to packages of eBooks in certain subject areas. These are available to libraries or to individuals.

For more information please contact webmaster.ebooks@tandf.co.uk

We're continually developing the eBook concept, so keep up to date by visiting the website.

www.eBookstore.tandf.co.uk

For Product Safety Concerns and Information please contact our EU representative GPSR@taylorandfrancis.com
Taylor & Francis Verlag GmbH, Kaufingerstraße 24, 80331 München, Germany

www.ingramcontent.com/pod-product-compliance
Ingram Content Group UK Ltd.
Pitfield, Milton Keynes, MK11 3LW, UK
UKHW020012200926
475702UK00014B/1845
9781138788954